T0356472

Praise for *The Generalist Advantage*

"A compelling case for why organizations should value breadth over depth. *The Generalist Advantage* by Dr. Mansoor is a masterclass in leadership! If you want to future-proof your career in the age of AI, this book is your ultimate guide."

—Dominic Carter
Executive Vice President, The Sun

"Forget being a specialist! It's time to embrace your inner 'renaissance person.' We've long celebrated specialists, but with this book, Mansoor has redefined what expertise really looks like. A super-interesting read!"

—Dorie Clark
Executive Education Faculty, Columbia Business School, and Wall Street Journal *best-selling author of* The Long Game

"Refreshing and original...Many people believe that specialization is key to success, when the opposite is true. Dr Mansoor's years of research and experience make him the perfect guide for navigating the world of generalist leadership."

—Bjorn Billhardt
CEO, Abilitie (a global leadership development firm), and coauthor of The 12 Week MBA

"I cherish this book because it puts words on the life I have lived. Mansoor not only validates being a generalist (why) and frames types of generalists (what), but also suggests skills and actions to be an effective generalist (how)."

—Dave Ulrich
Rensis Likert Professor, Ross School of Business, University of Michigan, and Partner, The RBL Group

"Every chapter pushes you to rethink your approach to leading and scaling an organization, leveraging the generalist mindset. An insightful 2×2 matrix categorizes four types of generalists that we often see at work: shallow, domain, skill, and ultra generalists. It is a must-have for every leader's bookshelf."

—Rob Cross
Senior Vice President of Research, Institute for Corporate Productivity, Professor of Global Leadership, Babson College, and coauthor of The Microstress Effect

"As a former professional international rugby player, I've seen firsthand the importance of having a diverse range of skills. Mansoor Soomro's *The Generalist Advantage* provides a powerful framework for understanding the benefits of generalism in both sports and business."

—Rory Underwood
MBE DL, England Rugby's Record International Try Scorer, Royal Air Force (RAF) Fast Jet Pilot, and Founder/CEO of Wingman

"Dr. Mansoor Soomro delivers a masterful guide to navigating the complexities of modern leadership. His deep research and compelling case studies offer a powerful framework for embracing versatility in the AI era. This book is an essential read for any leader looking to develop a generalist mindset."

—Dr. Marshall Goldsmith
Thinkers50 #1 Executive Coach and New York Times *bestselling author of* The Earned Life, Triggers, *and* What Got You Here Won't Get You There

"In a world where organizations are experiencing unprecedented change, Professor Soomro lucidly illustrates the importance and advantage of being a generalist. Chock-full of engaging examples, this book is a must-read for us to stay relevant."

—Hatim A. Rahman
Associate Professor, Kellogg School of Management at Northwestern University and author of Inside the Invisible Cage: How Algorithms Control Workers

"By applying the Generalist Quotient assessment, HR and L&D executives can play a more strategic role in driving organisational success. The framework of four types of generalists (shallow, domain, skill, and ultra generalist) at work can be readily integrated into training programs, helping teams drive peak performance."

—Jordan Workman
HR Business Partner, Aston Martin Lagonda Ltd.

"Mansoor Soomro has crafted a practical guide for leaders who want to excel in the future of work. *The Generalist Advantage* offers a clear road map, and it's a powerful resource for anyone ready to rethink the traditional path to success."

—Erin Meyer
Professor of Management Practice, INSEAD, New York Times *bestselling author of* The Culture Map, *and coauthor of* No Rules Rules

"Sick of feeling pigeonholed? It's time to embrace your generalist advantage. Dr. Mansoor is a remarkable researcher and a captivating keynote speaker who brings fresh perspectives to leadership and AI. His thought leadership is driving a new understanding of how organizations can thrive; this book is a testament to that."

—Jason Averbook
Senior Partner, Global Lead Digital Transformation, Mercer and Forbes Human Resources Council Member

"This fascinating book makes a powerful claim to rehabilitate the generalist. The author depicts the generalist as holding a portfolio of skills to address the changing nature of our environment. This is certainly an important consideration for managers who want to stay relevant in this context."

—Thomas Roulet
Chaired Professor of Organisational Sociology & Leadership, Judge Business School & King's College, University of Cambridge, and author of The Power of Being Divisive: Understanding Negative Social Evaluations

"As a military leader, I recognized the importance of having a diverse and adaptable team. Our people are our power. Mansoor Soomro's book *TGA* is a must-read for anyone looking to develop leadership in dynamic, high-pressure environments."

—Lieutenant Colonel Andy Black
Head of Army Engagement for North of England, Headquarters North, Ministry of Defence UK

"Mansoor Soomro's work is a valuable addition to the generalist/specialist debate and creates a useful framework for firms in transition, preparing themselves for a high-tech future."

—Yuri Bender
Editor-in-Chief, Professional Wealth Management, Financial Times

"Occasionally, dearly held beliefs need to be challenged. This is what Mansoor Soomro does when he suggests that generalists can outplay specialists in the age of AI. A compelling hypothesis!"

—Christian Stadler
Professor of Strategic Management, Warwick Business School, and coauthor of Open Strategy: Mastering Disruption from Outside the C-Suite

"Mansoor Soomro has written a game-changing book for business leaders. The Near Future Readiness Index (NFRI) mentioned in the book is a valuable resource for any organization looking to thrive in the 21st century."

—Justin Rix
Partner, People Advisory, Grant Thornton UK LLP

"In a world full of distractions, it's hard to lose sight of what is important, and what is coming next. This book is a practical guide to help leaders become more well rounded and ready for whatever the future throws at them!"
— **Alex Whiteleather**
L&D Strategist and Managing Director of Abilitie Europe

"As organizations reimagine their operating models in response to advances in remote work, artificial intelligence, and skills-based resourcing strategies, it will be more important than ever to have generalist leaders."
—**Phil Kirschner**
Founder and Principal Consultant, PK Consulting, and Ex-Associate Partner, McKinsey & Company

"Dr. Mansoor Soomro is knowledgeable, thoughtful, forward-thinking, and erudite in his approach. This book is remarkable, both in terms of hypothesis and implementation."

—**Leo Ulph**
Presenter, BBC

"Soomro makes us rethink the limitations and strengths of generalists by explaining how they spur innovation, bridge communication gaps, and make sense of complexity. Find out to what extent you are (or should be) a shallow, domain, skill, or ultra-oriented generalist."
—**Ian P. McCarthy**
W.J. VanDusen Professor of Innovation & Operations Management, Beedie School of Business, Simon Fraser University

"*The Generalist Advantage* provides a compelling framework for unlocking the potential of generalists, especially in the AI-driven world. This book is a must for both leaders and organizations aiming to stay ahead of the curve."
—**Paolo Aversa**
Professor of Strategy, King's College London, and Associate Editor of Journal of Management Studies

"*The Generalist Advantage* is a game-changing book for our era of specialization. More than just informative, it's an inspiring manifesto for leaders who want to unleash their full potential and succeed in uncertain times."
—**Des Dearlove**
Cofounder, Thinkers50

"Very interesting read! Backed by extensive research and packed with actionable insights, *The Generalist Advantage* outlines models and theories that executives can leverage to maximize both individual and team productivity."

—Imran Saeed
Head of Treasury & Corporate Finance, Middle East & Africa,
Siemens Energy LLC

"Captivating read! *The Generalist Advantage* book by Mansoor shows what it takes to rise above mediocrity and lead organizations that thrive and endure for the long haul. Contrasting generalists' edge over specialists, this book provides rich insights and actionable leadership wisdom."

—Shaz Ansari
Professor of Strategy and Innovation at Judge Business School,
University of Cambridge

"Soomro makes the timely and valuable case that specialization in academia and business has gone too far, arguing not only the value of generalism but also offering practical advice on how to develop oneself as a generalist."

—Martin Reeves
Chair of Boston Consulting Group (BCG) Henderson Institute
and coauthor of The Imagination Machine

The
Generalist
Advantage

The Generalist Advantage

PROVEN FRAMEWORK TO EXPLORE
THE POTENTIAL OF 4 TYPES OF
GENERALISTS AT WORK

MANSOOR SOOMRO, PHD

WILEY

Library of Congress Cataloging-in-Publication Data Applied for:

Print ISBN: 9781394276400
ePDF ISBN: 9781394276424
epub ISBN: 9781394276417

Cover design by Wiley

SKY10099577_030725

Dedicated to Khizr and Hamdan

I am so proud of you. You two inspire me every day!

May this book excite your adventures and help you towards a fulfilling life.

Brief Contents

Foreword   xxi

PART I   THE GENERALIST ADVANTAGE   1

Chapter 1   Embracing the Generalist Mindset   3

Chapter 2   Redefining Expertise in a Shifting
            Landscape   17

Chapter 3   The Age of AI and the Rise of
            Generalists   35

PART II   BECOMING A GENERALIST   53

Chapter 4   Four Types of Generalists at Work   55

Chapter 5   Domain and Skill Variation of Different
            Generalists   95

Chapter 6   The Generalist's Role in Innovation
            and Problem-Solving   131

Chapter 7   The Generalist Advantage in
            Action—Case Studies   167

PART III SELF-ASSESSMENT 181

Chapter 8 The Generalist Quotient (GQ)™ 183

Afterword 185

Acknowledgments 187

About the Author 191

Glossary 193

Further Reading 197

Index 217

Contents

Foreword   **xxi**

Why Read This Book?   *xxiii*

How to Read This Book?   *xxvi*

PART I   **THE GENERALIST ADVANTAGE**   **1**

Chapter 1   **Embracing the Generalist Mindset**   **3**
                 Who Is a Generalist?   3
                 Who Is Not a Generalist?   6
                 Debunking 10 Myths of Generalists   8
                 Six Superpowers of Generalists   13

Chapter 2   **Redefining Expertise in a Shifting**
                 Landscape   **17**
                 Generalist vs Specialist: Key Differences   17
                 Near Future Readiness: What and How?   19
                     Near Future vs Future   20
                     What Is Near Future Readiness?   20
                     How Can Individuals Cultivate Near
                         Future Readiness?   22
                     How Can Businesses Cultivate Near
                         Future Readiness?   22
                 Generalists and Near Future Readiness   23
                 Near Future Readiness Index (NFRI)™   24
                 Defining the Generalist Advantage (TGA)™   28

Chapter 3 The Age of AI and the Rise of Generalists 35

Balancing Complementary with
Contrasting Skills 35

Portable Skills as the Key to Professional
Resilience 39

Portable Skills and Professional Resilience 41

How to Develop Portable Skills? 42

The Power of Versatility in the Era of
AI Revolution 45

The Challenge: What AI Does
Exceptionally Well 46

Where Humans Maintain Unique Value:
The Power of Versatility 46

Overcoming Disciplinary Blind Spots 48

Strategies to Overcome Blind Spots 49

Way Forward on Seeing Beyond Blind Spots 51

PART II   BECOMING A GENERALIST 53

Chapter 4 Four Types of Generalists at Work 55

Are All Generalists the Same? 55

Shallow, Domain, Skill, Ultra (SDSU)™
Generalist Framework 57

SDSU Framework Based on Portable Skills
and Cross-industry Adaptability 58

SDSU Framework Based on Expertise
and Perspectives 60

SDSU Framework Based on Skills
and Domains 61

Possible Paths of the Generalist
Advantage (TGA) 64

Typical path 1: When people switch
their companies early in their careers 64

Typical path 2: When people switch
their companies a bit later in their careers 65

Type I: Shallow Generalist (S) 66
Who Is a Shallow Generalist? 66
Characteristics of a Shallow Generalist 68
Pains and Gains of a Shallow Generalist 68
How Not to Become a Shallow Generalist 68
Where Do Shallow Generalists Thrive? 69
Type II: Domain Generalist (D) 71
Who Is a Domain Generalist? 71
Characteristics of a Domain Generalist 72
Pains and Gains of a Domain Generalist 73
How to Become a Domain Generalist 73
Where Do Domain Generalists Thrive? 74
Type III: Skill Generalist (S) 76
Who Is a Skill Generalist? 76
Characteristics of a Skill Generalist 78
Pains and Gains of a Skill Generalist 78
How to Become a Skill Generalist 79
Where Do Skill Generalists Thrive? 80
Type IV: Ultra Generalist (U) 82
Who Is an Ultra Generalist? 82
Characteristics of an Ultra Generalist 86
Pains and Gains of an Ultra Generalist 86
How to Become an Ultra Generalist 86
Where Do Ultra Generalists Thrive? 88
Summary of Strengths, Risks, and Organizational
Aspects of Generalists 90

**Chapter 5 Domain and Skill Variation of Different
Generalists 95**
Law of Specialist Saturation (LOSS)™ 95
Why Is It a "LOSS"? 99
LOSS Scenarios 100
Ability to Work Outside the Domain 101
Why Does Working Outside the
Domain Matter? 103
How Can Organizations Encourage Leaps
Outside the Domain? 105

Top 60 Domains for Developing TGA   106
Bonus: Emerging/Nascent Domains
     (Fit for AI Era)   109
Ability to Acquire New Skills   110
    Why Does Acquiring New Skills Matter?   112
    How Can Organizations Encourage a Culture
     of Upskilling and Re-skilling?   114
Hard vs Soft Skills of Generalists   115
Disciplinary Strokes of Generalists   120
    How Can Generalist Leaders Take Advantage
     of These Four Approaches?   122
    Power of the Trans-disciplinary Mindset   123
Top 40 Skills for Developing TGA   125
    Bonus: Emerging/Nascent Skills
     (Fit for AI Era)   128

Chapter 6   **The Generalist's Role in Innovation
and Problem-Solving**   **131**
Generalists Dealing with Uncertainty   131
    How Does Foresight Help Ultra Generalist
     Leaders in Preparing for Uncertain Times?   137
    Generalist-led Case Studies for
     Uncertain Events   139
Generalists Tackling with Complexity   141
    How Does Holistic Thinking Help
    Ultra Generalist Leaders in Solving
    Complex Problems?   146
    Generalist-led Case Studies for Complex
     Problems   148
Innovation Ins and Outs of Generalists   149
    Innovation Management Practices for
     Generalists   154
    Generalist-led Innovation Case Studies   156
Problem-Solving Modes of Generalists   157
    Problem-Solving Approaches of Generalists   163
    Generalist-led Problem-Solving
    Case Studies   164

Chapter 7 The Generalist Advantage in Action—Case Studies **167**

Case Study 1: Shallow Generalist as a Leader |
Analysis till Paralysis 167

The Case of Ben Bennett: Analysis Paralysis
in the Face of Disruption 167

Early Success: The Rise of a Meticulous
Leader 168

Changing Tides: Emerging Disruption 168

The Perils of Perfectionism 169

The Cost of Indecision 169

Results 169

Discussion Questions 170

Case Study 2: Domain Generalist as a Leader |
Cross-industry Adaptability 170

The Case of Rebecca Martinez:
Leveraging Cross-Industry Insights for
Transformational Growth 170

Early Influences: Foundations in the
Nonprofit Sector 171

Pivot to Tech: Embracing a Culture of Agility 171

The Test: Revitalizing a Legacy Business 172

Transferring Learnings: Driving Change at
DB Transportation Corp 172

Results 172

Discussion Questions 173

Case Study 3: Skill Generalist as a Leader |
Applying Unrelated Skills 173

The Case of Ali Shaikh: The Power
of Unrelated Skills in a Dynamic
Environment 173

Early Influences: A Developer and a
Hobbyist 174

The Benefits of Unrelated Skills 174

Applying the Unexpected: Innovation at
Miro Electronics 174

Results 175

Discussion Questions 176

Case Study 4: Ultra Generalist as a Leader |
    Thriving in Uncertain Times   176
  The Case of Adele Ortiz: Leading with
    Resilience and Adaptability in a World
    of Disruption   176
  The Value of Multi-Domain Expertise   177
  Resilience in Uncertain Times   177
  Results   178
  Discussion Questions   178

PART III   SELF-ASSESSMENT   **181**

Chapter 8   The Generalist Quotient (GQ)™   **183**
  What Is a Generalist Quotient?   183
  Where Can I Check My Generalist Quotient?   183
  How Can the Generalist Quotient
    Self-Assessment Help Me?   184

Afterword   **185**

Acknowledgments   **187**

About the Author   **191**

Glossary   **193**

Further Reading   **197**

Index   **217**

Foreword

Experts are overrated! Moreover, expertise is often equated with success, so the generalist concept may seem out of place.

Yet, in the tapestry of human endeavor, a thread exists that weaves through the fabric of history, connecting individuals who defy the confines of narrow expertise. This thread speaks to the power and resilience of the generalist, those who embrace the breadth of interests, knowledge, skills, and experiences that transcend the boundaries of any single discipline or expertise.

For me, writing this book taught me that when we are told to "narrow our focus" or to "stay in our lane," we miss out on something profoundly special. Our greatest strengths often lie in that willingness to dance on the borders of multiple fields, finding unique synergies that drive real-world impact. That is the beauty of *the Generalist Advantage (TGA)*. My life, my career, my persona, and my choices, in one way or another, have all directed me to write this book.

As a proud generalist, I seamlessly blend industry and academic experiences. I bring expertise across multiple functional areas—including finance, marketing, human resources, and technology. While I am an introvert by nature, I am a confident and compelling keynote speaker, capable of captivating large audiences.

There is, of course, no single pathway for every generalist out there. Some of you might take these ideas and become the most unconventional and successful CEOs ever. Others might kick-start incredible creative projects, inspire the next generation of multifaceted learners, or become those problem-solving superheroes every team needs. And you know what? You might do all those things over the course of one (just one) beautifully diverse life!

What I can promise is this: the generalist path is anything but ordinary! It will challenge you, push you beyond neat categorizations, and sometimes

"the generalist path is anything but ordinary!"

make you doubt yourself. There will be times when the voices whispering to "pick a lane" will come back again, louder than before. But that's what makes the triumph so sweet. Learning to tell your story authentically, showcasing your multifaceted value, and navigating a world built for a different kind of thinking—that's where the real fulfillment of the generalist lies. Seriously, I hope this book can become like a giant "permission slip" to embrace those side hustles, random bursts of curiosity, and your general all-over-the-place brilliance.

If you ask me, this book, *The Generalist Advantage*, is a celebration of this timeless archetype, a testament to the profound impact and enduring relevance of those who dare to venture beyond the confines of specialization. In these pages, you will embark on a journey to uncover the hidden treasures of versatility, adaptability, and creativity that lie at the heart of the generalist mindset.

Generalists often underrate themselves, not knowing that integration is their superpower. Imagine a symphony conductor who understands acoustics, psychology, and leadership. Their baton orchestrates harmony, transcending musical notes to evoke emotions. Or the environmentalist who merges biology, economics, and policymaking. Their solutions address climate change holistically, leaving no stone unturned. Imagine a physicist who can paint, a chef who can code, and a historian who can design user interfaces. It is possible—and what it requires is a voracious appetite for learning, a refusal to be confined by silos.

As you journey through the pages that follow, not only seek to understand the power of the generalist but also embrace the potential within us to embody this archetype. Drawing upon insights from a diverse array of disciplines, rooted from psychology to philosophy, *The Generalist Advantage* offers a holistic exploration of what it means to embrace breadth over depth, cultivate a curiosity that knows no bounds, and thrive in an ever-changing landscape of opportunity and challenge, especially in the age of artificial intelligence (AI).

From the classroom to the boardroom, from the laboratory to the studio, the generalist mindset offers a unique perspective to rise above the limitations of siloed thinking. Let us cultivate the courage to embrace uncertainty, the humility to acknowledge our limitations, and the resilience to persevere in the face of adversity. For it is in the diversity of our experiences, the richness of our perspectives, and the multiplicity of our empathy that we find the true measure of our success, personally and professionally.

Why Read This Book?

There are two key reasons why I encourage you to read this book:

a. This book reveals the incredible *power of generalists*, what I call *the Generalist Advantage*, helping you understand why they will thrive in today's dynamic world.

b. This book offers a *practical framework* that classifies four types of generalists in the workplace, providing valuable insights for generalists (and specialists) on how to leverage *the Generalist Advantage* to achieve greater personal and professional success.

I have always been a collector. Not of things, mind you, but of interests. As a child, I adored building blocks one day and meticulously dissecting my toy cars the next day. My college years were a whirlwind too as I enjoyed studying medicine but at the same time, I loved mathematics. The pattern continued well into my professional life—an interest in coding here, a fascination with behavioral psychology there, and an impromptu passion for public speaking otherwise. I started my career working at *Siemens*. Being a sizable multinational organization, I enjoyed working there in multiple roles in diverse functions: technology operations, human resources, marketing, and financial management.

And while all this filled me with joy, it also brought a strange sort of anxiety. The world around me seemed to have clear lanes carved out for success. To excel, the logic was to choose a specialty, a single path, and become the absolute best within that narrowly defined territory. The whispers were insidious, "Mansoor, you are spreading yourself too thin!" The implication was clear—my curiosity, this messy collection of interests, might leave me with an enjoyable life, but one less likely to leave a significant mark.

Somewhere deep down, I felt something wasn't quite right. *Was I doomed to forever apologize for loving to learn across wildly different fields?* It took around eight years of soul-searching, conversations with inspiring individuals, and stumbling upon fascinating research for the fog to finally lift. It wasn't that I lacked focus; it was that my focus took a different form. My attention flowed from one passionate pursuit to another, and as counterintuitive as it seemed, threads began to emerge. For example, an idea from my public speaking interest unlocked a problem in my leadership style. My knowledge of psychology gave me surprising insights into my business events. Instead of my diverse interests diluting my abilities, they seemed to cross-pollinate, leading to innovative solutions and a worldview richer than I could have imagined.

At work, I used to ask myself: *Do generalists or specialists have a higher chance of becoming a part of the top management, especially the chief executive officer (CEO) or the managing director (MD) in their organization?* Taking the example of a hospital, can a medical doctor as an expert on medicine perform better as the CEO of a large hospital? Or can someone with good leadership and management experience excel in running a large size hospital? As you probably know, in a majority of organizations and industries, the focus lies overwhelmingly on the specialist model. Success stories in organizations often then highlight laser-focused determination, not the winding adventure and exploration of generalists.

Moving forward, I tried to find an answer to this question while undertaking an academic pursuit—my PhD. Right from the initial months of my PhD research, I studied biographies, human personalities, and organizational mantras to understand who is more successful in personal and professional life, a generalist, or a specialist. Even now, working in academia at the *Teesside University International Business School* in the United Kingdom, leading the Future of Work research unit, I research on similar lines to understand *whether generalists are more innovative than specialists* and *whether generalists are more visionary than specialists, as well as whether generalists can outperform specialists as better leaders.*

Introspecting myself further, I am the person at conferences and events who bounces from conversation to conversation, soaking up bits of knowledge like a sponge. One minute I am talking about business sustainability, the next I am arguing about the most powerful engine in an automobile. Fortunately, or unfortunately, I get excited about a ridiculous number of things. Everyone kept telling me, "Find your niche!" and "You can't be good at everything, you know?" At first, I bought into it. But then it took me a while to realize that those voices were not correct. It was not that I lacked potential; it was that I needed a different way to see the world. The fact is, my "all over the place" brain did not just fuel random hobbies, but, somewhere beneath the surface, connections were happening.

The turning point was realizing that I wasn't alone. Throughout history, there have always been *generalists*—sometimes also called *Renaissance polymaths, cross-disciplinary scientists*, and *multi-hyphenate entrepreneurs*. In the modern world, with its dizzying speed of artificial intelligence (AI), this generalist perspective is not merely quirky; it's very much necessary. More than ever, we need adaptable problem solvers, unorthodox thinkers who connect the seemingly unconnected, and lifelong learners who can thrive in a world of constantly shifting knowledge and skill sets.

Despite the demand, it is not easy to become a generalist. We lack the *framework* and *tools* to understand this generalist path thoughtfully. This is why I want you to read this book as it provides a research-backed framework (*the Generalist Advantage Framework*) and a pragmatic set of tools (*Generalist Quotient Self-Assessment*) to help you identify and develop your generalist talent.

> **❝We lack the *framework* and *tools* to understand this generalist path thoughtfully. ❞**

Inside this book, you will find:

- ◆ *A practical framework:* Make use of a *2×2 TGA™ (the Generalist Advantage)* framework to maximize your learning, identify the overarching themes of your interests, and translate your eclectic background into compelling narratives that showcase your value.
- ◆ *Workplace strategies:* Discover *SDSU™ (shallow, domain, skill, ultra generalist)* strategies to deal with negative perceptions of the generalist path, effectively communicate your capabilities, and find environments where your unique skill set is celebrated.

♦ *Psychological insights:* Learn how generalists can counter the diminishing productivity of specialists using *LOSS™ (Law of Specialist Saturation)* and develop an attitude and aptitude for pattern recognition across fields.

How to Read This Book?

This book argues the case for *the Generalist Advantage* and explores the potential of *four types of generalists at work*. At the heart of *The Generalist Advantage* lies a celebration of curiosity—the insatiable thirst for knowledge and understanding that drives us to explore the world around us.

This book has three parts with eight chapters. I would urge my readers to approach each chapter with a sense of wonder and curiosity, eager to uncover new insights and perspectives that may challenge their preconceived notions. No wonder, books are more than ink on paper; they are gateways to imagination. All three parts and eight chapters follow a gradual progression, beginning with theoretical concepts and culminating in practical applications.

The first part of "The Generalist Advantage" (Chapters 1 to 3) focuses on the "why" of this advantage; the second part, "Becoming a Generalist" (Chapters 4 to 7), elaborates on the "how" of this advantage; and the third part, "Self-Assessment" (Chapter 8), provides an opportunity to take a short online assessment in attempting to understand the type of generalist one resembles the most. Within these pages lies a treasure trove of ideas, waiting to spark your imagination, challenge your assumptions, and expand your horizons about the advantage generalists have in organizations.

> **"Within these pages lies a treasure trove of ideas, waiting to spark your imagination, challenge your assumptions, and expand your horizons"**

I suggest that readers can benefit the most by reading this book in three phases:

Phase 1: Read the book *in the flow it's written* (Chapter 1 to Chapter 7) to understand the significance and classifications of generalists.

Phase 2: Complete the *self-assessment online* (QR code and link mentioned in Chapter 8). It will give you some idea of which type of generalist category best represents you, and what can be your strongest and possibly not-so-strong areas.

Phase 3: Reflecting on the results of the self-assessment, pay more attention to the generalist type you currently are, and the generalist type you can transition to. Once the gap is clear, *read again* Chapters 4 to 7 to drive an action plan for yourself.

Based on your self-assessment results, create a plan to address your areas of growth. In other words, develop a plan to leverage *the Generalist Advantage*. This might involve setting mid- to long-term targets, seeking additional training, identifying some courses, or finding a mentor. Also, it is important to track your progress on this generalist journey. Periodically, revisit your self-assessment and track your progress toward your targets. This will help you stay motivated and be more conscious of your development.

Albert Einstein famously said, "If you can't explain it simply, you don't understand it well enough." While writing this book, my kids, Khizr and Hamdan, would often look over and ask me what certain words or terms meant, such as "Generalist... What is that? Who is that?" I tried a few times to simplify my answers, using examples from their magical world. For instance, I explained that a generalist is like a superhero with many different superpowers instead of just one. Over time, I realized that these *childlike* (mind you, not *childish*) insights can offer clarity for us grown-ups too—especially for managers and leaders in the workplace. So I've included some of the explanations I shared with my kids throughout this book in a box under the heading "Explain It to Kids." I hope you'll enjoy reading and connecting with them!

PART I

The Generalist Advantage

CHAPTER 1

Embracing the Generalist Mindset

Who Is a Generalist?

A *generalist* is someone who possesses a wide range of interests, knowledge, abilities, or experiences (as opposed to a *specialist*, who carries a deep focus on a specific interest, knowledge, ability, or experience).

Explain It to Kids

Generalist: is a superhero who knows a little bit about a lot of things, someone with many different skills instead of just one!

Whether it's embracing diverse skills or understanding different industries, generalists play a crucial role in our ever-evolving world. Generalists tend to have a diverse set of interests and abilities, allowing them to adapt and excel in various situations or roles. They often thrive in environments that require flexibility, creativity, and the ability to connect ideas from different fields.

Generalists are the ones with a big appetite for knowledge and/ or experience. They do not like to stick long to one subject—instead, they like to sample a little bit of everything. In terms of profiles, this could signal a historian who likes to do coding, a technology geek who also likes biology, or a mathematician who takes a keen interest in subjectivity. That's what we're talking about while referring to a generalist. One of the key traits of a generalist is curiosity—they are genuinely curious about a wide range of subjects, fields, and hobbies. They do enjoy dabbling, but more than that they authentically find value and excitement in learning from many different domains.

Moreover, generalists are masters of mash-ups. Instead of seeing knowledge in neat little boxes, generalists see it all jumbled together. They make crazy connections that other people miss, such as seeing how fixing a car has something in common with treating a patient or solving an accounting problem. And here is the best part—when faced with a new challenge, they're less likely to get stuck with the same old approach. They pull from different things they've learned, experiment way more, and often end up surprising themselves (and everyone else on their team) with unexpected solutions leading to multiple possibilities. In simple words, generalists love to be part of the "why not?" crew (*who see opportunities first*) vs the what-if crew (*who see impediments first*).

In terms of teamwork, generalists thrive in diverse teams, talking to anyone from engineers to accountants to lawyers to marketers with ease. A generalist is like a powerful translator having knowledge and experience in multiple languages, who can bridge connections between people who specialize in specific languages. In fact, generalists help specialists understand each other better! Not a lie, generalists have more power to do magic in organizations.

Generalists are also called *multi-potentialite* (having multiple creative passions), *Polymath* (having diverse learning points on their learning curve), and *multi-hyphenate* (having several jobs and professions). There are various historical and contemporary examples of famous personalities who qualify the generalist mark: (a) *Oprah Winfrey*: multi-hyphenate who built a media empire encompassing production, acting, publishing, and philanthropy—her ability to connect with audiences draws from all of it; (b) *Steve Jobs*: while associated with Apple, he fostered his generalist perspective through calligraphy, Eastern philosophy, and design thinking, fueling his iconic innovations; and (c) *Elon Musk*: serial entrepreneur across varied industries (technology, space exploration, infrastructure). These wide experiences enable them to approach problems from unconventional perspectives.

There is also an interesting concept known as a *T-shaped professional*, a concept popularized by *Tim Brown*, the CEO of IDEO, which suggests that T-shaped professionals combine deep expertise in one area (the vertical line of the T) with a broad understanding of multiple areas (the horizontal line of the T). I will explain later in the second part of this book that the topology of generalists today calls for more than just a T-shape expansion.

The main thesis of this book is that the world needs more generalists. Big messy problems? Those are a generalist's playground! Generalists are valued for their interdisciplinary approach, which enables them to see the big picture, identify patterns, and solve complex problems that may span multiple domains. In fact, if you or your team are stuck and lack fresh ideas, call a generalist rather than a specialist!

Let's picture these four business scenarios to understand how generalists thrive at work:

Scenario 1: The Intrapreneur
◆ *Role:* director
◆ *Generalist strengths:* Instead of starting their own thing, they bring an entrepreneurial spirit inside an established organization. Their ability to spot connections between different departments or industries inspires them to spearhead internal initiatives. For example, they might suggest new products or services, or lead internal innovation programs.

Scenario 2: The Visionary Strategist
◆ *Role:* chief innovation officer
◆ *Generalist strengths:* Pulls on broad industry knowledge, understanding of customer behavior trends, and awareness of technological disruptions to outline new competitive directions for a company. They might have held different positions earlier, even outside the domain, granting them a fresh view of how the company can reinvent itself.

Scenario 3: The Cross-Functional Liaison
◆ *Role:* product development lead
◆ *Generalist strengths:* Possesses a high-level understanding of both technical and creative processes. They seamlessly act as a bridge between marketing, design, and engineering teams, translating their unique viewpoints. This ensures everyone stays on the same page and prevents costly siloing.

Scenario 4: The Entrepreneur

◆ *Role:* start-up founder

◆ *Generalist strengths:* Early-stage businesses require wearing many hats—and generalists thrive in such chaos! They navigate marketing, customer service, rudimentary accounting, and product development in the initial stages before bringing in specialist support. Their adaptable skills often become a core pillar of a company's early success.

Who Is Not a Generalist?

Someone who is not a generalist is typically referred to as a specialist. Specialists focus on a narrow area of interest, knowledge, ability, or experience, to develop proficiency in a specific field or subject. Specialists are also known as *experts* and *niche leaders*.

Explain It to Kids

Specialist: is also a superhero but with one special skill—they know a lot about one thing, such as a doctor for animals or a chef for desserts!

Unlike generalists, specialists may have limited exposure to or interest in areas outside their specialized field or domain. They excel in roles requiring *highly specialized knowledge* (like an aircraft pilot) or *technical expertise* (like a nuclear power plant engineer) and may find it challenging to adapt to tasks or responsibilities outside their narrow focus. While specialists bring expertise to their respective fields, they may benefit from collaborating with generalists who can offer broader perspectives and interdisciplinary insights.

Defining who is *not* a generalist is trickier than defining a generalist. Here are a few examples to illustrate who is not a generalist:

◆ *The master of a craft:* An individual focusing obsessively on mastering a single craft is out of the generalist league. Their depth within their domain is incredible, but they are intentionally not focused on breadth.

- *The comfort zone clinger:* They resist learning new things outside their expertise. New problems feel intimidating because they might require stepping outside their known skills. This rigid mindset inhibits the cross-pollination of ideas that generalists thrive on.
- *The information silo seeker:* Their world is defined by their narrow field, and they view other domains with disinterest or even condescension. This limits their perspective, stifling collaboration, and their ability to connect seemingly unrelated concepts.
- *The established paradigms favorer:* Some individuals prefer operating strictly within known models and systems within their field. Limited exploration beyond this paradigm inhibits innovative leaps that often result from synthesizing new or adjacent information, an approach generalists favor.

Overall, there are two main considerations connected with the generalist-specialist debate: *degrees of generalist-ness* and *contextual relativity*. First, in terms of "degrees of generalist-ness," we are not living in a binary world with an on/off switch. There are all sorts of shades of gray in between. Someone can be highly specialized in one field but still maintain some generalist traits and tendencies in other areas of life. Like most personality traits, being a generalist exists on a spectrum, or a continuum. We all have both specialized and generalist tendencies. Some people lean heavily toward the generalist side, while others incorporate broader learning into a primarily specialized identity. This is where the degree of generalist-ness comes in. Also, some of us begin as focused specialists and find ourselves drawn to learning a wider range of things later on. For example, scientists might get frustrated with their linear research subject and apply that rigor to study something far different from their expertise and domain.

Next, in terms of "contextual relativity," while an exceptional individual within one field might possess more openness to broader ideas compared to those around them, they themselves might be relatively less generalist when evaluated against their industry as a whole. For example, a highly skilled engineer at a big tech company is surrounded by specialists. Still, compared to others in their field, this engineer might be the resident generalist who excels at seeing how systems interact. Moreover, it is not that generalists are always better and they can excel in every field. For example, a heart surgeon in an operation room in a hospital takes the lead based on its laser-focused specialization in heart-related surgical procedures, which is a case where contextual specialists are clearly preferred.

It is also interesting to relate the generalist-specialist debate with the notion of evolution and learning. People *can* and *do* transition, depending on exposure to new problems, life experiences, or intentional cultivation of new areas of interest. Our brains are incredibly powerful and wired to make connections in unexpected ways when intersecting with a particular opportunity or crisis. Also, there is no single right way to be a generalist! Realistically, a lot of this depends on personality. Some people simply love diving deep into one topic, while others feel alive to jump-start new learning paths constantly. Both are amazing in their own way, and both play crucial roles in successful companies, handling both large-scale and intricate projects.

> **❝People *can* and *do* transition, depending on exposure to new problems, life experiences, or intentional cultivation of new areas of interest. ❞**

In terms of *specialism* and *mastery*, there is another interesting concept known as *the 10,000-hour rule*, a concept popularized by Malcolm Gladwell claiming that extensive practice (in the form of 10,000 hours) is essential for mastering any field. I, along with several other scholars, argue that the 10,000-hour number is arbitrary and doesn't apply universally. Different skills may require varying amounts of practice, depending on their complexity, the individual's starting point, and innate talent. In the third chapter of this book, I will explain why, in the age of AI, mastery is no longer essential.

> **❝in the age of AI, mastery is no longer essential. ❞**

Debunking 10 Myths of Generalists

Jack-of-all-trades, master of none is the most deceptive statement that we have been listening to for ages. This myth suggests that one should not be a generalist. Let's bust this myth!

Successful generalists never claim that they are proficient at anything and everything. While possessing wide-ranging knowledge and exposure, generalists often cultivate proficiency in selected areas. Their multidimensional skill set is a significant strength, not a weakness! In other words, generalists may have interests at multiple places, but they can *zero in* when they need to. Plus, the things they learn in one area tend to make them even better at another! There is not much to believe that generalists are mostly superficial, and specialists (experts) are mostly needed to solve real business problems. On the contrary, imagine a world where being a jack-of-all-trades is the ultimate power move. We're living in that world right now!

Various other common myths about generalists hold little to no significance or value in real life. Let's debunk some of the most persistent myths about generalists:

Myth 1: Generalists are less productive than specialists.

◆ *Reality:* Productivity is about increasing output over the given set of inputs. With rapidly changing fields, technology disruptions, and global issues demanding cross-domain solutions, generalists have the potential to be more productive as they can pivot easily and join seemingly unrelated trends. Moreover, diversity of knowledge breeds innovation, enhancing business productivity.

◆ *Example:* A project manager with a background in general management may be perceived as less valuable than a project manager with specialized expertise in a particular industry, such as health care or finance. However, the generalist project manager brings a versatile skill set and broad perspective that can be applied to diverse projects and industries, adding to outputs and productivity at work.

Myth 2: Generalists lack focus and direction.

◆ *Reality:* Interest in many things doesn't equal scatterbrained. Good generalists make connections, transferring knowledge between fields.

◆ *Example:* An entrepreneur who has launched successful ventures in various industries, including technology, hospitality, and retail, may be viewed as lacking focus or direction by some. However, this entrepreneur demonstrates adaptability and a willingness to explore new opportunities, leveraging their generalist mindset to identify untapped markets and innovate across different sectors.

Myth 3: Generalists are not good decision-makers.

◆ *Reality:* While some struggle to decide which interest to explore first, a mature generalist has greater self-knowledge. Knowing diverse skills gives them the power to make more informed decisions. Also, there is a difference between indecision and deliberate multi-interest. True generalists strategically embrace the power of diversity for the pursuit of their greater goals. They might seem directionless on the surface, but there's an underlying drive behind their exploration.

◆ *Example:* An entrepreneur builds multiple revenue streams (blog, product, services). His generalist nature lets him make better decisions in navigating changing markets—if one stream slows down, his "portfolio mentality" creates flexibility that a single-focus businessperson may lack.

Myth 4: Generalists are not effective team players.

◆ *Reality:* Being great in a team doesn't just rely on subject expertise. Generalists flourish as empathetic listeners, facilitating dialogues between those with divergent views. They're excellent collaborators, recognizing diverse talents and bridging divides within teams.

◆ *Example:* A product manager with experience in three diverse domains of software development, construction management, and event planning has better empathy based on his or her learning from different industry sectors with their different workplace challenges. Such leaders are great team sport members, and they often thrive by working in heterogeneous teams.

Myth 5: Generalists cannot be good mentors at work.

◆ *Reality:* While traditional mentorship follows the master-apprentice model, generalists excel as "exploration guides." They help mentees identify connections between areas of interest, develop effective learning strategies, and embrace challenges with resilience. They don't offer all the answers, but they have the tools to figure things out—incredibly valuable in its own right.

◆ *Example:* A divisional director having worked in different business units (such as finance, marketing, and information technology) possesses learning from different fields, which is a powerful attribute for mentoring and coaching. Such generalist leaders take pride in cross-disciplinary innovation and have a lot to offer as mentors.

Myth 6: Generalists are largely extroverts.

◆ *Reality:* Absolutely not true! There are introverted generalists, just like extroverted generalists, thriving in different senior and junior roles in organizations. These introvert generalists channel their wide-ranging interests inwards by finding focus within outlets simultaneously.

◆ *Example:* A marketing professional who is skilled as a generalist in digital marketing, content creation, branding, and market research may be an introvert who mostly enjoys working behind the scenes. However, this individual's diverse skill set as a generalist still allows him or her to be an introvert in reaching out to customers and other stakeholders.

Myth 7: Generalists are mostly mediocre in performance.

◆ *Reality:* This boils down to how we define success and excellence. If it's based solely on traditional markers of niche mastery, then sure. However, it ignores the inherent strengths generalists develop: innovative problem-solving, pattern recognition, and sense-making—hardly the hallmarks of mediocrity!

◆ *Example:* A generalist middle manager in a mid- to large-size company has stretched targets and is meant to carry a high bias for results and performance. This is important for him or her to climb the corporate ladder of success even more than a specialist, as generalists often charter their unique career pathways moving laterally. Moreover, this manager pursuing a work life driven by continuous learning and tackling big interdisciplinary challenges is far from mediocrity.

Myth 8: Generalists are only good at entry-level positions.

◆ *Reality:* While early in their careers, generalists may take on unrelated roles for experience, their ability to adapt and learn propels them into unique senior positions. Companies are recognizing the value in leadership who understand the big picture and bridge teams with disparate expertise.

◆ *Example:* CEOs, being part of the senior management, cannot survive without being generalists. They are often expected to oversee department areas and functions without specialized knowledge and experience in all those areas.

Myth 9: Generalists only fit into start-up environments.

◆ *Reality:* Certainly, a start-up environment is often a generalist's playground. With very limited resources at the start of any business, entrepreneurs must take the lead in multiple job roles themselves as a one-man show. Mostly, SMEs rely on generalists for bundled support instead of keeping a specialist for each role. Yet, established companies increasingly leverage innovation for that generalist ability of their executives to disrupt routines and generate solutions that would go unnoticed within siloed departments.

◆ *Example:* A generalist human resource executive in an established multinational company is a great fit, as large corporations have added complexity and layers where generalist leaders can excel more as they can wear multiple hats working with different business functions.

Myth 10: Generalists are easily replaceable.

◆ *Reality:* Highly skilled generalists with proven value-add within companies or projects are the opposite of replaceable. Their unique lens, coupled with the ability to collaborate effectively across different silos, makes them irreplaceable as connectors and knowledge integrators.

◆ *Example:* A head of department in a pharmaceutical firm who has past exposure from varied industry domains (working in pharma companies, hospitals, and NGOs) will have a unique approach to solving problems, team management, and business development. Replacing this head with a similar generalist profile will not be easy, making generalist careers more indispensable.

Those are some of the myths that often plague generalists. I am of the view that old prejudices do fade, and new ones emerge, and as leaders in organizations, it is important to dissect these myths with a stroke of practicality. However, *cultural context* matters here a lot. Some organizational cultures celebrate "lifelong craftsmanship," making the generalist path less understood. It's all about how generalists frame their talents, emphasizing value rather than letting outdated stereotypes rule the day.

Let's get specific! Did a particular myth resonate? In the next chapter, we will look into more real-world situations of how these myths get busted every day.

Six Superpowers of Generalists

Now that we have cleared up some of the misconceptions around the generalists, it's time to understand the real power of generalists. In modern work environments emphasizing complexity and innovation, the generalist's *mindset* and *skill set* offer immense value. They foster collaboration, excel in rapidly changing conditions, and act as catalysts for fresh ideas and solutions, just to mention a few arguments advocating the power of generalists in the workplace.

Superpower 1: Generalists Spur Innovation

Instead of solely relying on breakthroughs within fields, successful leaders understand that innovation occurs at intersection points—and generalists excel here. Known as *outside inspiration*, they pull ideas from unrelated sectors, bringing novel approaches that specialists with *tunnel vision* easily miss. For example, generalist leaders from the product management team at Dyson revolutionized vacuums using cyclone technology inspired by industrial sawmills—definitely not a typical approach within appliance design.

Superpower 2: Generalists Are Bridge Builders

A team of specialists can struggle to translate their knowledge to colleagues outside their niche. On the contrary, generalists speak many languages—enhancing collaboration and preventing misunderstandings. Generalists are team translators as they help break silos in organizations. Moreover, they connect ideas and resources across departments, maximizing existing resources instead of reinventing the wheel in every corner of a company. For example, at Apple, marketing needs tech insights for a new campaign. A generalist project manager who is good at marketing media and has a reasonable understanding of leading tech platforms can facilitate that knowledge exchange between marketing and information technology departments, which can eventually pull a powerful campaign for the organization, something that they made use of in the launch of Apple Vision Pro spatial computing glasses.

Superpower 3: Generalist Value Foresight

Beyond tracking specific topics, generalists recognize *bigger-picture patterns* others miss. They see market shifts before they go mainstream and prepare teams earlier. They are good at spotting trends, fashion, and fads. Diverse knowledge of generalists lets them spot potential disruptions or hidden issues. For example, generalist business leaders may sense regulatory changes by monitoring policy conversations even if not directly in their field. This can then give the company an incredible kick start in the market, especially in highly competitive cut-throat markets (such as Samsung in smartphones, Uber in ride-hailing, and Wingstop in the fast-food market).

Superpower 4: Generalists Are Brilliant Adapters

Specialists are great when processes are static, but generalists excel in fluid situations. In terms of problem-solving agility, the diverse knowledge of generalists fuels adaptable solutions. In the face of tech disruption, a generalist might propose solutions drawing from social trends analysis that a tech-focused team would overlook. For example, when Airbnb emerged, their generalist leaders embraced hospitality plus technology while traditional hotels struggled to adapt.

Superpower 5: Generalists Champion Resilience

The COVID-19 pandemic made it clear that businesses with diversified revenue streams and the ability to go digital survived better. A company mindset led by generalists naturally builds this, even unknowingly. In other words, generalists' *comfort with the unknown* helps companies see calculated risk as healthy experimentation rather than danger. In fact, it opens opportunities others, too fearful, simply never attempt. More or less, a generalist perspective does well by building resilience while thinking beyond one industry's norms. For example, Peloton Interactive, originally a fitness equipment company, transformed into a fitness and streaming company during the pandemic. Peloton saw a significant increase in demand for its home fitness products as gyms closed. The company's revenue more than doubled in 2020. Their generalist leaders not only offered interactive bikes but also offered virtual (synchronous and asynchronous) workout classes, which led to a significant increase in subscriptions and sales. This helped the company bounce back and build resilience.

Superpower 6: Generalists Foster Learning Culture

Certainly, employees mimic leadership. Seeing leaders value exploration keeps teams dynamic and discourages complacency. When curiosity permeates a company, everyone is open to learning beyond their defined job titles. Simply put, when people have a broader understanding of the business, everyone makes better decisions and feels less isolated. It creates a sense of *collective brain trust*, which boosts morale. It works like a nitro boost! For example, teams at OpenAI are mostly generalist in nature as they are composed of members from diverse backgrounds, including computer science, neuroscience, engineering, and ethics, to promote cross-pollination of ideas and a high-octane learning culture. Employees are encouraged to explore new projects and switch teams based on their interests and expertise, promoting a learning agenda and drive.

For sure, generalists are not *know-it-all freaks*. Sure, they know a bunch of things, but that doesn't make them experts on every other thing. The best generalists are super-curious and love learning from anyone, including specialists. In summary, generalists bring versatility, adaptability, and fresh perspectives to leadership roles. Why would anyone not want to capitalize on these six superpowers?

Chapter 1 Takeaways

- It is time to embrace a mindset that values breadth more than depth.
- It is incorrect to say that generalists lack focus, do not have "real" expertise, or cannot drive results.
- In today's fast-evolving environment, we need rapid learners—and generalists fare better than specialists in unlearning and relearning.

CHAPTER 2

Redefining Expertise in a Shifting Landscape

Generalist vs Specialist: Key Differences

Generalists and specialists represent two distinct lines to acquiring knowledge and leveraging experience. Specialists see generalists' leaps as recklessness. Generalists see specialists' caution as an obstacle to progress. Likewise, specialists are baffled by how generalists arrive at a conclusion seemingly out of thin air. Generalists think the specialist's obsession with details is pure madness. Let's start with a contrasting snapshot, as outlined in Table 2.1, of how both are different in terms of their individual strengths and limitations.

> **❝Specialists see generalists' leaps as recklessness. Generalists see specialists' caution as an obstacle to progress.❞**

In terms of strengths, generalists thrive on curiosity, but specialists favor mastery. In terms of limitations, generalists may lack focus, but specialists, on the other hand, may be excessively focused. Let's apply these strengths and limitations to the workplace environment. The key differences between generalists and specialists go beyond basic definitions and include nuances of how they think and function in the world. Here are some key differences between them in terms of the impact they have on the workplace.

Breadth vs depth: Generalists possess a broad range of knowledge and skills across multiple disciplines or domains. They prioritize

Table 2.1 Conceptual differences between a generalist and a specialist

	Generalist	Specialist
Strengths	• Adaptability • Innovation • Insatiable curiosity	• Deep understanding • Technical expertise • Mastery of methods
Limitations	• May lack focus on specialized areas • Can be an overwhelming experience at times	• May miss the bigger picture • Can be inflexible at times

breadth of understanding over depth in a specific area. Specialists, on the other hand, focus on acquiring deep expertise in a narrow field or subject area. They prioritize depth of understanding within their specialized domain.

Versatility vs specialization: Generalists are versatile and adaptable, able to apply their skills and knowledge in a variety of contexts and situations. They excel at connecting ideas from different fields and disciplines. Specialists are highly specialized in a specific area, often possessing in-depth knowledge and expertise that is valuable within their narrow field. They may have limited applicability outside of their specialized domain.

Problem-solving approach: Generalists tend to approach problems with a broad perspective, considering multiple factors, perspectives, and solutions. They are adept at synthesizing information from different sources and disciplines to address complex challenges. Specialists approach problems with a narrow focus, leveraging their deep expertise to analyze issues within their specialized domain. They may excel at finding solutions within their area of expertise but may struggle to see the bigger picture or consider alternative approaches.

Learning approach: Generalists prioritize learning across a wide range of subjects and disciplines, often seeking out diverse experiences and opportunities for personal and professional growth. Specialists focus their learning efforts on acquiring in-depth knowledge and expertise within their specialized area, often through formal education, training, and experience.

Career opportunities: Generalists may pursue diverse career paths and opportunities, as their broad skill set and adaptable mindset allow them to transition between different roles, industries, and functions. Specialists often pursue careers within their specialized

Table 2.2   Workplace application differences between a generalist and a specialist

	Generalist	Specialist
Core focus	Breadth	Depth
Knowledge structure	Versatile	Specialized
Problem-solving	Multifactor and cross-domain approach	Targeted and well-established approach
Learning mindset	Perpetual learning to acquire knowledge	Expertise-learning to fill knowledge gaps
Work style	Thrives in dynamic environments juggling multiple projects	Excels in detail-oriented environments with established routines

field, leveraging their deep expertise to advance their careers and make significant contributions within their narrow domain.

For ready reference, these five workplace application differences between generalists and specialists are summarized in Table 2.2. Research on career goals suggests that *individual preferences, motivation*, and *circumstances* are equally important when we look at the path people take in their careers. To that, both generalists and specialists play important roles individually and in organizations, each bringing unique strengths and perspectives to the table. However, the future belongs more to generalists, as will be explained more in this chapter.

Near Future Readiness: What and How?

The world of work is changing too much (*magnitude of change*) and too fast (*speed of change*). A lot of jobs are being displaced due to AI's influence, including the roles of *blue-collar jobs* (manual labor workers), *white-collar jobs* (managerial staff), and *open-collar jobs* (freelance professionals). The concept of a monthly salary will become obsolete soon as remuneration options will be shorter (such as week or hour-based) or otherwise project-based (as seen with the freelance, or gig economy). Our workweek concept will be also shorter and different from the standard nine-to-five, five days a week work model, promoting hybrid working, flexible working, four-day working week, and six-hour working model as the norm. With these shifting landscapes and changes, it is difficult to rely on experts as their expertise might not be

Table 2.3 Differentiation between near future and future

Near Future	Future
• Anticipated and somewhat predictable time frame, usually a few years to a decade. • Changes during this time likely emerge from trends already in motion.	• Open-ended and mostly speculative time frame, usually over a decade. • Changes include disruptions that are hard to define now, shifts stemming from breakthroughs not yet invented, or societal changes whose path is unpredictable.

needed the same way moving forward. Now, is exactly the time when generalists will rise!

> **❝it is difficult to rely on experts as their expertise might not be needed the same way moving forward. ❞**

NEAR FUTURE VS FUTURE

To help leaders navigate through these uncertain times, a *Near Future Readiness Index (NRFI)* is presented in this chapter. I arrived at this index while interviewing over 370 middle and senior executives from 265 companies during the pandemic. Learning from the pandemic, we have seen that planning too far in the future is not very helpful, and instead planning for mid-term (near future) is more needed. Table 2.3 shows what is implied by the terms "near future" and "future".

WHAT IS NEAR FUTURE READINESS?

Near Future Readiness refers to the ability of individuals and organizations to anticipate, adapt to, and thrive in an increasingly uncertain and rapidly changing but predictable time frame. It encompasses a range of skills, mindsets, and capabilities that enable individuals and organizations to navigate complex challenges, seize opportunities, and remain resilient in the face of ongoing or upcoming uncertainty.

Near future readiness is important as it allows for:

- ◆ *Anticipation:* Actively scanning for disruptions, shifts in customer needs, and changes within or adjacent to one's industry.

- *Agility:* Responding quickly and creatively to uncertainty, with an ability to pivot based on new information and context.
- *Resilience:* Not merely bouncing back from challenges but developing strategies to withstand setbacks and come out stronger.

Some of the key aspects of near future readiness include:

- *Strategic foresight:* Anticipating near future trends, opportunities, and challenges and developing strategies to address them proactively is a key attribute. Near future ready individuals and organizations invest in strategic planning, scenario analysis, and trend forecasting to inform decision-making and guide mid-term planning (not long-term planning). This includes considering best-case, worst-case, and most likely outcomes.
- *Tactical adaptability:* The ability to change plans and strategies quickly in response to shifting circumstances on the ground is important in preparing for the near future. It requires a clear understanding of overall goals, combined with flexibility in the methods used to achieve them. Successful tactical adaptability relies on good situational awareness and the ability to make informed decisions under pressure.
- *Ecosystem thinking:* Viewing the business as part of a larger ecosystem helps. Near future ready individuals understand interdependencies and leverage collective intelligence. They collaborate with start-ups, industry peers, and academia in cocreating solutions and sharing knowledge. This diversification attitude often chalks out novel revenue streams, along with expanding adjacent product lines.

Of course, developing near future readiness is not easy, and it has its own share of challenges. The first challenge is that of *analysis till paralysis*. Being constantly focused on scanning mode can turn into procrastination. So it is better to balance awareness with decisive action. The next challenge is that of *downplaying complexity*. Near future readiness means tackling problems at the systems level, not just through quick fixes. The third challenge is that of the *burnout trap*. Near future-minded leaders always find their minds jogging on anticipating problems. This proactive mindset may lead to some level of distress and discontentment.

One way to address these challenges is to proactively cultivate near future readiness on both *individual* and *organizational* levels. As near future readiness requires a commitment to continuous personal and professional development, individuals and organizations must be proactive in acquiring new knowledge, skills, and competencies to stay ahead of the curve in a rapidly evolving world. Let's look at what individuals and businesses can do differently to be near future ready.

HOW CAN INDIVIDUALS CULTIVATE NEAR FUTURE READINESS?

- *Build your curiosity muscle:* Deliberately seek out information that lies outside your comfort zone. Sample a wide range of podcasts, talks, or newsletters across domains to see what sparks your interest.
- *Develop meta-skills:* Focus on problem-solving processes, resilience, adaptability, and creative communication skills beyond mastery of a specific task.
- *Always be a beta version:* Embrace constant evolution—the current edition is never a final edition.

HOW CAN BUSINESSES CULTIVATE NEAR FUTURE READINESS?

- *Hire with diversity in mind:* Seek out generalist skill sets—teams with varied talent and a proven ability to learn go a long way.
- *Prioritize knowledge flow:* Invest in systems encouraging communication between teams, especially in breaking down silos that hinder growth.
- *Build innovation spaces:* Create physical or virtual environments where cross-functional teams experiment without traditional pressure. This requires accepting some calculated failure for the sake of big potential results.

In addition to this, classification or *type of industry* plays a key role here in understanding and achieving the near future readiness. For instance, in the fast-moving telecommunications industry or high-velocity e-commerce industry, the near future might be months rather than years! While more stable industries such as health care may have larger windows to describe the same near future-ness.

Generalists and Near Future Readiness

Near future readiness is about *planning* as well as *experimentation*. In terms of planning, businesses scream for better research to make investments in talent upskilling and upgrading organizational infrastructure. Generalist leaders due to their wide interests have better insights, which helps in planning. In terms of bold experimentation, businesses are demanding a greater tolerance for failure and a willingness to pivot if their early bets go wrong. Generalists here again, due to their exploratory mindset, can help steer course corrections quickly. In an ever-evolving world, being near future ready is crucial for maintaining a competitive edge. *So are generalists more ready than specialists for the near future?* Let's consider these two scenarios:

Scenario 1: Generalists and Extrapolating Current Trends

- *Business focus:* To emphasize the evolution of existing technologies, societal shifts, and economic conditions. Also, to extrapolate what we see now into how it might shape things soon.
- *Generalist role:* They thrive here! Analyzing a diverse set of current data from varied fields helps them piece together how markets, technologies, or even cultural forces are about to change. Strategic planning relies on this skill.
- *Example:* A tech firm's generalist foresees not just AI growth, but also societal fatigue with screens, and starts a research & development (R&D) lab. This R&D initiative seeks more natural tech interaction methods, well before a market demand even exists clearly.

Scenario 2: Generalists and Envisioning Disruptive Events

- *Business focus:* To encompass *wildcards* (power moves) and *black swan* (major surprise) events outside what current trend charts suggest. Also, to envision truly transformative disruptions or radically different ways of existing.

- *Generalist role:* Their ability to synthesize unexpected connections becomes crucial. Imagining potential scenarios based on a combination of possibilities *(new tech + policy change = ??)* makes them valuable futurists and scenario planners.
- *Example:* An automotive company sees growing e-bike use + climate policy pressures. A generalist-led initiative helps pivot research toward smaller, urban-focused vehicle solutions.

Overall, generalists excel at near future readiness for three main reasons. Generalists are *pattern seekers*. Their diverse knowledge base lets them spot connections and weak signals others miss, giving early warning of change. Generalists are above-average *idea adapters*. Pulling from different domains, they fuel innovative solutions in unexpected ways. They often transfer a concept into a totally new setting when specialists get stuck. Generalists, by and large, enjoy being *comfortable with the unknown*. For them, constant learning means not only embracing change but being energized by it. Generalists often don't cling to outdated or conventional models like those averse to navigating unknowns might.

Near Future Readiness Index (NFRI)™

Recognizing the distinction between the future and the near future, as well as the importance of being prepared for the latter, it is time to introduce the *Near Future Readiness Index (NFRI)*. This index, grounded in research, identifies crucial indicators essential for navigating the near future. Its purpose is to assist leaders in preparing for both negative (and positive) events or situations within a *predictable time frame*.

Explain It to Kids

Near Future Readiness: NFRI is being ready for the cool new things that are coming soon, such as flying cars or robot helpers!

In studying over 265 companies during the pandemic, the three key aspects of near future readiness (strategic foresight, tactical adaptability, ecosystem thinking) and five key differences between generalists and specialists (core focus, knowledge structure, problem-solving, learning

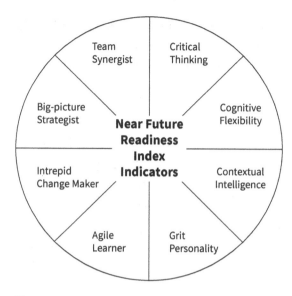

Figure 2.1   Eight indicators of Near Future
Readiness Index (NFRI).

mindset, and work style), I have come to these eight Near Future
Readiness Index indicators as sketched in Figure 2.1: *critical thinking,
cognitive flexibility (thinking), contextual intelligence (application),
grit personality, agile learner, intrepid change maker, big-picture strategist,* and *team synergist.*

Just in case you were wondering what these eight indicators are
and why are they important for near future readiness, I have tabu-
lated *"what (it is)"* and *"why (is it important)"* in the Near Future
Readiness Index, presented in Table 2.4. I have added some examples from the corporate environment too, to help you relate to the
importance of these indicators in today's workplace.

In terms of measuring this index, quantitative data (surveys) and
qualitative data (interviews) were used to get people's perceptions
of preparedness and to assess how companies respond to hypo-
thetical immediate future scenarios, revealing underlying biases. In
addition to that, skill set audits with a mix of manufacturing and
service-based companies were utilized to map what expertise exists
across organizations. Over 370 middle and senior executives from
265 companies during the pandemic were studied to conceive and
propose this index.

In constructing the Near Future Readiness Index, the objective is not to devise a single metric but rather to gauge a *composite score* that is built on key parameters of leadership. For instance, adaptability

Table 2.4   Near Future Readiness Index (NFRI)

Near Future Readiness Index (NFRI)			
NFRI Indicators	What (is it)?	Why (is it important)?	Examples (from my research)
1. **Critical thinking**	Assessing information, identifying problems, and proposing solutions	To understand the big picture and diverse viewpoints	A marketing director used critical thinking to reassess a declining product's performance by analyzing customer feedback, market trends, and competitor strategies.
2. **Cognitive flexibility**	Shifting perspectives and approaching problems from different angles	To learn new skills quickly, and adjust strategies readily	When a global pandemic forced a sudden shift to remote work, a company's CEO with cognitive flexibility quickly adapted the company's operations, implemented new policies, and ensured employee well-being.
3. **Contextual intelligence**	Understanding how knowledge applies in different settings	To make relevant decisions based on situational factors	A sales executive applied contextual intelligence by tailoring their pitch to align with a client's pain points, increasing the relevance and impact of their solution.
4. **Grit personality**	Sustaining effort despite difficulties and maintaining goals	To push through setbacks and gain resilience	Demonstrating perseverance and grit, a research & development (R&D) officer pushed through multiple design failures and setbacks over months, refining the prototype until it met market demands.

Near Future Readiness Index (NFRI)			
NFRI Indicators	What (is it)?	Why (is it important)?	Examples (from my research)
5. **Agile learner**	Embracing continual learning and mastering new information efficiently	To seek out diverse learning opportunities, and readily absorb new skills	A product manager exemplified agile learning by quickly mastering new AI tools to enhance product development, applying insights from recent failures to improve future iterations.
6. **Intrepid change maker**	Embracing innovation and venturing into uncharted territory	To challenge the status quo, propose and implement new solutions	An automobile company CEO acted as an intrepid change maker by boldly announcing a vision to transition the entire fleet to fully electric vehicles within five years, defying industry norms.
7. **Big-picture strategist**	Envisioning overall goals and aligning individual projects to a broader strategy	To develop comprehensive plans, consider diverse factors and stakeholders	A strategic marketing director of an fast-moving consumer goods (FMCG) company acted as a big-picture strategist identifying emerging market segments and developing innovative marketing campaigns for its products to retain leadership in the FMCG industry.
8. **Team synergist**	Building relationships and leveraging diverse strengths for synergy	To communicate effectively, foster collaboration and teamwork	A software development manager exemplified team synergy by fostering open communication and collaboration among developers, quality assurance, and user experience (UX) design teams, encouraging diverse perspectives in sprint planning meetings.

as a parameter is about the capacity to learn new skills, shift directions, and embrace change swiftly with less resistance than those clinging to the status quo. Similar to that, innovation as a parameter focuses on the ability to generate, develop, and implement novel solutions. This goes beyond mere ideas, incorporating a bias for action.

In terms of application, this index is essentially focused on *individuals* (leaders at the workplace), but it can also be applied to an *organizational* and an *industry* level. In terms of individual level of application, this index highlights where to upskill, re-skill, and unskill. It can lead to more tailored learning opportunities with a near future mindset for generalists. In terms of organizational level of application, this index provides a benchmark for strategic shifts. It identifies where investments are needed in terms of skill gaps and team structures. In terms of industry level of application, this index offers insights into evolving sectors and helps predict where growth is most likely to occur. It also can gauge resilience against shocks and can allow policymakers to target investment in future-proofing different industry sectors. However, this index is largely subjective as it is based on qualitative indicators that would best depict near future readiness and its orientation in terms of what and why.

Defining the Generalist Advantage (TGA)™

Returning to the debate on generalists versus specialists, a pertinent question arises: *which group is better equipped for the near future?* It is clear that generalists and specialists operate quite differently. In this section, I've sought to establish *the Generalist Advantage (TGA)* by applying the previously proposed *Near Future Readiness Index (NFRI)*. Using the eight key indicators identified for the near future, I have compared and contrasted the strengths of generalists and specialists.

Readiness can manifest in both positive and negative forms. Positive readiness signifies preparedness and adaptability to seize opportunities, while negative readiness may reflect a state of being overly reactive or resistant to change, hindering progress and innovation. In Table 2.5, I have added positive or negative readiness manifestations for generalists and specialists, based on the eight NFRI indicators, and have suggested the underlying logic that explains the choice of positive or negative form.

Explain It to Kids

The Generalist Advantage: TGA is all about how being good at different things helps people solve problems. In other words, it is about connecting different pieces in cool ways, like a puzzle master!

By definition, *the Generalist Advantage (TGA)* refers to the benefits gained from having a broad skill set and diverse domain exposure, allowing individuals or organizations to adapt to various roles, think creatively, solve problems, and build resilience in dynamic environments.

Table 2.5   Deriving the Generalist Advantage (TGA) through the Near Future Readiness Index (NFRI)

The Generalist Advantage (TGA)		
Near Future Readiness Index (NFRI) indicators	Readiness of a generalist for the near future	Readiness of a specialist for the near future
1. **Critical thinking**	*Readiness: Positive* Sees patterns across things and asks why things are done the way they are.	*Readiness: Positive* Deeply understands how their stuff works and analyzes problems within their own area.
2. **Cognitive flexibility**	*Readiness: Positive* Switches gears easily, is open to trying new ways, and is comfortable figuring things out on the fly.	*Readiness: Negative* Sticks to proven methods and prefers a known process over experimenting with new approaches.
3. **Contextual intelligence**	*Readiness: Positive* Takes ideas from anywhere and sees how stuff might work in unexpected ways.	*Readiness: Negative* Uses its niche knowledge in its expert context, but seems puzzled when faced with the multiplicity of contexts.
4. **Grit personality**	*Readiness: Positive* Not afraid of failure, learns from mistakes, and is motivated by the challenge, even when it's difficult.	*Readiness: Positive* Wants to get it right almost every time and focuses intensely on overcoming specific obstacles within their field.

(continued)

Table 2.5 *(continued)*

The Generalist Advantage (TGA)		
Near Future Readiness Index (NFRI) indicators	Readiness of a generalist for the near future	Readiness of a specialist for the near future
5) **Agile learner**	*Readiness: Positive* Gets enough to get started and is not like a perfectionist, who wants to know everything up front.	*Readiness: Negative* Takes time, and wants to master the basics before going wild with new tools or concepts.
6. **Intrepid change maker**	*Readiness: Positive* Excited by shake-ups, sees problems as opportunities, and craves change.	*Readiness: Negative* Champions change within their specific field of expertise only, and that too at a relatively slow pace.
7. **Big-picture strategist**	*Readiness: Positive* Thinks about the whole system (sees the forest for the trees), how the pieces fit, and where there might be issues later.	*Readiness: Negative* Focuses on making its own piece work the best it can, and sometimes ignores the larger system needs.
8. **Team synergist**	*Readiness: Positive* Great at spotting gaps and seeing where people with different strengths can plug in.	*Readiness: Negative* Prioritizes finding the right expert for a specific task, and is more concerned about results than the team bonding process.

In terms of near future readiness, generalists score higher than specialists in navigating in times of uncertainty, identifying nascent (emerging) trends, leading potential disruptions, and highlighting emerging opportunities for product and market developments. Generalists are the best form of *systems thinkers*—who see the whole system instead of mere parts. Perceiving interconnected elements and anticipating cascading effects help generalists in their decision-making and problem-solving.

A generalist's main advantage largely boils down to cross-disciplinary innovation and interdisciplinary communication. In terms of cross-disciplinary innovation, generalists leveraging insights from multiple fields identify novel solutions and synthesize new models, disrupting outdated industry practices. In terms of interdisciplinary communication, generalists invest in effective communication and knowledge translation across specializations which bridges gaps, facilitates team success, and accelerates project outcomes.

Table 2.5 distinctly indicates *the Generalist Advantage*, showing that generalists are more ready for the near future based on all eight NFRI indicators *(critical thinking, cognitive flexibility, contextual intelligence, grit personality, agile learner, intrepid change maker, big-picture strategist, and team synergist)*, whereas specialists are largely ready for the near future in terms of two NFRI indicators *(critical thinking and grit personality)*. This defines *the Generalist Advantage* as a unique asset that only generalists have, which is presented even more vividly in Figure 2.2.

The Generalist Advantage is a strategic asset characterized by diverse experience, cross-domain knowledge, and cognitive agility. Generalists excel in pattern recognition, creative problem-solving, and navigating complexity. Their capacity to connect disparate concepts fuels innovation, adaptability, and interdisciplinary collaboration, offering a distinct competitive edge in dynamic environments (especially in the age of AI). Simply put, this advantage arises from the ability of generalists to leverage their diverse backgrounds and versatile mindset to excel in various contexts and situations.

NFRI Indicators	Generalist	Specialist
1) Critical thinking	✓	✓
2) Cognitive flexibility	✓	✗
3) Contextual intelligence	✓	✗
4) Grit personality	✓	✓
5) Agile learner	✓	✗
6) Intrepid change maker	✓	✗
7) Big-picture strategist	✓	✗
8) Team synergist	✓	✗

The Generalist Advantage

Figure 2.2 Defining the Generalist Advantage (TGA).

From an organizational standpoint, there are several benefits of cultivating *the Generalist Advantage*. However, the advantages associated with the generalist mindset can be amplified through a deliberate focus on skill development, cross-functional project experience, and embracing diverse learning opportunities. Some of the elements to think about here are:

◆ How to design employee skill development programs in line with the advantage of generalists?
◆ How leadership training with adaptive capacity can be developed by taking advantage of generalists?
◆ How organizational resilience factors can be assessed with the generalist mindset?

There are a good number of research studies investigating the link between generalist-led businesses and disruptive innovation. These studies, mostly empirical, show that the following four business situations can be a good start to magnify *the Generalist Advantage*:

◆ *Leadership roles:* Generalist leaders equipped with a multi-perspective understanding can be a leadership compass in guiding strategy, innovation, and cross-functional collaboration within organizations.
◆ *Unstructured problems:* Facing ill-defined, ambiguous challenges with undefined best practices requires the out-of-the-box thinking of a generalist.
◆ *New product development:* Generating fresh product or service concepts through drawing on diverse inspiration sources becomes a key generalist strength.
◆ *Change management:* Generalists excel in anticipating the ripples of change across teams and adapting processes to foster resilience during periods of transition.

Overall, *the Generalist Advantage* empowers individuals to thrive in today's multifaceted and interconnected world by leveraging their diverse skills, adaptable mindset, and interdisciplinary approach to problem-solving. It is a boon in a variety of contexts, from business and innovation to education and leadership, enabling generalists to make meaningful contributions and achieve success across diverse domains. In today's interconnected world, having a good understanding of various topics can be advantageous, and the key then is to leverage your diverse strengths to contribute effectively to your team and organization.

"A specialist might find themselves becoming more generalist later in their career, or a generalist might resort to becoming a specialist along the line."

It is also important to understand that the *transition* between generalists and specialists is possible. People learn and change! A specialist might find themselves becoming more generalist later in their career, or a generalist might resort to becoming a specialist along the line. However, the prospects of shifting from specialist to generalist make more sense, and that is where *the Generalist Advantage* comes in.

Chapter 2 Takeaways

- ◆ Experts are overrated! Generalists are more ready for the near future.
- ◆ Utilize the NFRI™—Employ the Near Future Readiness Index to evaluate your preparedness for the future of work.
- ◆ Embrace the TGA™—Understand and apply the principles of the Generalist Advantage to maximize your potential at work and in life.

CHAPTER 3

The Age of AI and the Rise of Generalists

Balancing Complementary with Contrasting Skills

Let's start with some artistic exploration. Let's talk about colors. There are warm colors (such as red and yellow) and cool colors (such as green and blue). Understanding warm and cool colors helps artists create mood and balance in their compositions. Warm colors stir up passion and energy, while cool colors express composure and calmness. The same is the case with complementary and contrasting skills at the workplace. These skills can be placed next to each other with a small differential or can be quite apart creating a strong contrast.

Artists often use complementary colors, but using contrasting colors can create a different visual impact. For example, placing red and green together can intensify both hues. Van Gogh's *Starry Night* painting demonstrates this contrast nicely, by using yellow and blue shades. Whether you're an artist, a problem solver, or a communicator, embracing both complementary and especially contrasting skills enhances your journey through life.

Put simply, a *skill* is the ability to perform a task with proficiency. In today's age of AI, success relies on empowering individuals to collaborate effectively with intelligent systems—demanding a new, collaborative skill set. While AI can process vast amounts of data and perform complex tasks, it often lacks the human judgment, creativity, and critical thinking necessary for nuanced problem-solving and innovative solutions.

35

Complementary skills (also known as *related skills*) are those abilities that complement or enhance each other when combined. These skills tend to align well with each other and contribute to a synergistic effect when applied together. In other words, these are skills that naturally enhance and support each other when combined. They build on a similar foundation of knowledge or aptitude, often flowing together effectively in task execution. Think of them as puzzle pieces with similar edges: they interlock with ease, offering greater strength and functionality than in isolation.

For example, creative skills and analytical thinking skills are complementary skills applied in the workplace. Generating innovative ideas and solutions, and then analyzing and evaluating them to determine their feasibility helps leaders at work. Some more examples of complementary skills could be:

- *Project manager with strong communication skills:* Fosters team cohesion and clarity for smoother project execution.
- *Teacher with skills in educational technology:* Creates more engaging and interactive lessons for students.
- *Salesperson with customer service understanding:* Builds longer-term relationships, not just one-off transactions.
- *Web designer with basic user experience (UX) principles:* Creates more functional, not just beautiful, experiences.

Complementary skills work best for *specialists* and *experts* as they solidify their specific domain and develop more skills by enriching their radius around their desk and team. It does contribute to collective success but only by leveraging the unique strengths of individual team players.

Explain It to Kids

Complementary skills: are like puzzle pieces—each one is different, but together they fit perfectly to make something awesome!

On the other hand, *contrasting skills* (also known as *unrelated skills*) are those abilities that contrast or differ from each other in nature or approach. These skills provide diversity and balance within a team or individual, offering different perspectives and approaches to problem-solving and decision-making. In other words, these skills are mostly drawn from seemingly oppositional domains or ways of thinking. Their strength comes from the synergy of differences, challenging existing perspectives when combined. Think of them as different puzzle sets entirely: when you force them together, an unexpected new image emerges.

Explain It to Kids

Contrasting skills: are like yin and yang, opposites that balance each other out, making you stronger!

Examples of contrasting skills include strategic thinking skills and tactical execution skills. Developing long-term plans and vision, and then executing the details and tactics to achieve those goals are highly valuable in conjunction. Some more examples of contrasting skills are:

- ◆ *Data analyst with storytelling skills:* Extracts compelling, human-centered narratives from raw information.
- ◆ *Engineer with artistic sensitivity:* Designs not just functional products, but ones with intuitive user appeal.
- ◆ *Social worker with business experience:* Creates more successful programs driven by both efficiency and deep community understanding.
- ◆ *Writer with a background in biology:* Crafts science articles with both accuracy and creative engagement.

Contrasting skills work best for *generalist-type profiles.* These skills are valuable because they provide alternative viewpoints and complementary approaches to tackling challenges, leading to more robust and well-rounded solutions.

As you can see, complementary skills work together harmoniously to enhance each other's effectiveness, while contrasting skills provide diversity and balance by offering different perspectives and approaches. Both types of skills are valuable in their own right and can contribute to individual and team success when leveraged appropriately. In the age of artificial intelligence, where technology can take care of basic tasks and humans can work on superior tasks, recognizing and understanding the complementary and contrasting skills between humans and various AI tools, technologies, and platforms can lead to more effective collaboration, decision-making, and problem-solving in a variety of contexts.

For both specialists and generalists, a balance between these two skill types is beneficial—as both complementary and contrasting skills play a pivotal role in various aspects of life, both personally and professionally. In terms of individuals, for generalists especially, developing a blend of both expands their capacity to take on complex projects with fresh perspectives. In terms of teams, a mix of complementary and contrasting skills within a team fosters innovative problem-solving, prevents blind spots, and builds overall resilience for generalists.

Some practical applications, where both these skills can help include: *job searches*—leaders understand how seemingly connected and distinct experiences build a unique profile through complementary and contrasting skill pairings, and then they highlight those overlaps strategically; *self-development*—leaders target growth across areas that complement what you're already good at, while deliberately choosing stretched skills that contrast to open new territory; *team building*—leaders seeking well-rounded groups look beyond a narrow list of job requirements, considering transferable skills and how individuals might build on each other's strengths and differences in a team.

It is also important to note that this isn't just about having skills in a bucket—it's about how you apply and integrate them strategically toward a goal. You can think along these lines to get started:

◆ Do you have a particular task, specific job, or project in mind where you can make use of complementary skills?

- Can you think of your favorite movie, book, painting, historical figure, or fictional character that serves as the closest example of contrasting skills and how these skills can be of great importance considering the contrasts?
- How about an example from your own life when contrasting skills unexpectedly gave you an advantage?

Portable Skills as the Key to Professional Resilience

Are you...

- *aiming for a career shift? or feeling stuck in a career path?* If yes, your portable skills can help as you can identify the hidden transferable gems in your past work.
- *looking to strengthen specific skills? or job hunting in a volatile market?* If yes, your portable skills can help again as you can highlight your resilience narrative based on transferable skills, not just specific past work titles.
- *interested in selling yourself better? or interested in upskilling to safeguard your future?* If yes, your portable skills can help as you can map which one of your transferable skills offers the broadest protection against shifts in demand, and which ones are most valued by employers in the current times.

Explain It to Kids

Portable skills: are like special tools in your backpack that you can use no matter where you go, helping you solve problems and make new friends!

So, do you possess portable skills? *Portable skills* (also known as *transferable skills* or *universal skills*) are abilities that aren't confined to a single job, role, or industry. They help you thrive in varied tasks and make you adaptable across different career paths. Think of them as the foundation you take with you from experience to experience, rather than hyper-niche skills tied to one specific task. For example, there are three portable skills that are valuable for almost all career combinations, especially generalists:

Portable Skill 1: Communication and Influence

- *Aim:* The ability to convey ideas clearly to others.
- *How to develop these skills:*
  - Practice articulating ideas clearly and effectively in conversations, presentations, and meetings.
  - Hone your writing skills by drafting emails, reports, and other written documents with clarity and precision.
  - Listen attentively to others, ask clarifying questions, and demonstrate empathy and understanding in your interactions.
- *Application areas:*
  - A project manager effectively communicating project goals to team members.
  - A customer service representative empathetically addressing customer concerns.
  - A marketing specialist crafting persuasive messages for a campaign.

Portable Skill 2: Problem-Solving

- *Aim:* The ability to find solutions to complex or difficult issues.
- *How to develop these skills:*
  - Generate innovative ideas, approaches, and solutions by thinking outside the box and challenging conventional wisdom.
  - Make well-informed decisions by weighing options, considering consequences, and balancing risks and rewards.
  - Resolve conflicts and disagreements constructively by listening to all parties, finding common ground, and seeking win-win solutions.
- *Application areas:*
  - A cashier quickly devising a workaround when the point-of-sale system shuts down.
  - An accountant creating a more efficient filing system to improve transparency.

- An executive in a political campaign constructing a database to enhance voter outreach.

Portable Skill 3: Critical Thinking

◆ *Aim:* The ability to analyze information objectively to produce refined judgments.

◆ *How to develop these skills:*

- Analyze information, evaluate evidence, and draw logical conclusions to solve complex problems.
- Embrace change and uncertainty with an open mind and be willing to adjust your approach and priorities as needed.
- Bounce back from setbacks and challenges with resilience and perseverance, maintaining a positive attitude and sense of purpose.

◆ *Application areas:*

- A teacher tailoring a curriculum to meet students' unique needs.
- A union representative advocating for factory workers' safety and well-being
- An employee challenging popular opinions in meetings to ensure sound decisions.

PORTABLE SKILLS AND PROFESSIONAL RESILIENCE

Portable skills act as a bedrock of professional resilience, especially in the fast-paced AI-powered era. These skills are not specific to a particular job or field but are valuable in a wide range of situations. Portable skills can increase the overall value of an individual when working with machines, robots, and algorithms. The concern of whether AI will *replace* or *displace* jobs can be best countered by investing in portable skills.

> **"Portable skills can increase the overall value of an individual when working with machines, robots, and algorithms."**

Employers across industries are looking for transferable strengths to thrive in the unprecedented age of *human–computer interaction (HCI)*. For example, your ability to communicate, work in teams, or think critically as part of your portable skill set makes you a valuable addition regardless of your technical experience. So, developing portable skills is essential for career growth, adaptability, and success in today's dynamic AI-paced environment.

If you are still not convinced, here are four reasons why one should invest in portable skills:

- *Career resilience:* The job market is dynamic, or rather unpredictable. Job markets shift, industries emerge and vanish—your ability to adapt is no longer merely an asset; it's survival. Having some good portable skills in your pocket can improve your career resilience.
- *Career transitions:* Switching fields? In today's era of AI-driven enterprises, you don't need to stay in your lane in terms of your career path. And if you decide to take a transition, your portable skills can become the bridge. Proving a relevant skill you already possess is crucial when entering a new arena. These portable skills ensure you aren't locked into a single career track, making you more adaptable in uncertain times.
- *Technology proofing:* Tasks and roles are getting automated, but it's the core human element of how to problem-solve creatively, collaborate, teamwork, and the like, that's most future-proof. Portable skills in the form of human or softer skills add to resilience in the technology-driven landscape.
- *Interdisciplinary fit:* Portable skills facilitate interdisciplinary teamwork, enabling individuals to work effectively with colleagues from diverse backgrounds, disciplines, and perspectives. Individuals with portable skills can foster synergy within multidisciplinary teams and organizations.

HOW TO DEVELOP PORTABLE SKILLS?

Developing portable skills makes you a lifelong learner, embracing new challenges and knowledge acquisition easier. It opens up broader life opportunities. In essence, portable skills (such as communication, influence, problem-solving, and critical thinking) serve as a linchpin of professional resilience, enabling individuals to navigate uncertainty, seize opportunities, and thrive in an ever-evolving work environment. To develop portable skills, I suggest you can make good progress following these three steps:

1. Identify Your Existing Strengths
   - Think of projects, even outside formal jobs, where you solved a problem, led a team, etc. What skills did you use? I am sure you will find real success.
   - In terms of formal education, pursue courses or certifications on portable skills, such as communication skills, problem-solving, and critical thinking.
   - Try some self-assessments, online tools, or career counselors that can help pinpoint hidden abilities you take for granted but are highly portable. Toward the end of this book, there is a link to the *Generalist Quotient Self-Assessment*, which can help you in ascertaining the skills gap.
   - Practice self-reflection and introspection to recognize areas for personal and professional development.
2. Seek Growth Opportunities
   - Volunteer, take a class, or seek diverse challenges outside your comfort zone to force those skills to sharpen. These new activities will help you take the leap.
   - Gain on-the-job learning experience by actively participating in a variety of tasks and projects. Seek out diverse experiences and opportunities for learning and growth.
   - Self-study, read books, watch tutorials, and practice skills independently.
   - Job shadowing and cross-training help! Even briefly engaging with other departments helps cultivate an understanding of how your skills transfer elsewhere.
   - Solicit feedback from others, and use it as an opportunity for self-improvement.
   - Seek out projects at work that tap into underutilized or new skills while remaining in your position. These stretch assignments can provide a new opportunity.

3. Showcase Strategically
- In terms of résumé and cover letters, don't just list skills, weave in narratives and examples demonstrating them in action.
- In terms of interviews, practice stories showing how you used communication to handle a conflict, and adaptability to learn on the fly.

By developing portable skills, you can enhance your employability, adaptability, and effectiveness in a variety of roles and contexts, setting yourself up for success in your career and beyond. The *eight NFRI indicators* mentioned in the previous chapter are all portable skills, and, as shared earlier, generalists perform better than specialists against most of those near future readiness indicators.

If you are a generalist, your diversified interests constantly help you build multiple portable skills, which then make you naturally more resilient. Call it the generalist edge, but each time you acquire a new portable skill, you demonstrate your versatility and adaptability to potential employers, which then adds to your career resilience.

Figure 3.1 describes the spectrum of these three skills that we have discussed in this chapter so far: *complementary skills, contrasting skills,* and *portable skills.* As you can see, portable skills are the

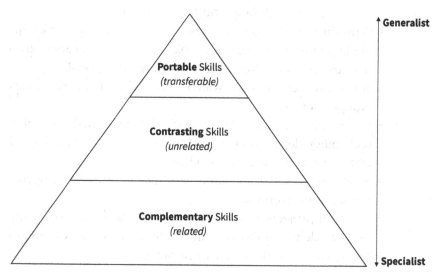

Figure 3.1 Skills pyramid for generalists.

most valuable, and generalists tend to work on them better. Specialists, on the other hand, work closely on accumulating more complementary skills. In terms of investment, portable skills demand more time and effort to develop than contrasting skills, and in a similar tone, gaining contrasting skills requires more time and effort than complementary skills. The pyramid shape here with portable skills at the very top indicates the scarcity of portable skills, especially in comparison with contrasting and complementary skills.

I wish you luck in investing more in your portable skills, as a way to reap the full benefits of *the Generalist Advantage.*

The Power of Versatility in the Era of AI Revolution

In the age of AI, versatility is king, and this book, *The Generalist Advantage*, can help you unlock that versatility. As you progress further in this book, you will:

1. Discover the evolving work landscape in the AI era and how to thrive in it as a generalist executive;
2. Get hands-on strategies for developing a generalist mindset and moving away from traditional specialization;
3. Learn how organizations can harness the incredible potential of generalist leaders, enabling them to outsmart their competition in the age of AI-driven productivity.

Versatile individuals are quick to embrace new technologies, including AI and automation, and adapt their workflows and processes to leverage these tools effectively. For example, a versatile manager with marketing and technology skills in a marketing agency adopts AI-powered analytics tools to analyze customer data, identify trends, and optimize advertising campaigns in real time, allowing them to deliver more targeted and personalized marketing messages to their clients' audiences.

Likewise, versatile leaders demonstrate agility in decision-making, leveraging AI-driven insights and data analytics to make informed decisions quickly and effectively. For example, a versatile supervisor with retail, admin, and analytical skills in a retail chain uses AI-powered predictive analytics to forecast inventory and customer prospects. The firm can reduce or increase stock levels by analyzing historical sales data (such as customer feedback) and peripheral factors (such as weather disruption).

The rise of AI presents both threats and immense opportunities, with versatility being our greatest human "superpower" against potential disruption. Let's take a closer look at what AI does well, and where humans can maintain their uniqueness.

THE CHALLENGE: WHAT AI DOES EXCEPTIONALLY WELL

- *Pattern recognition:* AI excels at processing vast amounts of data, pinpointing trends humans might miss.
- *Automated routine:* Anything structured and repetitive will soon become the domain of increasingly complex AI systems.
- *Precision execution:* AI is flawless when following well-defined rules with predictable inputs.

WHERE HUMANS MAINTAIN UNIQUE VALUE: THE POWER OF VERSATILITY

- *Adaptability to the unexpected:* While AI thrives on predictability, humans excel at tackling surprises, anomalies, or shifting goals that trip up machines.
- *Creative connections:* Combining seemingly unconnected concepts and drawing insights from unrelated fields is where innovative breakthroughs truly lie, and this is where our messy brains shine.
- *Social and emotional intelligence:* AI might predict buying trends, but can't replicate the depth of empathy and nuanced communication needed for strong leadership, complex client relationships, and powerful team dynamics.
- *Ethical guidance and contextual analysis:* AI needs input to learn its values. Understanding nuanced biases, social implications, and making wise decisions beyond pure computation relies on human moral reasoning.

Versatility is a great business advantage. In this AI-driven era, versatility is a survival strategy. Embracing AI's potential while nurturing our uniquely human abilities and its versatility ensures success and resilience. Here are three functional business problems in the context of AI, with the perspective of how being versatile is powerful:

Problem #1 Marketing: AI generates content at scale, but lacks real-world context and emotional resonance.

Solution: Versatile business leaders appreciate AI augmentation, but they understand that AI can displace but not replace them. Versatile executives using their creative, humor, and cultural skills can make the marketing experience relatable.

Problem #2 Manufacturing: Fully automated lines with AI-enabled options at times can face costly shutdowns when faced with unexpected problems such as supply glitches, novel issues, and the like.

Solution: Versatile business leaders are trained for adaptive troubleshooting across multiple stages of the line and understanding the root causes of problems for faster recovery and prevention.

Problem #3 Customer services: AI-powered chatbots disappoint with their lack of real comprehension and frustrate us when our needs are complex.

Solution: Versatile business leaders with emotional and technology skills remain crucial for complex sales deals, building true partnerships, and providing personalized service at the highest level.

AI continues to develop at an astonishing pace. What makes us *uniquely human* may need new definitions over time. This makes ongoing investment in the hardest-to-replicate skills even more crucial for long-term success. Generalists, of course, will do far better than specialists and experts in the era of AI, due to their versatile profiles. As a professional, some of the points to ponder, irrespective of your current profile and persona, are:

> **"AI continues to develop at an astonishing pace. What makes us *uniquely human* may need new definitions over time."**

♦ *Your industry:* Examine which roles in your wider industry rely dangerously on routine tasks, as AI is replacing those roles first.

Next, identify which roles are nonroutine as this is where the demand for versatility will grow.

♦ *Current business problem:* Identify where a "human element" injection might yield greater success than the pure AI or technology solution.

♦ *Future planning:* Brainstorm a resilient company culture, emphasizing the skills to make you AI compatible instead of fearing it!

In summary, the power of versatility in the era of the AI revolution lies in the ability of individuals and organizations to adapt, integrate, collaborate, learn, and make decisions effectively in a rapidly changing and technology-driven environment. By embracing the versatility of generalist leaders and leveraging the capabilities of AI, firms can unearth growth opportunities and realize sustainable development in the digital age.

Overcoming Disciplinary Blind Spots

Disciplinary blind spots, the limitations imposed by our narrow focus within a specialized field, are an ever-present danger for individuals, teams, and organizations. No wonder generalists enjoy having fewer disciplinary blind spots than specialists.

Explain It to Kids

Blind spot: is something you don't see, even though it's right in front of you!

At this point, you might be thinking, "But why do blind spots exist in the first place?" Based on my research with middle and senior executives, over the last eight years, here are three main reasons I have found:

♦ *Cognitive ease:* Our brains crave efficiency. Once deeply immersed in one way of thinking, it's mentally taxing to change gears. We fall back on the familiar, missing opportunities outside that paradigm.

- *Specialization rewards:* Academia and businesses alike create structures that emphasize focus on increasingly niche topics for advancement. A broader view is mostly seen as a "nice to have," not a core part of success.
- *Language barriers:* Even when using similar words, there are nuances across fields. This causes misunderstandings, a false sense of common ground, and prevents interdisciplinary breakthroughs that rely on precise terminology. For example, in one client meeting, I learned that the jargon *POC* stands for *proof of concept*, whereas, in another functional gathering, it was a short form for *principles of controlling*.

STRATEGIES TO OVERCOME BLIND SPOTS

Overcoming disciplinary blind spots is essential for individuals and organizations to effectively navigate the complexities of the modern world, especially where interdisciplinary collaboration and holistic thinking are increasingly valued. You can make your life easier by recognizing that individuals from different disciplines bring unique perspectives, approaches, and insights to the table.

In meetings, most of the time, it looks as if the other person with another department were trying to create blockades, but in reality, both individuals represent different disciplines and have their own standpoints, which may be a blind spot for the other party. Sometimes what you need in this situation is called *epiphany*—a sudden and profound realization or insight, often resulting from a combination of reflection, intuition, and new information. This epiphany then helps overcome blind spots.

To overcome disciplinary blind spots, it is important to encourage open dialogue, collaboration, cross-training, and up-skilling among team members from diverse backgrounds to leverage the full spectrum of knowledge available. The philosophy of *boundary-spanning leadership* is instrumental here. It is a concept that encourages leaders to serve as boundary spanners, who can bridge gaps between different disciplines, departments, and stakeholders. In other words, it is about equipping leaders with the skills and tools needed to facilitate collaboration, communication, and alignment across diverse groups and perspectives.

Here's a multipronged approach to overcoming blind spots at work:

Cultivate Intellectual Humility

- *Acknowledge:* Your expertise has limits! This makes you open to having a *beginner's mind* for outside concepts, sparking that sense of wonder needed to spot insights the specialists may not even notice. *Intellectual humility* then is the awareness of one's limitations in knowledge and the openness to new ideas and perspectives.
- *"Explain it to a child" exercise:* This approach forces simplification of complex concepts from your field. Doing so often highlights where assumptions are built in that an outsider would question, exposing your blind spots.

Seek Discomfort Learning

- *Taste, don't gorge:* Pick areas far outside your comfort zone, such as listening to a different kind of podcast. You will learn that your assumptions may not all hold ground, especially in areas outside your expertise.
- *Attend outlier events:* A physicist at a poetry slam, a marketer at a geology conference—exposing yourself to the thought patterns of other groups is surprisingly powerful.

Build a Diverse Network

- *Informal mentors:* Don't ask people to teach you their whole field, but ask for the *stupid questions* they were afraid to ask when starting out. This helps deconstruct the way information is organized.
- *Online forum lurking:* Read how those in seemingly distant fields discuss current events, social trends, etc. This reveals their lenses, helping you spot limitations in your own by contrast.

Practice Cross-Pollination

- *Concept mashups:* Force a connection (however crazy) between your work and the opposite extreme, such as biology + music, accounting + design philosophy. The results may be absurd, but it trains the brain to seek those links.
- *Collaborate strategically:* Work on multidisciplinary teams intentionally. Observe how people problem-solve differently and identify gaps in understanding. This builds your mental translation tool set.

WAY FORWARD ON SEEING BEYOND BLIND SPOTS

It is time for real practice then! You can try overcoming blind spots, as part of working on *the Generalist Advantage*, by following these six steps:

1. Pick a problem you're currently stuck on. I bet by drawing insights from an unlikely discipline, we can see it anew.

2. Are you a manager? You can identify where structural changes in a workflow process can bring together perspectives that often are disconnected—this is where blind spots become business liabilities.

3. Want to grow personally? Create a *learning adventure list* to push your mind off the well-worn path.

4. Build tolerance for failure. Cross-disciplinary innovation is riskier. Create space for experimentation, where success isn't narrowly defined. This helps teams in spotting those insights locked outside traditional boundaries.

5. Reward the outsider question. Leaders valuing those challenging assumptions help the team fight that urge for confirmation bias within their discipline. This makes it psychologically safe for the person asking, "But, is that even the right question?"

6. Celebrate accidental discovery. Sometimes, when specialists stumble into each other's territory, something truly amazing happens. Foster a culture where that's rewarded! For example, in medicine, antibiotics were created by accidental contamination of penicillium mold in a culture dish in a laboratory, and today antibiotics are one of the most prescribed drugs.

By working on these steps, individuals and organizations can overcome disciplinary blind spots and unlock the full potential of interdisciplinary collaboration, innovation, and problem-solving. Remember, overcoming disciplinary blind spots requires humility, curiosity, and a willingness to collaborate—the ingredients that successful generalists work on religiously, and hence generalists can perform far better here than specialists.

Largely, in the age of AI, businesses are becoming increasingly interconnected and holistic, with technology driving seamless integration across various functions and disciplines. As leaders strive to break down silos and reduce gaps between departments, the ability to overcome disciplinary blind spots has never been more critical. These blind spots, where expertise in one area can limit understanding in another, can hinder innovation and adaptability. Generalists, as compared to specialists, are better off here in overcoming these blind spots, and by virtue of this, they are more prepared to prosper with AI advancements.

Chapter 3 Takeaways

◆ As artificial intelligence (AI) continues to reshape professions and industries, the role of humans is going to be even more significant.

◆ There is going to be an increasing need for balancing complementary skills (related skills) with contrasting skills (unrelated skills), and generalists are uniquely positioned to thrive with this balance.

◆ As AI automates specialized tasks, portable skills (transferable skills) will become the cornerstone of professional resilience, and generalists tend to carry more portable skills in their tool kits than specialists.

PART II

Becoming A Generalist

CHAPTER 4

Four Types of Generalists at Work

Are All Generalists the Same?

The first part of this book introduced *the Generalist Advantage (TGA)*, building the premise that generalists have a greater chance of leading in the near future (especially in the age of AI). In other words, the first part of the book focused on the "why" part of *the Generalist Advantage—why* should one be a generalist?

Once you have understood the incredible power of generalists, the next step you would like to take is to become one. In this second part of the book, I have tried to expand the "how" part of *the Generalist Advantage—how* can one be a generalist?

Even more, through my research shared in this book, I want to help my readers explore the different types of generalists we see at work, and given those classifications of generalists, how can one generalist type be better than another? In case you are already a generalist, you would still love to understand the different kinds of generalists, and you would still love to understand which of the generalist types resonates with you more closely.

As described earlier, generalists are people with a wide range of interests, knowledge, abilities, or experiences. Think of a liberal arts graduate with a background in literature, history, and science who pursues a career in marketing, where they apply their diverse skill set to develop creative campaigns and engage with a wide range of audiences. However, my curiosity in writing this book has been to understand whether there are any exciting distinctions in terms of how generalists manifest themselves and whether there are different types generalists can be classified into. In effect, are all generalists the same? I am amazed to have come to realize, in the process of writing this book, that there are different generalist flavors, and each of them is unique.

As you read further, it is a good time to ponder these two questions:

- Are you energized by many interests at once, or are you a *one deep obsession at a time* person?
- Think of your most recent accomplishment, or a recent innovation you have been part of: Was it due to your *technical knowledge/skill*, or was it due to your ability to make connections from *different industries*, or was it your *big-picture thinking* that reframed the problem itself?

As a head start, answering these two questions for yourself will expose (in part) the type of generalist thinking you lean toward.

So are all generalists the same? Let's try to see this with the lens of *scope, focus,* and *personality.* In terms of *scope*, generalists can be *"multi-potentialities"* who are driven by enthusiasm for a wide range of skills. It is like Leonardo da Vinci with mastery of art, science, and invention, who took joy in sampling varied disciplines. Similar to multi-potentialities, generalists can be *"scanners"* who focus on varied systematic or ad hoc experiences. They like diving deep into a topic for a definite period and then pivoting entirely. This one is like Elon Musk whose ventures span a wide range, from electric vehicles (Tesla) to commercial space travel (Space X) to clean energy (Solar-City) to brain–computer interfaces (Neuralink).

In terms of *focus*, generalists can be *translators* bridging the communication gap between specialists speaking different languages. This generalist turns complex jargon from niche fields into actionable points for collaboration. For example, a freelance digital nomad who embraces remote work opportunities and leverages their diverse skill set in areas such as graphic design, content writing, and project management to pursue a flexible and fulfilling career. On the other front, generalists can be *innovators* focusing on finding unexpected applications, rethinking usual approaches with unconventional tools, and breaking the rules. For example, an urban planner who combines principles of architecture, engineering, sociology, and environmental science to design sustainable and livable cities that meet the needs of diverse communities and stakeholders.

In terms of *personality*, generalists can be *visionaries* focusing on big-picture strategies, spotting overarching trends and future implications. They may draw in specialists based on their vision, acting as a charismatic idea hub that needs a team to execute. For example, a business consultant who specializes in helping companies develop long-term strategic plans and navigate industry disruptions by leveraging their broad knowledge of business operations, market dynamics, and emerging technologies. Alternatively, generalists can be *creative,* drawn to artistic pursuits, combining flair across different media, storytelling methods, or design principles. For example, a multimedia artist who combines visual design, storytelling, and technology to create immersive and interactive experiences that engage audiences across different platforms and media.

These are just a few examples of the diverse types of generalists who exist in various professions and industries. Each type of generalist brings its unique strengths and perspectives to the table, contributing to the richness and diversity of our collective knowledge and expertise. Mind you, I am not talking about the effectiveness of generalists (or specialists) yet, as their effectiveness can depend on specific circumstances, including the pace of change in the field and the nature of the work. To that point, one thing is for sure—*all generalists are* not *the same!*

Shallow, Domain, Skill, Ultra (SDSU)™ Generalist Framework

This discussion is not just about boxes, but more about blends! Also, it is important to understand that interests evolve. Over time, generalists may move between their wide range of interests. This doesn't mark failure as a generalist, but growth in defining a certain ability, strength, or characteristic at a certain time.

In this vein, the term *portfolio career* is also popular these days. A portfolio career is a way of working where an individual has multiple sources of income and doesn't rely on a single, traditional full-time job with one company. This includes freelancing, the gig economy, and side hustles with a viewpoint like that of a generalist—people can be good in multiple areas and can work in different domains without being fixated on one job or role. Portfolio careers are becoming increasingly common, making them a great way to design a fulfilling and adaptable work life.

After studying the various flavors of generalists in my eight years of research on the topic, I was drawn to the point that there could be three ways to understand the classification of different types of generalists:

Basis 1: portable skills and cross-industry adaptability

Basis 2: expertise and perspectives

Basis 3: skills and domains

Let's explore each of these foundations one by one, introducing the *SDSU framework* along the way.

SDSU FRAMEWORK BASED ON PORTABLE SKILLS AND CROSS-INDUSTRY ADAPTABILITY

To start with, the two most important criteria helping us understand the potential of generalists are their portable skills and their cross-industry adaptability.

- *Portable skills* have value and utility beyond the single circumstance where they were initially developed. They can be applied across different contexts or situations. In today's rapidly changing job market, the portability of skills is a highly valued asset. It helps people navigate career paths with more ease and gives employers access to flexible talent.
- *Cross-industry adaptability* refers to the ability to take knowledge, skill, and behavior (KSB) gained in one industry and successfully apply them in a different, sometimes vastly dissimilar, industry. Cross-industry adaptability is also crucial in today's evolving job market as it helps foster innovation, resilience, and competitiveness in an ever-evolving business landscape. It enables individuals and organizations to leverage diverse experiences and insights to drive growth, solve complex problems, and create sustainable value.

Explain It to Kids

Cross-industry adaptability: is like being someone who can change into different costumes and work in different kinds of situations!

Based on the two criteria of portable skills and cross-industry adaptability, and the research that I have done with more than 370 individuals, I would like to present in this chapter the *SDSU™ framework*. It is a framework based on the four types of generalists that we often see at work: shallow generalists, domain generalists, skill generalists, and ultra generalists (hence the term SDSU). This framework in 2×2 matrix form is represented by Figure 4.1, which will guide you throughout this book.

Figure 4.1 divides the generalist types into four quadrants: shallow generalist, domain generalist, skill generalist, and ultra generalist. This framework categorizes four types of generalists based on two dimensions: portable skills (y-axis) and cross-industry adaptability (x-axis). To recall, portable skills refer to the number of transferable skills a person has that can be applied across different contexts, while cross-industry adaptability measures the ability to switch between various industries.

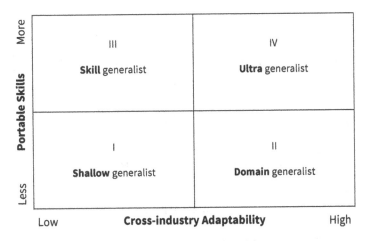

Figure 4.1 SDSU Framework based on portable skills and cross-industry adaptability.

Quadrant I represents shallow generalists, who possess few portable skills and have low adaptability across industries. Quadrant II, domain generalists, also have limited portable skills, but these limited skills are highly adaptable in multiple industries due to their wide domain experiences. Quadrant III, skill generalists, possess many portable skills but may not be as adaptable across different industries, due to their narrow domain experiences. Finally, quadrant IV, ultra generalists, combines both high adaptability and a large number of portable skills, making them capable of navigating various industries while applying a wide range of skills effectively.

SDSU FRAMEWORK BASED ON EXPERTISE AND PERSPECTIVES

Next, let's reframe the 2×2 *SDSU framework* classifying four types of generalists based on two other criteria, as shown in Figure 4.2: expertise (plotted on the y-axis) and perspectives (plotted on the x-axis). The expertise criterion ranges from deep to wide, while the perspectives criterion spans from narrow to broad.

◆ *Expertise* refers to the level of mastery developed through experience, education, training, and practice. Expertise is important as it is often paralleled with task efficiency and performance excellence.

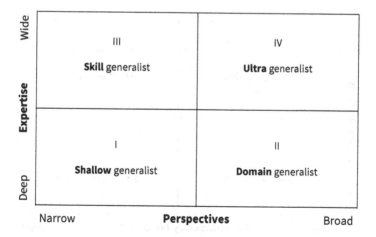

Figure 4.2 SDSU Framework based on expertise and perspectives.

♦ *Perspectives* represent the range of viewpoints an individual can bring to problem-solving or decision-making scenarios. Perspectives are crucial as they indicate the ability to draw on different ways of thinking, allowing for a more holistic approach.

This then implies that shallow generalists have deep expertise (expert thinking) and narrow perspectives (siloed approach). On the contrary, ultra generalists have wide expertise (generalist thinking) and broad perspectives (collaborative approach). Naturally, domain generalists have broad perspectives (taking benefit of a few domains in their portfolio), and skill generalists have wide expertise (taking benefit of a few skills in their portfolio).

SDSU FRAMEWORK BASED ON SKILLS AND DOMAINS

Explain It to Kids

Domain: is like a special playground where you can play with your favorite games and activities, and each playground is different!

In my research studying generalists and specialists alike, I discovered that there is a third and perhaps the most important way to classify generalists, which is by classifying the generalists into four types (and four quadrants) in terms of skills and domains. Table 4.1 attempts to draw more sense into the four quadrants along with a baseline example from the accounting profession. Here, *few* means two or three, and *multiple* means over three. So, a few skills mean two or three skills, and multiple skills mean more than three skills. In other words, ultra generalist is essentially a combination of both domain and skill generalist, as ultra generalist has the advantage of both multiple domains and multiple skills.

Each type of generalist is positioned in a distinct quadrant according to these two dimensions: skills and domains (industries):

♦ *Shallow generalist (quadrant I):* They possess one *major* skill in one *major* domain (industry), typically holding frontline positions. The first type of generalist is not a generalist per se,

Table 4.1 Defining the four types of generalists

No.	Generalist type	Skills	Domains	Example (education, experience)	Progression level	Growth potential
I	Shallow generalist	1 Skill	1 Domain	Accounting skills in an engineering firm	Mostly frontline	Limited
II	Domain generalist	1 Skill	Few domains	Accounting skills in engineering, travel, and pharmaceutical firms	Mostly middle	Moderate to high
III	Skill generalist	Few skills	One domain	Accounting, taxation, project management skills in pharmaceutical firm	Mostly middle	Moderate to high
IV	Ultra generalist	Multiple skills	Multiple domains	Accounting, taxation, project management, problem-solving skills in pharmaceutical, banking, retail, and health care firms	Mostly senior	Exceptional

as it is part of the specialized cadre. Moreover, based on the 2×2 *SDSU framework*, shallow generalists have very few portable skills (skills that can be transferred) and very low cross-industry adaptability (ability to work in different industries).

♦ *Domain generalist (quadrant II):* They have one *major* skill but experience in utilizing that skill set across a few domains (industries), often occupying middle management roles. With reference to the 2×2 *SDSU framework*, domain generalists have very few portable skills (skills that can be transferred) but high cross-industry adaptability (ability to work in different industries).

♦ *Skill generalist (quadrant III):* They have few skills under their belt but experience in using them within a *singular* domain (industry), also typically holding middle management positions. Based on the 2×2 *SDSU framework*, skill generalists have many portable skills (skills that can be transferred) but low cross-industry adaptability (ability to work in different industries).

◆ *Ultra generalist (quadrant IV):* Finally, ultra generalists possess multiple skills across multiple domains, often reaching senior executive levels. In terms of the 2×2 *SDSU framework*, ultra generalists have many portable skills (skills that can be transferred) and high cross-industry adaptability (ability to work in different industries).

Now that we know the skill–domain split of each of the four types of generalists, the *SDSU* 2×2 framework can be elaborated further by showing skills on the y-axis and domains on the x-axis. Quadrant I (shallow generalist) is the least favorable quadrant, and quadrant IV (ultra generalist) is the most favorable quadrant. In line with this discussion of skills and domains, the *SDSU* 2×2 framework can be presented more clearly in Figure 4.3.

In chess, an astute player knows the strength of each piece on the chess board and its right timing with the right moves. Likewise, it is worth knowing about each of the four quadrants, or each of the four types of generalists, especially in terms of their transitions. This framework provides a useful tool for understanding and assessing the generalist capabilities of individuals in the workplace. Here are a few more points to bear in mind, as part of this framework:

◆ Shallow generalists are also known as hyper-specialists.

◆ Domain generalists are also known as industry generalists

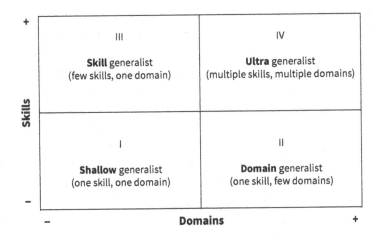

Figure 4.3 SDSU Framework based on skills and domains.

- Skill generalists are based largely on education-related credentials.
- Domain generalists are based largely on work-related experiences.
- Ultra generalists = skill generalists + domain generalists
- Quadrant I is the least favorable quadrant.
- Quadrant IV is the most favorable quadrant.

Possible Paths of the Generalist Advantage (TGA)

My academic research (on the topic of generalists vs specialists) and my industry experience (of working alongside various generalists and specialists) have led me to believe that there are two main paths that one can take while investing in *the Generalist Advantage*: path 1 *(when people switch their companies early in their careers) and* path 2 *(when people switch their companies a bit later in their careers)*.

As a researcher and executive educator at the *Teesside University International Business School* in England, UK, I was awarded the Inter-Act Storytelling Fellowship in 2022 based on this philosophy of path 1 and 2 of generalists. This fellowship under the auspices of the Made Smarter Innovation Network of *UK Research and Innovation (UKRI)* and *Economic and Social Research Council (ESRC)* recognized the contribution of my work titled "The Generalist-Specialist Paradox."

TYPICAL PATH 1: WHEN PEOPLE SWITCH THEIR COMPANIES EARLY IN THEIR CAREERS

a) shallow → domain → skill → ultra (they become domain generalists first and skill generalists later)

It is normally easy for people to generalize their domains first (by moving to new employers based on the same skill set) before they generalize themselves in terms of different skills (acquiring new skills while staying with the same employer), as skill set building takes more time investment. Let's say they have learned accounting skills so they will want to stick to this skill (accounting) and apply it in different domains (industries), as it comes more handy and can be readily taken advantage of. Figure 4.4 shows how the transition of four types of generalists will turn out in the case of typical path 1, i.e. *shallow → domain → skill → ultra*. Please note that the progress an individual or

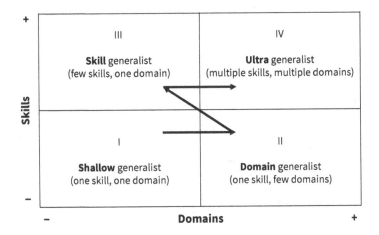

Figure 4.4 Transition of four types of generalists under typical path 1 (when people switch companies early in their careers).

a generalist makes from quadrant I (shallow generalist) to quadrant IV (ultra generalist) here is called *the Generalist Advantage (TGA)*, represented by inverted Z arrow(s) at the center of the 2×2 matrix. *Typical path 1 is the default path, and this book takes this track as the main approach.*

TYPICAL PATH 2: WHEN PEOPLE SWITCH THEIR COMPANIES A BIT LATER IN THEIR CAREERS

b) shallow → skill → domain → ultra (they become skill generalist first and domain generalist later)

Path 1 is the default track for a majority of us as managers and leaders worldwide. However, there can be another typical path where people transition to skill generalist first and domain generalist next, trying to stay within the same company and working on cross-functional opportunities, gaining diverse skills but staying in the same domain (industry) for a relatively longer period of time, which is explained now in typical path 2. Figure 4.5 shows how the transition of four types of generalists will turn out in the case of typical path 2, i.e. *shallow → skill → domain → ultra. TGA* here will work in an "N" rather than "inverted-Z" direction. In either case, it will not make much difference in the strategies and approaches that are mentioned later in this chapter for each type of generalist.

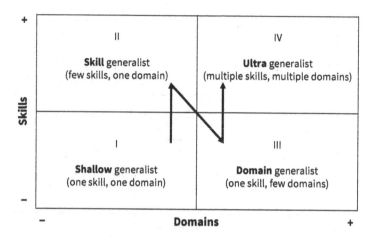

Figure 4.5 Transition of four types of generalists under typical path 2 (when people switch companies a bit later in their careers).

Apart from typical path 1 and 2, there could be other combinations where you may not necessarily start from being a shallow generalist, as you may already be a domain or a skill generalist. Those other combinations could look something like this: (a) if you are already an accomplished skill generalist, you need to take the transition to a domain generalist and then ultra generalist (skill → domain → ultra), or (b) if you are already an accomplished domain generalist, you need to take the transition to a skill generalist and then ultra generalist (domain → skill → ultra).

Now that you have captured some idea about the *SDSU framework* classifying generalists into four types (shallow, domain, skill, ultra), and the possible paths of *TGA, the Generalist Advantage* (typical path 1 and 2), it is time to look into each of the four types of generalists individually, before doing a summative analysis toward the end of this chapter.

Type I: Shallow Generalist (S)
WHO IS A SHALLOW GENERALIST?

A shallow generalist (also known as a hyper-specialist) is someone who has one major skill predominately in one domain/industry, as presented in Table 4.2:

Table 4.2 Defining a shallow generalist

No.	Generalist type	Skills	Domains	Example (education, experience)	Progression level	Growth potential
I	**Shallow generalist**	1 Skill	1 Domain	Accounting skills in an engineering firm	Mostly frontline	Limited

Here one skill is to the level of mastery. In other words, it's one major or one primary skill that a shallow generalist has mastered, i.e. one core skill with a view to take it to the level of perfection. It often carries a negative connotation within discussions of *the Generalist Advantage*, but it is a usual way to take a start on the journey to becoming a generalist. The perceived *shallowness* here implies a lack of varied skills across several domains.

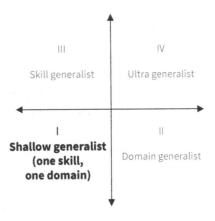

Shallow generalists are specialists who are *master of one* in the *jack-of-all-trades, master of none* proverb. They dive deep and contribute substantially to any single field. However, this is often a case of unreliable expertise. Unreliable as it may give the appearance of understanding complex subjects, but understanding of complex topics cannot be sufficient without a reasonably good understanding of surrounding topics (nuances that generalists master). This at times can cause miscommunications or costly mistakes. In terms of career development, it kills the exploration phase. To be successful as a generalist, breadth over depth is the goal, and shallow generalists are far from it. In fact, sampling many 'shallow dips' is better than a deep dive as it provides a sound breadth that helps personally and professionally, especially in the long run.

In terms of cross-pollination, shallow generalists have less rigorous expeditions into unfamiliar fields, which affects in terms of building mental connections. Remarkably, surface-level knowledge of generalists sparks a creative thought process that specialists, bound by orthodoxy, lack. Likewise, in terms of agility and rapidly changing markets, an initial "broad but not super deep" work package can be helpful in solving a wide and complex range of problems. Generalists here offer solutions that have more chances of pushing the needle in terms of momentum, which deep expertise of shallow generalists often cannot.

Despite the criticism, this *shallowness* can be a current necessity (for example, an individual may try to position themselves in a certain field due to early career mapping), but it cannot be a strategic advantage.

CHARACTERISTICS OF A SHALLOW GENERALIST

The three main characteristics of a shallow generalist are:

Deep expertise: Shallow generalists possess in-depth knowledge and honed skills in their specific field. Their niche area allows them to solve complex problems, recognize subtle patterns, and provide unique insights not found in generalists on that topic.

Attention to detail: Shallow generalists understand that every detail matters in their field. Their meticulous approach ensures accuracy, thoroughness, and quality output. Their work is often trusted due to the consistency of their precision.

Focus: Shallow generalists are passionate about their chosen focus and are highly dedicated, able to persevere through challenges and complex projects within their domain.

PAINS AND GAINS OF A SHALLOW GENERALIST

Table 4.3 explores the trade-offs inherent in the shallow generalist approach.

HOW NOT TO BECOME A SHALLOW GENERALIST

As shown in Figure 4.2, shallow generalists have deep expertise (expert thinking) and narrow perspectives (siloed approach)—the bottom left quadrant. In terms of *the Generalist Advantage*, this is not a good place as their growth is limited, and their progression mostly

Table 4.3 Pains vs gains of a shallow generalist

Pains (Shallow generalist)	Gains (Shallow generalist)
• Big-picture thinking: Shallow generalists often fail to see the broader implications of decisions or strategies.	• High credibility: In contexts where specialized expertise is valued, shallow generalists are seen as more credible due to their forte.
• Interdisciplinary collaboration: Shallow generalists often struggle to collaborate and communicate with people from different fields.	• Confidence: Shallow generalists tend to be more confident in their competence in a specific area or domain.
• Flexibility: Shallow generalists are largely inflexible, and they are not able to pivot and take on new challenges or opportunities in rapidly changing environments.	• Career in specialized industries: Shallow generalists having deep expertise can grasp career advancement opportunities in industries that value specialized knowledge.

hits the ceiling of frontline management (as opposed to senior management). Here are a few ways to address this:

1. *Explore diverse topics:* Engage in reading, attending seminars, or taking online courses in various subjects to gain exposure to different fields and disciplines.
2. *Develop versatility:* Emphasize adaptability and versatility in your skill set, allowing you to perform adequately across a range of tasks or roles.
3. *Network and collaborate:* Interact with individuals from different backgrounds and industries to exchange ideas and insights, broadening your perspective and knowledge base.
4. *Stay informed:* Stay up to date on current events, trends, and developments across multiple domains to maintain a general awareness of various topics.

WHERE DO SHALLOW GENERALISTS THRIVE?

Shallow generalists thrive in environments where deep knowledge and niche skills add unique value, solve complicated problems, and drive innovation. In the near past, demand for shallow generalists has been rising, as we have been living in the world of experts and specialists. However, in the near future (artificial intelligence era), the demand for shallow generalists will decline over other types of generalists (domain generalist, skill generalist, and ultra generalist). Here's a breakdown of where shallow generalists fit well, with reference to industry sectors and workplace environments:

Industry Sectors (Where Shallow Generalists Best Fit)

♦ Technology:
  • Software development (specific coding languages, database architecture, cybersecurity)
  • IT infrastructure (network specialists, cloud computing experts)
  • Artificial intelligence (machine learning engineers, data scientists)
♦ Health Care:
  • Medical specialties (cardiology, oncology, neurology)
  • Pharmaceutical research (specific disease areas, drug development)
  • Medical technology (radiologists, surgical robotics specialists)
♦ Sciences:
  • Research (specific fields such as molecular biology, astrophysics)
  • Environmental science (climate modeling, ecological impact analysis)
  • Forensics (DNA analysts, crime scene reconstruction)

Workplace Environments (Where Shallow Generalists Best Fit)

♦ Large Corporations:
  • Shallow generalists best fit in large organizations with well-defined departments and complex projects, requiring deep expertise (examples: technology consultant specializing in a specific software implementation, quality auditor focusing on a particular industry niche)
♦ Highly Regulated Industries:
  • Shallow generalists succeed in fields with strict regulations and standards (examples: aviation engineer overseeing safety certifications, patent attorney with in-depth knowledge of intellectual property law).
♦ Research & Development:
  • Cutting-edge R&D departments often require shallow generalists to tackle intricate challenges and explore uncharted

territories (examples: microbiologist working on novel vaccine development, software engineer developing advanced AI algorithms).

Type II: Domain Generalist (D)
WHO IS A DOMAIN GENERALIST?

A domain generalist (also known as an industry generalist) is someone who has one major skill but exposure to a few different domains/industries, as presented in Table 4.4:

Let's start with these two questions:

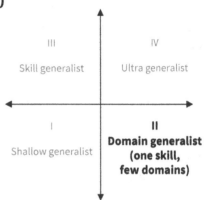

◆ Are you facing a complex business problem within your industry but are looking for out-of-industry solutions? A domain generalist perspective might reveal unseen angles.

◆ Do you want to build a dynamic team alongside specialists? Here again, the domain generalist with their niche skill set but diverse industry exposures can cultivate a growth mindset in the team, drawing experience from different industries.

Domain generalists' adaptability is impressive as it offers distinct advantages in today's fast-paced business landscapes. Typically, a domain generalist has a comprehensive understanding of various industries and their sectors, including their operations, trends, challenges, and opportunities.

Table 4.4 Defining a domain generalist

No.	Generalist type	Skills	Domains	Example (education, experience)	Progression level	Growth potential
II	**Domain generalist**	1 Skill	Few domains	Accounting skills in engineering, travel, and pharmaceutical firms	Mostly middle	Moderate to high

They can connect dots and bridge relationships between industries, their sectors, and subsectors. Their flexible application of a singular skill set helps them apply the same level of expertise in varied scenarios while navigating through different industries. In terms of cross-industry insight, this type of generalist leverages knowledge from adjacent or disparate industries for inspiration. They bring novel perspectives to the team and wider organization by recognizing inherent patterns and outside practices.

Domain generalists play a crucial role in driving innovation, growth, and competitiveness within their respective industries by leveraging their deep cross-industry expertise to seize opportunities for business progression. Business and management consultants (from the likes of McKinsey & Company, Boston Consulting Group, Bain & Company, and Accenture) perform very well in this space. They provide expertise and guidance to clients across different industries and sectors, requiring them to have a broad knowledge base that can be applied to solve various business challenges and opportunities.

Domain generalists are "innovation catalysts" as they identify gaps, potential synergies, and overlooked opportunities by viewing the industry through a wider lens. They spark unique collaborations and foster creative problem-solving. In addition to that, domain generalists are "anticipating disruptors" as they recognize seismic shifts, regulatory changes, and emerging technologies influencing their industry early on. They help organizations stay ahead of the curve rather than being blindsided by change.

CHARACTERISTICS OF A DOMAIN GENERALIST

The three main characteristics of a domain generalist are:

Industry knowledge and exposure: Domain generalists have a good understanding of the inner workings, trends, and dynamics of selected industries, acquired through their rotation in different industry sectors.

Identifying external opportunities: Domain generalists excel at industry-specific challenges and capitalize on emerging opportunities, proving to be highly informed problem solvers and outside-in innovation catalysts.

Networking and relationship-building: Domain generalists have a strong network of contacts and relationships between different industries, allowing them to collaborate, share insights, and stay informed about industry best practices.

PAINS AND GAINS OF A DOMAIN GENERALIST

Table 4.5 explores the trade-offs inherent in the domain generalist approach.

HOW TO BECOME A DOMAIN GENERALIST

Becoming a domain generalist involves developing an understanding of different industries or sectors, as well as acquiring cross-expertise across various areas within those industries or sectors. Here's how one can become a domain generalist:

1. Map Your Landscape:
* *Identify micro-niches:* Subsectors, key processes, and interconnected roles within industries. Visualize their relationships across industries, not just your current place within an industry.

Table 4.5   Pains vs gains of a domain generalist

Pains (Domain generalist)	Gains (Domain generalist)
• Generalization risk: Having exposure to different industries, domain generalists might risk generalizing their experiences to a stand-alone industry issue on hand.	• Enhanced Team Communication: As the translators across specialties, domain generalists facilitate project cohesion and mitigate issues before they snowball.
• Limited specialization: While domain generalists possess a broad understanding of industries, they may lack deep specialization in a specific area, which can limit opportunities where specialized expertise is needed.	• Spotting emerging opportunities: Domain generalists see where untapped market shifts are headed and new products are needed, ahead of those trapped in old patterns of thinking.
• Overwhelming scope: The exposure required to become a domain generalist can be overwhelming, especially in rapidly evolving industries with complex dynamics and regulations.	• Flexibility: Domain generalists are flexible, and by learning from different industries, they can navigate changes, disruptions, and challenges well.

- *Learning from the ground:* Shadow people in different areas of the industry, even at entry level, to understand pain points and daily workflows you might otherwise be blind to.
2. Strategic Learning Plan:
   - *Industry newsletters and reports:* Consume information beyond your usual sources. Seek out viewpoints from adjacent sectors to see where yours connect/fall behind unexpectedly.
   - *Industry conferences:* Seeking out talks and events focused on aspects of an industry you barely interact with yields novel insights. For instance, an accountant at a design-focused conference gains new marketing potential awareness.
3. Diversify Your Projects and Activities:
   - *Cross-functional collaboration:* Volunteer for projects outside your primary role in the organization, exposing you to new challenges and ways of thinking within your industry first.
   - *Side gigs outside your company:* Freelance work, side hustles, and consultancy work with other industries can render experiential lessons on the vast differences between different industries—something that internal work mostly obscures.

WHERE DO DOMAIN GENERALISTS THRIVE?

Domain generalists thrive where adaptability and the ability to connect the dots across disciplines are valued. Their broad perspective and willingness to tackle different challenges make them highly adaptable in evolving work environments. Moreover, domain generalists because of their adaptive leadership style are ideal for leading cross-functional teams, promoting a culture of agility, breaking down silos, and steering initiatives with cross-sector impact. Here's a breakdown of industry sectors and workplace environments where domain generalists excel:

Industry Sectors (Where Domain Generalists Excel)

- ◆ Cross-Industries:
  - Domain generalists' broad understanding of different business sectors makes them ideal for teams working across business

units in different industries. They bridge communication gaps and facilitate collaboration (for example, banking, retail, customer service, engineering, and aviation industry).

♦ Emerging Industries:
   • When a field is new or undergoing significant transformation, domain generalists with a strong learning capacity can quickly grasp overarching concepts, explore new technologies, and adapt to changing landscapes (for example, AI and robotics, biotechnology, quantum computing, space exploration).

Workplace Environments (Where Domain Generalists Excel)

♦ Start-ups and Small Businesses:
   • In early-stage or small companies, domain generalists are invaluable due to their adaptability and multitasking abilities. They often wear many hats, handling a variety of roles such as marketing, operations, and customer service (for example, a domain generalist well versed in the energy sector, understanding policy, technology, and societal impact of renewables can be a great fit for a sustainability start-up).

♦ Fast-Paced and Dynamic Environments:
   • Domain generalists handle change and ambiguity well. They excel in industries with constant innovation, evolving customer needs, or rapid market shifts where their flexibility is an asset (for example, a technology enthusiast having domain exposure to programming languages, data centers, and networking protocols can provide versatile solutions in the IT market, as this environment shifts faster than any one niche technology expertise can keep up with).

♦ Consulting:
   • Consultants address diverse client needs. Domain generalists can effectively analyze overarching problems, identify key areas for improvement, and offer strategic insights drawn from their broad experience in different industries (for example, business process improvement consultant looking at process improvement best practices from across industries).

◆ Mergers and Acquisitions:
  • Domain generalists offer nuanced insight during mergers, strategic partnerships, and new market expansions. They spot cultural integration risks and identify hidden growth potential others might overlook (for example, an investment banker as a domain generalist can advise companies on deal strategy, valuation, finding potential buyers or acquisition targets, negotiation, and seeing the entire transaction through).

Type III: Skill Generalist (S)
WHO IS A SKILL GENERALIST?

A skill generalist is someone who has a few different skills predominately in one domain/industry, as presented in Table 4.6:

Let's start with these two questions:

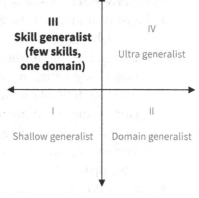

◆ Are you stuck on a project due to a constrained skill set? Skill generalists can approach your current problem-solving workflow and expose the additional skills that could spark surprising progress.
◆ Does your team work mostly in pigeonholes? Here again, skill generalists can help by developing a team of diverse talents to break from pigeonholing, which also translates into better future-proofing of your team.

Skill generalists often excel at adapting to new roles, projects, and challenges by leveraging their broad skill set. They are catalysts for problem-solving. Their skills can be *soft skills* (leadership skills) as well as *hard skills* (technical skills).

Skill generalists are best known for their *cognitive adaptability*— the ability to change and modify thinking strategies and behaviors in response to new information. In terms of skills, they rapidly pick up

Table 4.6 Defining a skill generalist

No.	Generalist type	Skills	Domains	Example (education, experience)	Progression level	Growth potential
III	Skill generalist	Few skills	1 Domain	Accounting, taxation, project management skills in pharmaceutical firm	Mostly middle	Moderate to high

new concepts, navigate unfamiliar knowledge territory, and apply existing learnings in novel ways. They continuously work on learning new skills and expanding their skills tool kit beyond their prime expertise. In short, they invest in a thinking to think and learning to learn mindset.

In terms of teamwork and mentorship, skill generalists' willingness to guide others by sharing insights based on their multiple skills and facilitating collaborative problem-solving spaces is commendable. In fact, recognizing strengths or skills across team members to leverage unique contributions for the collective team goal is their priority. They are known for active listening as they seek diverse subject-matter viewpoints, recognizing value in the experience and insights of others. This is crucial for bridging divides between team members or stakeholders with seemingly differing agendas.

In terms of honing their own skills, skill generalists benefit from the "teach as you learn" approach. Whether explaining something to a peer or journaling their thought process, their approach forces them to distill complexities and expose misunderstandings. The teach as you learn approach is a powerful learning strategy. Skill generalists use it for both strength development and areas of improvement. In terms of solidifying knowledge, explaining a concept to someone else, even if you're still learning it yourself, requires one to organize, structure, and clarify one's understanding. Teaching helps us identify weaknesses faster, as we get to see the gaps where more practice or clarity is needed.

Skill generalists are excellent collaborators in cross-functional teams, as they can apply different skills to cross-functional team challenges and performance. Moreover, due to their flexible skill set, they can also perform exceptionally well in hybrid roles (face-to-face + remote). For instance, a growth marketer with skills in data analytics, content creation, and campaign management, a community manager blending customer service, content creation, and online engagement skills, a marketing coordinator handling social media, website updates, and customer communications, and an operations assistant involved in logistics, administration, and customer support.

In short, becoming a skill generalist requires dedication, continuous learning, and a commitment to personal and professional development. While there may be challenges and sacrifices along the way, the gains of becoming a skill generalist, including leadership potential, can lead to rewarding career opportunities and personal growth in the long run.

CHARACTERISTICS OF A SKILL GENERALIST
The three main characteristics of a skill generalist are:

Diverse skill set: Skill generalists possess a range of skills across different areas, including technical, creative, analytical, interpersonal, and leadership skills.

Problem-solving abilities: Skill generalists excel at analyzing complex problems, identifying root causes, and developing innovative solutions by drawing on their diverse skill sets and multiskilled perspectives.

Communication and collaboration: Skill generalists possess strong communication and collaboration skills, enabling them to work effectively with differently skilled and talented individuals.

PAINS AND GAINS OF A SKILL GENERALIST
Table 4.7 explores the trade-offs inherent in the skill generalist approach.

Table 4.7   Pains vs gains of a skill generalist

Pains (Skill generalist)	Gains (Skill generalist)
• Time and effort: Developing a range of skills requires time, effort, and dedication. Skill generalists may need to invest resources in education, training, and practice to acquire and master multiple skills.	• Leadership growth: Carrying multiple skills in their tool kit makes skill generalists leaders who are in high demand, and employers and management will want to invest in their growth.
• Skill maintenance: Once skill generalists acquire a set of skills, they will also need to invest time and effort in maintaining and updating them to stay current and relevant in a rapidly changing world.	• High performers: Skill generalists are well suited for leadership roles, as they possess a broad range of skills and knowledge that enable them to lead teams, drive change, and achieve business objectives effectively.
• Feeling overwhelmed and burnt out: Trying to juggle multiple skill development initiatives simultaneously can lead to feeling overwhelmed and burnt out for skill generalists.	• Unlocking career agility: Job role switching inside the organization becomes relatively easy for skill generalists as they fit in easily in different functions and business units. Job searching also becomes favorable as it is less niche-dependent.

HOW TO BECOME A SKILL GENERALIST

Becoming a skill generalist means intentionally cultivating a wide range of abilities, while perhaps not reaching top-level expertise in all. Also, it is important for those who wish to become a skill generalist to acquire a diverse range of skills, as early as you can in your career. Considering the pains and gains listed, here is how one can become a successful skill generalist:

1. Embrace the Learning Mindset
   - *Curiosity-driven exploration:* Follow passions beyond job description. Experiment with varied online courses, tutorials, etc. The thrill of gaining competence itself becomes the drive, not merely the end goal.
   - *Sampling mentality:* It's about breadth, initially focusing more on the process of acquiring varied skills, and less on reaching perfection. This playful discovery helps you find unexpected hidden talent pockets.
   - *Focus on foundations:* Early on, prioritize grasping core concepts to spot how knowledge transfers. For instance,

web designing helps if you later dabble in graphics, even if that isn't your specialization area.

2. Strategic Skill Development
   - *Map existing strengths:* What do you learn quickly? Are you drawn to creative tools, systems thinking (one needs to understand parts to understand the system), client liaison roles, and the like? This points you toward how wide-skill generalist you naturally are.
   - *Target cross-discipline synergies:* Prioritize developing skills that complement each other. For instance, coding while also dabbling in user experience (UX) design. This lets you build stacks of useful competencies that compound in power.
   - *Emphasize transferables:* Actively seeking new experiences for the transferable meta-skills (problem-solving, communication, project iteration cycles) is how you make diversity a tool, not scatterbrained chaos.

3. Practical Application is Key
   - *Project mindset:* Frame each skill, no matter how basic, as part of a potential future project. For example, learning to cook isn't about that meal, but adaptability on a tight budget.
   - *Seek micro-opportunities:* Small side hustles and freelance tasks force applications of varied skills in a low-risk setting. The pressure brings focus, which the classroom lacks.
   - *Document your process:* Blog, journal, or diarize your journey. Articulating what you learn helps solidify it, spotting patterns you may miss, and serves as proof of the learning path for yourself and your organization.

WHERE DO SKILL GENERALISTS THRIVE?

Skill generalists thrive in environments where their versatility and ability to wear many hats are valued. They excel in roles demanding a mix of technical, creative, and interpersonal skills, providing a valuable, adaptable resource for various organizations. Here's a breakdown of where skill generalists thrive, along with industry sector and workplace examples:

Industry Sectors (Where Skill Generalists Excel)

◆ Technology and Digital Industries
  • The constant evolution of technology necessitates those who can learn, adapt, and master new tools and skills quickly (for example, skill generalists capable of web design, basic coding, data analysis, and digital marketing are in demand).

◆ Education and Training Industries
  • Educators, especially those developing multidisciplinary or skills-focused programs, benefit from a diverse skill set (for example, skill generalists who can design curricula, create engaging materials, and use various teaching and facilitation methods will be valued more).

◆ Creative Industries
  • Creative fields such as filmmaking, game design, or experience design benefit from skill generalists who possess different skills and can draw inspiration from diverse sources. They can bring unexpected combinations of expertise to create unique and engaging experiences (for example, skill generalists can bridge areas such as graphic design, photography, writing, and basic video editing skills for creativity).

Workplace Environments (Where Skill Generalists Excel)

◆ Product Development
  • Product managers often wear multiple hats—design, marketing, and technology (for example, a factory manager, as a skill generalist, can help synthesize requirements, communicate with engineers, understand user needs, and help deliver the right offering to clients).

◆ Customer Services
  • Skill generalists are adept at handling various customer needs and adapting their approach (for example, a customer experience executive, as a skill generalist, may showcase a broad skill set—strong communication, technical troubleshooting, problem-solving, and empathy, which can be highly regarded by clientele).

- Freelance Work
  - Skill generalists are well suited for freelance careers. As freelancers often work on a variety of projects for different clients, they require having a diverse skill set that can be applied across different contexts (for example, a freelance graphic designer may also possess skills in web design, branding, and digital marketing).
- Executive Coaching
  - Executive coaches are professionals who help others achieve goals and often draw on multiple skills: communication, goal setting, strategy, and even some creative coaching techniques (for example, an executive coach, as a skill generalist, can help a CEO clarify their vision, evaluate strategic options, and make sound decisions aligned with their company's long-term goals).

Type IV: Ultra Generalist (U)
WHO IS AN ULTRA GENERALIST?

An ultra generalist is someone who has multiple skills in multiple domains/industries, as presented in Table 4.8:

Is the "ultra" path for you? Consider these three questions:

- Does knowledge excite you as much as its application? Pure love of learning is core to ultra generalist mentality, with output sometimes less clear-cut than specialists and other types of generalists who follow existing paths.
- Are you comfortable being wrong? Experimentation and failures along the way

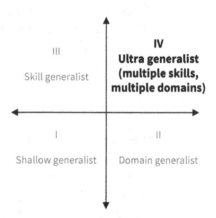

66 Are you comfortable being wrong? Experimentation and failures along the way are necessary stepping stones. 99

Table 4.8   Defining an ultra generalist

No.	Generalist type	Skills	Domains	Example (education, experience)	Progression level	Growth potential
IV	**Ultra generalist**	Multiple skills	Multiple domains	Accounting, taxation, project management, problem-solving skills in pharmaceutical, banking, retail, and health care firms	Mostly senior	Exceptional

are necessary stepping stones. The ultra generalist learns through audacious ventures.

♦ Is your legacy beyond your work? Ultra generalist aptitude often draws those seeking to have broad societal influence in contrast with those who have a niche focus.

An ultra generalist with a broad range of skills across multiple disciplines is the supreme level of a generalist, implying a level of proficiency in various fields. Based on their diverse industry experience, they can act as valuable consultants—who advise companies from a wide range of industries, on a wide range of issues, such as strategy development, market analysis, operational efficiency, and regulatory compliance. Likewise, based on their wide range of skills, they enjoy leadership beyond technical skills and roles. Ultra generalists are known for building those transferable *meta-skills* in an intentional way.

Ultra generalists are by definition *polymaths* and *Renaissance thinkers*. These individuals may work independently or within organizations, pursuing intellectual exploration across fields. They often contribute as authors, speakers, consultants, and futurists, sharing insights from their cross-disciplinary perspectives. At times, ultra generalists might face skepticism in organizations with rigid structures as they may not immediately understand their value. In that case, ultra generalists often need to prove themselves by demonstrating tangible outcomes and the unique impact they provide. However, they are polymaths, as they blend in science, arts, philosophy, and other disciplines, and they seek interconnections at a grand scale.

Some examples of ultra generalists include:

- *Leonardo da Vinci:* He was the epitome of blending art, science, and engineering. His breadth sparked insights no single scholar of his time could achieve. He excelled as a painter, sculptor, architect, engineer, scientist, and inventor.
- *Elon Musk:* He favors generalist roles, big-time. His early success relied on spotting potential links between software, payment systems, and space flight, that entrenched beyond a single sector. Now, Elon Musk is known for his significant contributions to the fields of aerospace, automotive, energy, and transportation.
- *Steve Jobs:* Ultra generalists often thrive at the intersection of the technical and the everyday user experience, like him. He was not an engineer, yet had a deep understanding of technology with a design-minded focus that drove Apple.

It is also important to acknowledge that ultra generalists have unconventional career paths. Many ultra generalists forge unique careers tailoring their interests. They might combine freelancing, teaching, and consulting with a passion project, creating a fulfilling and multifaceted professional life. So much so, that ultra generalists can perform well in nonprofit and social impact organizations too. These organizations having limited resources value versatile employees. Ultra generalists can take on administrative tasks, fundraising, communication, and program management, which is a fantastic package for nongovernmental organizations (NGOs). This sounds good, but ultra generalists need a lot of self-direction. Over their unconventional career, they demonstrate high levels of self-motivation and the ability to manage their own learning and career paths proactively. As they are nonlinear thinkers, their comfort with ambiguity is their superpower. Besides, they can entertain seemingly unrelated concepts simultaneously, forging unexpected intellectual connections beyond traditional pathways.

Moreover, ultra generalists are meta-skill focused. More than specific knowledge, they master learning itself. Rapid knowledge acquisition, complex pattern recognition, and creative synthesis in problem-solving become their most vital skills, and like a second skin to them. They like exploration sprints as they dedicate specific time to researching unfamiliar concepts. The key then is to avoid endless learning paralysis and setting actionable and achievable goals. They are rapid idea generators, for sure. If quick, outsider-perspective brainstorming is needed, assigning team members brief forays outside their domain does this. They may return with not fully realized solutions, but they certainly have a spark that others would not generate.

In terms of acceptance, ultra generalists are often misunderstood by traditionalists, as they struggle with roles in rigid workplaces. This is compounded by their inability to fit into standard educational pathways or specialization-heavy cultures. In terms of focus, ultra generalists can find themselves down endless rabbit holes. So it requires deliberate focus to turn grand insights into actionable plans others can implement, as "pure idea generators" often fail to bridge that gap. In terms of communication across paradigms, they at times feel frustrated when explaining concepts leaping across disciplinary boundaries to a wider organization. Here, ultra generalists must learn to distill complexity without oversimplification for impact.

So yes, ultra generalists capture the essence of pushing *generality* to its outer limits. They can improve communication across siloed teams hindering innovation. They can help in product strategy, bringing in outside industry viewpoints to expose unseen paths. From a business and leadership perspective, ultra generalists bring a unique set of skills and perspectives to the table. They are well suited for leadership roles that require strategic thinking, innovation, and the ability to navigate complexity and uncertainty. Through their versatility, ultra generalists can lead to significant contributions and impact in various fields and industries. Also, what's even better is that being an ultra generalist could be the best way to future-proof your career. To take a head start on becoming an ultra generalist, you can map out your portable skills within your area and adjacent sectors, which in turn will make you more resilient.

CHARACTERISTICS OF AN ULTRA GENERALIST

The three main characteristics of an ultra generalist are:

Cross-functional breadth: Ultra generalists have a vast and comprehensive breadth of skills that can be applied to multiple business functions, including HR, finance, marketing, IT, and general management.

Multidisciplinary expertise: Ultra generalists excel at integrating insights from different fields of study to solve complex problems, generate innovative ideas, and drive collaboration in various manufacturing, services, and hybrid industries.

Versatility: Ultra generalists are highly adaptable and flexible in acquiring and applying skills to a wide range of roles, projects, scenarios, and environments. Their "order through chaos" philosophy proves to be successful in making connections and synthesizing information, in an attempt to work across diverse domains.

PAINS AND GAINS OF AN ULTRA GENERALIST

Table 4.9 explores the trade-offs inherent in the ultra generalist approach

HOW TO BECOME AN ULTRA GENERALIST

Becoming an ultra generalist is a daring but highly rewarding path filled with unique challenges and extraordinary potential. Here's how one can become an ultra generalist, along with its pains and gains from a business and leadership perspective:

1. Embrace the Pursuit of Knowledge
   - *Insatiable curiosity:* Be driven by the need to understand, uncover, and connect ideas—the thrill is in the learning, not solely the results it will achieve later.
   - *Intellectual play:* View learning as experimentation, with joy in exploring even if there's no immediate return. This combats frustration when outcomes differ from what specialists have clearer road maps toward.
   - *Cross-paradigm exploration:* Blend the arts, sciences, technology, etc. Seek out contrasting worldviews to deliberately

Table 4.9 Pains vs gains of an ultra generalist

Pains (Ultra generalist)	Gains (Ultra generalist)
• Slower early output: Ultra generalists undergo a real test of patience as their results take longer than focused specialist paths. Having small proof-of-concept projects showcasing their unique ability before fully sketched solutions can be helpful.	• Futurists: Ultra generalists spot major trends years ahead due to their wide lens, unclouded by existing market constraints. This becomes a leadership superpower in times of accelerated change.
• Loneliness of the path: Ultra generalists have wide-ranging curiosity, and they may struggle to find others who share their specific combination of interests or those who understand the way their mind jumps between topics. This can make it difficult to cultivate deep intellectual connections.	• Disruptors: Ultra generalists are radical innovators as their unlikely connections often create novel value. While not every idea pans out, the unique angles offered are how organizations stay one step ahead, avoiding being disrupted by what they didn't see coming.
• Social acceptance: Ultra generalists are often misunderstood in traditional work environments as "flighty" or "lacking focus." Learning to communicate your value sporadically becomes crucial.	• Silo breakers: Ultra generalists are ultimate collaborators, seeing how teams with specialized know-how can create something bigger than their single-skill silos. In bridging gaps, they win hearts as silo breakers and change agents.

challenge preexisting mental models and break linear thinking.

2. Master Meta-Learning Skills

- *Rapid knowledge acquisition:* Develop systems for information intake, note-taking, and quick grasping of core concepts from varied domains. In this context, meta-learning is the process of learning how to learn. Meta-learning gives generalists an edge, allowing them to quickly absorb new information from a variety of domains.

- *Pattern recognition:* Consciously search for connections between seemingly unrelated areas. Train your mind through games, puzzles, and analysis of trends across wide sources.

- *Idea synthesis:* Practice bringing together discordant thoughts—force those unusual blends and analyze the insights born from the dissonance. This is how innovation beyond what silos create becomes possible.

3. Intentional but Nonlinear Path
- *Exploration seasons:* Dedicate time for deep dives into radically different topics without an immediate goal beyond acquiring that diverse foundation.
- *Connect to macro purpose:* Recall and reinforce the purpose as the end goal throughout. This will balance intellectual wandering with overarching questions and will help avoid drowning in information, giving focus to your explorations.
- *Embrace serendipity:* Serendipity is the occurrence of unexpected discoveries or accidental insights while seeking something else. Be open to chance encounters, and odd tangents in research. Let your intuition guide you sometimes—as an ultra generalist this leads to unique breakthroughs (which those tied to strict plans overlook).

WHERE DO ULTRA GENERALISTS THRIVE?

Ultra generalists thrive by disrupting the status quo and driving innovation. Ultra generalists, with their wide-ranging interests and the ability to connect disparate fields, thrive in environments that benefit from nontraditional thinking, innovative problem-solving, and adaptability to constant change. They are not meant for every environment, but in the right context, they can be game changers. Here's where they excel:

Industry Sectors (Where Ultra Generalists Excel)
- Multidisciplinary Industries
  - Areas bridging multiple disciplines value ultra generalists' ability to draw connections and see patterns others miss. Moreover, ultra generalists can handle ambiguity well and can manage complex and ambiguous roles spanning many industries. As an idea, multidisciplinary industries include biomimicry as it applies nature's solutions to engineering and design; cognitive science as it blends psychology, neuroscience, and computer science; and sustainability as it analyzes interconnected environmental, social, and economic factors. (For example, researchers as ultra generalists, in these uncharted territories, are well suited for

research projects involving complex, interlinked problems without preexisting solutions.)

- ◆ Future-Focused and Visionary Industries
  - Think tanks, foresight consultancies, and innovation labs work on visionary industries. Ultra generalists, within large companies following big-picture thinking, can synthesize complex information, anticipate trends, and propose novel solutions. They can serve as innovation catalysts within organizations. Where fields are continuously evolving and emerging, new ideas collide, and existing norms are never solidified. Here, an ultra generalist's unique mind finds an opportunity where specialists and other types of generalists only see fragments in isolation. (For example, future-focused companies often create roles specifically for ultra generalists to stimulate new ideas and challenge established approaches.)

Workplace Environments (Where Ultra Generalists Excel)

- ◆ Leadership and Management
  - Ultra generalists with their well-rounded knowledge and exposure are well positioned for leadership and management roles. They can leverage their broad perspective for strategic decision-making, spotting under-the-radar opportunities, and guiding organizations through complex transformations. In terms of long-term strategic leadership, navigating massive disruption (be it market shifts or unforeseen global crises) requires seeing not what is, but what's possible on the horizon through interconnected lenses others lack, and ultra generalists can do a fantastic job here. (For example, operations managers in a growing company need an understanding of various business functions, and department heads in mid-sized businesses can make better-informed decisions with skill and domain diversity.)
- ◆ Entrepreneurship
  - Starting multiple businesses requires diverse skills and comfort with uncertainty. Ultra generalists can move between industries, learning quickly and applying lessons from one

venture to another, and hence can be better entrepreneurs. They can navigate marketing, sales, finance, and operations as they build their ventures. (For example, an entrepreneur, as ultra generalist, wears many hats and needs to be proficient in various areas, such as business development, marketing, finance, operations, and customer service, to launch and grow their ventures successfully.)

♦ Project-Based Work
  ● Generalists often thrive in project-oriented settings where they can leverage their broad skill set to manage various project aspects, coordinate between stakeholders, and see projects through to completion. Ultra generalists are skilled at juggling various tasks and ensuring projects run smoothly. (For example, a construction site manager needs to possess a wide range of skills, including time management, problem-solving, communication, and technical expertise, to oversee construction sites, workers, and project stakeholders.)

Summary of Strengths, Risks, and Organizational Aspects of Generalists

Now that we have discussed each of the four types of generalists, it is time to summarize their key strengths and main risks in the workplace, along with their leadership succession patterns. Let's start with the bold facts as presented in Table 4.10.

Taking it further, let's compare the different flavors of generalists in terms of various organizational aspects, which is helpful for self-identification and understanding how to leverage their diverse mindsets, as outlined in Table 4.11.

Pragmatically speaking, this discussion about four types of generalists (shallow, domain, skill, and ultra) is more about a *spectrum* than it is about rigid boxes. Generalists can possess blends of traits and shifts on this scale, based on their personas and the projects they tackle.

> **❝ four types of generalists (shallow, domain, skill, and ultra) is more about a *spectrum* than it is about rigid boxes. ❞**

Table 4.10 Summary of strengths and risks of different types of generalists

Type of generalist	Skills-domains split	Strength	Risk	Leadership succession
Shallow generalist	One skill, one domain	Can impress others with trivia or depth	Risk of analysis till paralysis due to meticulousness	Career progression can halt at a certain point due to a lack of generalist skills
Domain generalist	One skill, few domains	Can understand moving parts of various industries to act as a bridge within the organization	Risk of being hindered by too many niche industry norms	Career progression through outside-in innovation due to their domain connections and correlations
Skill generalist	Few skills, one domain	Can facilitate cross-functional initiatives and projects based on their plural skill set	Risk of falling short compared to specialists and experts, in terms of subject-matter expertise	Career progression through inside-out innovation due to their portable skills
Ultra generalist	Multiple skills, multiple domains	Can adapt to a wide variety of roles and situations, especially in turbulent times	Risk of oversimplification and generalization if no strong collaborators to execute in their team	Career progression has no limits due to ultra generalist skills and domain exposure

Likewise, it is important to understand that the *maturity curve* applies here! A shallow generalist can evolve over time toward becoming a domain generalist or a skill generalist, or perhaps both. In the grand scheme of things, a mix of generalists at various levels, paired strategically with deep specialists (shallow generalists), is the way for innovative organizations to unlock their true potential!

Table 4.11   Summary of organizational aspects of different types of generalists

Organizational aspects	Shallow generalist	Domain generalist	Skill generalist	Ultra generalist
Focus	Surface-level focus	Industry focus	Skills focus	Industry and skills focus
Versatility	Specialization of skill and domain	Versatility over domains	Versatility over skills	Versatility over domains and skills
Interest, knowledge, and exposure	Limited	Wide-ranging	Wide-ranging	Vast and comprehensive
Collaboration	Limited ability to collaborate across domains and skills	Collaboration within industry sectors	Collaboration across various skill types	Facilitates multidisciplinary collaboration of skill set in different industries
Problem-solving	Limited problem-solving abilities	Industry-specific problem-solving	Skill-specific problem-solving	Exceptional problem-solving abilities, especially in uncertain times
Innovation	Innovation within the specialist area	Innovative thinking at the edge of industry parameters	Innovative thinking at the intersections of skills	Impressive innovation across diverse fields
Leadership potential	Leadership potential in the specialization area	Leadership potential in different industries context	Leadership potential in different skills context	Tremendous leadership potential, particularly in navigating through chaos
Typical roles	Operational leaders, departmental heads, technical specialists	Cross-sector leaders (manufacturing, services, hybrid industries)	Cross-functional leaders (HR, finance, IT, marketing functions)	Senior management leaders, consultants, advisors, futurists, thought leaders, entrepreneurs

Chapter 4 Takeaways

♦ All generalists are not alike! Study the SDSU™ framework, shallow, domain, skill, and ultra generalists, to understand the four archetypes of generalists at work.

♦ When people switch companies early in their careers, they become domain generalists before becoming skill generalists. This is typical career path 1, according to the Generalist Advantage.

♦ When people switch companies a bit later in their careers, they follow the opposite, which is they become skill generalists before becoming domain generalists. This is typical career path 2 in the Generalist Advantage.

♦ Advocate for generality, by promoting the value of generalists in organizations and encouraging a culture that values diverse skills and broad industry exposure.

Domain and Skill Variation of Different Generalists

Law of Specialist Saturation (LOSS)™

For the last 12 years, I have been facilitating leadership training workshops and delivering strategy keynotes in the UK, US, Middle East, and Far East Asia, for a good number of my *Fortune 500* clients. In conducting these programs, especially for the senior management cadre, I have realized that the question of or discussion around *productivity* always comes up. Based on that inference and my experience, I would like to introduce a law, which I dub the *Law of Specialist Saturation (LOSS)*. This law perfectly applies to the scenario of generalist and specialist leaders in the workplace. It represents the trend of diminishing productivity of specialists, which I believe can be aptly termed a "LOSS."

> ### Explain It to Kids
>
> **Law of Specialist Saturation (LOSS):** A law showcasing that if you stay an expert for long in one area and do not adventure in new areas, it will get tough for you to retain your position among your colleagues!

Imagine a situation where a specialist keeps pushing for deeper and deeper specialization. While this might lead to initial gains in a specific area, eventually:

- *Focus narrows:* The individual loses sight of the bigger picture and how their work connects to other departments or the overall company goals.
- *Adaptability suffers:* Rapid changes or unforeseen challenges become harder to navigate because the individual lacks the broader skill set of a generalist.
- *Innovation stagnates:* Overspecialization can lead to groupthink and a lack of fresh perspectives that fuel innovation.

Projecting the same scenario, a generalist can counteract this diminishing productivity of a specialist. Here is how a generalist can take charge:

- *Brings balance:* Generalists can bridge the gap between the specialists and other departments, fostering collaboration and a broader understanding.
- *Adaptability boost:* Generalists' broader skill set can help the team adapt to changing circumstances and identify new opportunities.
- *Sparks innovation:* A generalist's different perspective can challenge assumptions and lead to creative solutions within the specialist team.

The Law of Specialist Saturation states that while the initial introduction of specialists yields significant improvements in specific areas, beyond a certain point the marginal benefits of additional specialization decrease. Moreover, to sustain and enhance overall organizational performance, generalists are essential in optimizing business results. In other words, the *Law of Specialist Saturation* highlights the danger of overreliance on specialists and elevates the critical role of generalists in optimizing organizational performance.

Figure 5.1 sketches the LOSS mechanism over time. It illustrates the relationship between *productivity* and *career lifespan* for both specialists and generalists. It depicts two curves: one representing *specialist productivity* (solid line) and the other showing *generalist*

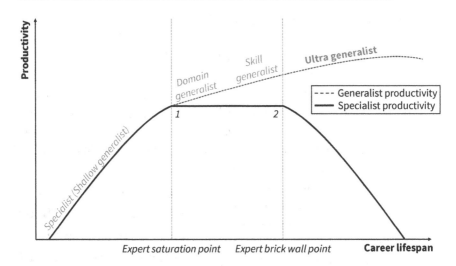

Figure 5.1 Law of Specialist Saturation (LOSS).

productivity (dashed line). The x-axis measures the career lifespan, while the y-axis indicates productivity levels. The diagram marks two key points along the career timeline: the "expert saturation point" and the "expert brick wall point," which help to differentiate the productivity trends between specialists and generalists.

For specialists, the productivity curve initially rises steeply as they gain deep expertise in a narrow field, reaching a peak at the *expert saturation point.* At this stage, their productivity levels off, indicating that additional experience or knowledge gains offer diminishing returns. When they reach the *expert brick wall point,* their productivity begins to decline, suggesting limitations in how their specialized skills can adapt to new challenges or fields, leading to a drop in effectiveness over time.

In contrast, generalists (including domain, skill, and ultra generalists) show a more gradual but sustained increase in productivity. Instead of plateauing, the generalist curve continues to rise beyond the *expert saturation point,* illustrating how their broader skill sets and adaptability allow them to maintain and even enhance productivity over a longer career lifespan. The ultra generalist's productivity trajectory extends the highest, demonstrating the potential for continuous growth through cross-disciplinary skills and experiences. This suggests that while specialists may initially excel in specific areas, generalists are better positioned to sustain long-term productivity across diverse roles.

Here are the key points in the LOSS diagram:

1. *Specialist Productivity (Solid Black Line)*
   Specialists excel in solving complex, niche problems that require a high level of technical knowledge. As more specialists are added, the incremental benefits decrease. This saturation occurs because the organization may become too siloed, and the additional specialists may have overlapping skills or redundant roles. Excessive specialization can lead to communication barriers and lack of cohesion, as each specialist focuses primarily on their specific area without considering the broader organizational context.

   > **"Excessive specialization can lead to communication barriers and lack of cohesion."**

2. *Generalist Productivity (Dotted Black Line)*
   Over time, the generalist's ability to integrate and optimize various aspects of the organization leads to sustained productivity. Generalists play a critical role in integrating the work of various specialists, ensuring that their efforts align with the organization's strategic goals. Generalists bring a holistic view, facilitating cross-functional collaboration and reducing silos. They can see the bigger picture and help prioritize initiatives that have the most significant impact on the organization.

3. *Expert Saturation Point (Dotted Grey Line)*
   Marks the time point where the productivity gains from a specialist start to stall or diminish slowly, emphasizing the limitations of a highly specialized approach.

4. *Expert Brick Wall Point (Dotted Grey Line)*
   Marks the time point where the productivity gains from a specialist take a nosedive and start to rapidly diminish, reinforcing the damage that has been done due to continued specialist approach.

It is interesting to note that the LOSS diagram shows two phases: *specialist saturation* and *generalist optimization*. In terms of specialist saturation, the productivity gains from a specialist diminish over time due to their narrow focus and potential for creating silos. Likewise, in terms of generalist optimization, a generalist maintains and enhances productivity over time through effective integration and strategic guidance. This diagram visually represents the principle that while a specialist leader provides significant initial productivity gains, a generalist leader is crucial for maintaining and optimizing productivity over the long term.

> **"productivity gains from a specialist diminish over time due to their narrow focus."**

WHY IS IT A "LOSS"?

I theorize it as a loss, as my research over the years has led me to believe that professionals largely work on *intentional specialization* first and then they look out for *planned exploration*. They mostly prioritize a path of deliberate specialization as a foundation but incorporate structured periods of cross-field exploration later. It is a *loss* as planned exploration is often late, and it results in specialists becoming complacent. Moreover, it does not allow generalists to flourish in good times in their careers to gain wider roots and ventures.

Typically, people build their careers by specializing first and generalizing later. One may argue that this depends on the specific needs of the company as some companies have highly specialized projects. But as a matter of fact, LOSS applies to both *highly specialized* and *general projects*. For example, in the case of a highly specialized project, a specialist might be ideal for the initial phase, but as the project progresses, introducing a generalist can ensure adaptability and long-term success. In the case of general projects, a generalist leader can be effective, utilizing a team of specialists to provide crucial in-depth expertise when needed. Here, a *brick wall specialist* is someone who thinks of generalizing only when they don't get promoted in their skill or domain. Just like a mid-life crisis, it should encourage self-reflection. This is another manifestation of the *loss*.

Generalists often have simplistic solutions to complex, deeply seated problems, but they are mostly correct with their apparently simplistic solution due to their broad understanding of things. They possess the *helicopter view* in most cases. The enigma of expertise suggests that while expertise in a specific domain can be valuable, it can also lead to tunnel vision and narrow-mindedness. Specialists may become so focused on their area of expertise that they overlook alternative perspectives or solutions.

The catch is that—specializing for too long without zooming out to spot overarching shifts risks missed opportunities and threats, and it leads to outdated strategies. In other words, there is a point at which the benefits of specialization plateau, and further specialization may not lead to significant improvements in performance or outcomes. Generalists can mitigate the effects of this law by working on breadth instead of mere depth, ensuring that they have diverse skill sets and domain exposure that enables them to adapt to changing circumstances and address a wide range of challenges.

Today's organizations scream for dynamic resource management, and in terms of human resource management, there is no better way to do this than by keeping a balance of generalists and specialists according to organizational needs. Research suggests that during periods of innovation and technical challenges, most organizations initially depend on specialists before shifting their focus to generalists. In contrast, during phases of strategic growth, they consistently emphasize the value of generalists. In terms of fortes, generalists outperform specialists in strategic planning and coordination, while specialists can better handle technical execution within their domains. Research shows that generalists work well in middle to senior management roles, and specialists often perform well in front and middle management roles.

LOSS SCENARIOS

Here are some real-world scenarios to illustrate how managers and leaders can leverage the *Law of Specialist Saturation*:

Scenario 1: Launching a New Software Product

A specialist with deep technical expertise is ideal for the initial development phase. They can ensure the product is built with a strong foundation and adheres to industry best practices. As user testing begins, a generalist can join the team. Research shows that a generalist can help bridge the gap faster between the technical team and potential users, ensuring the product is intuitive and user-friendly. Their broader perspective can also identify potential marketing or sales opportunities.

Scenario 2: Streamlining Manufacturing Processes

A specialist with a strong understanding of current manufacturing processes can lead the initial analysis. They can identify bottlenecks and areas for improvement. Once improvement plans are established, a generalist can be crucial for implementation. Research shows that a generalist can communicate more effectively with all levels of staff, manage change resistance, and ensure the new processes are adopted smoothly.

Scenario 3: Crisis Management

In a crisis situation, a specialist with relevant expertise (e.g. legal, financial, marketing) might take the lead for initial actions to mitigate immediate damage. As the situation stabilizes, a generalist can take charge of the recovery phase. Research shows that a generalist can better oversee communication, rebuild morale, and ensure the company learns from the crisis to prevent future occurrences.

By understanding the *Law of Specialist Saturation*, companies can create a more solid leadership baseline, leveraging on the strengths of generalists, and helping navigate the successful transition of specialists to generalists, resulting in a more productive and conducive work environment.

Ability to Work outside the Domain

- ◆ *Domain:* Your industry base (for instance, your industry through which you have gained most of your work experience).
- ◆ *Working outside:* Stepping into adjacent fields outside your industry base (for instance, collaborating on cross-industry projects, focusing on inter-industry experiences, or tackling unfamiliar problems that leverage your out-of-industry understanding).

So *working outside the domain* means possessing the adaptability to contribute effectively in fields beyond your primary expertise. Without an iota of doubt, the ability to work outside one's domain is increasingly valuable in today's interconnected and rapidly changing business environment. This capability allows individuals to leverage their expertise and adaptability to tackle challenges and contribute to projects beyond their primary area of specialization. A pertinent concept here is that of the *Medici Effect*, popularized by Frans Johansson. It is an effect that describes how groundbreaking innovations often arise at the intersection of different fields or unrelated disciplines.

Remember, being *domain-flexible* does not mean being *domain-shallow*. It requires individuals to actively maintain a level of curiosity and continuous learning outside their core focus, *along with their core area*. It is also not about neglecting deep expertise, but adding more sets of expertise to the arsenal. Experts in niche domains are also valuable, but deep expertise that is singular and too niche can be risky. However, those experts who can connect their specialization to a wider context will become uniquely valuable in the age of AI, which again requires the ability to work outside the domain.

Leaders who operate beyond their domain get more chances to develop their business acumen. Their ability to think holistically, learn continuously, and collaborate across domains (industries and sectors) drives long-term success and profitability. Here I present again the 2×2 *SDSU framework* represented in Figure 5.2, correlating ability to work outside the domain with success, establishing that:

I Shallow generalists have little to no success.

II Domain generalists have medium success.

III Skill generalists have low success.

IV Ultra generalists have high success.

In the bottom left, quadrant I (shallow generalist: one skill, one domain), individuals with the ability to work only in the base domain

III	IV
Low success (skill generalist)	**High** success (ultra generalist)
I	II
Little to no success (shallow generalist)	**Medium** success (domain generalist)

–   Ability to Work outside the Domain (Industry/Sector)   +

Figure 5.2 Outside-the-domain merits and generalists.

and that rely on one major skill experience little to no success, reflecting a complete lack of domain versatility. Moving to the bottom right, quadrant II (domain generalist: one skill, few domains), those with a moderate ability to transition between domains achieve medium success, with good domain adaptability. In the top left, quadrant III (skill generalist: few skills, one domain) shows that even with no ability to work outside their domain, some individuals still achieve a certain level of success—mostly low—due to their varied skills assisting in different functions in the same domain. In the top right, quadrant IV (ultra generalist: multiple skills, multiple domains) represents individuals with both a high ability to adapt across different domains and a high level of skill diversity, indicating high or pinnacle success.

WHY DOES WORKING OUTSIDE THE DOMAIN MATTER?

Large-size organizations benefit from outside-the-domain skills because they can access diverse perspectives, expertise, and fuse it with their strong internal systems, leading to a competitive advantage. However, it is not only large-size organizations that benefit from outside-the-domain skills. Let us take an example of a start-up and a consulting firm as a small to medium-sized organization.

Start-ups often operate with lean teams where employees are required to wear multiple hats and work across various domains. For instance, a start-up founder may need to handle product development, marketing, sales, and finance functions with internal and external teams simultaneously to navigate the challenges of building and scaling a new venture. Another case is that of consulting firms who work in small settings too. Consulting firms consciously employ professionals from diverse industries and domains and are tasked with solving complex business problems based on this beyond domain expertise, especially in conducting market research and designing strategic plans for clients that come from heterogeneous sectors.

Here are four good reasons why the outside domain matters, for all company sizes:

1. *Solving wicked problems:* Issues affecting society and business that rarely fit neatly into single domains are called wicked problems. Diverse, domain-flexible teams have a broader tool kit to create more robust solutions. Great leaders

look beyond their own companies to solve significant problems. These leaders tackle issues such as climate change, public health, and social inequality. They harness their networks to drive innovation. For example, a public health campaign designed by epidemiologists, but fueled by the storytelling skills of a social media expert, has a much greater reach and impact.

2. *Increased innovation:* Bringing in an outsider's perspective can help challenge assumptions and inspire fresh approaches in stagnant areas. A company can remap its internal values by taking inspiration from external teams and organizations. Outsider advantage can lead to renewed motivation, improved work quality, and higher goal attainment. For example, a company hires a consultant from the gaming industry to revamp its onboarding process, leading to new interactive onboarding that increases employee engagement.

3. *Adapting to change:* In a fast-paced world, organizations need people who can jump between tasks and evolve quickly. Working outside one's domain often involves collaborating with colleagues from diverse backgrounds and areas of expertise. Effective communication, teamwork, and interpersonal skills are essential for building trust, fostering collaboration, and driving collective success. For example, an accountant embraces automation within their field and starts to learn programming concepts that improve financial analysis beyond basic spreadsheets.

4. *Personal growth:* Leaving your comfort zone is intellectually stimulating! The learning agility of these individuals is high as they demonstrate a willingness to continuously learn and grow, adapting to new technologies and methodologies across industries. For example, electrical engineers working outside their typical domain in multiple industries build a richer skill set and are more engaged compared to their fellow engineers who have been fixated in a singular domain.

In each of these examples, individuals with the ability to work outside their immediate domain contribute to the success of their teams and organizations by bringing a combination of expertise, adaptability, problem-solving, collaboration, and learning agility to the table. Moreover, the world is moving toward cross-industry projects (collaboration across different departments and functions) between different industries and sectors. For example, a company may launch a sustainability initiative that involves input from internal operations, marketing, supply chain, external regulators, and stakeholders to implement environmentally friendly practices and reduce carbon emissions.

Explain It to Kids

Wicked problem: is like a maze that's really hard to solve because every time you think you've figured it out, it changes!

HOW CAN ORGANIZATIONS ENCOURAGE LEAPS OUTSIDE THE DOMAIN?

There are various strategies organizations can follow that can actively encourage those valuable leaps outside the domain. Here are a few moves that can help organizations take a head start:

Culture Shift
- *Celebrate versatile thinkers:* Spotlight success stories where cross-domain executives made the difference. This shows it's valued, not just a nice-to-have.
- *Embrace productive failure:* Create a safe space for taking calculated risks with projects requiring expertise-stretching. Don't just tolerate errors, focus on learning from them.
- *Remove departmental silos:* Encourage project-based mixing of people from across and outside the organization. Crowdsourcing is one of the ways, where organizations rely on outsiders to work with insiders.

Project Design
- *Intentionally hybrid teams:* When launching new initiatives, require a mixed-domain team where nobody can operate just within their comfort zone.

♦ *Outsider perspective through rotations:* Build in short stints for employees to shadow their role in another industry setting with a view to gaining fresh air and thinking.

♦ *Problem-based, not role-based, assignments:* Challenge people by putting them onto projects based on the problem statements, and see if you can pair teams based on mismatched industry skills—as it will improve their learning curve.

Development Opportunities

♦ *Outside domain learning sprints:* Offer short, high-impact programs or workshops where employees tackle issues slightly outside their usual work and domain.

♦ *Support external knowledge building:* Fund conferences, courses, or even just subscriptions in topics adjacent to people's roles in other industries and sectors—as it sparks unexpected connections.

♦ *Knowledge bazaar:* Set up informal peer-to-peer coaching sessions of employees with externals—people from outside your domain can share their best practices and challenges to create awareness of untapped talent.

Leadership Actions

♦ *Leaders set the example:* When managers participate in that industry-sharing bazaar or join initiatives outside their domain, it sets the tone for everyone.

♦ *Mentorship for lateral growth:* Pair people who are doers with those who are thinkers, and emphasize transferrable skills with those stronger in diverse domain knowledge.

♦ *Reward the connectors:* Highlight employees who create strong links between teams or successfully translate complex ideas, drawing from the multitude of their industry experiences.

Top 60 Domains for Developing TGA

These are various domains (industries and sectors) encompassing a wide range of fields, from technology to health care to manufacturing to education, that one can invest in to develop *the Generalist Advantage (TGA)*. As an ultra generalist, you can leverage on multiple domains. Having said that, each domain presents unique opportunities and challenges for leaders and managers to navigate. Here's a list of 60 domains (organized with some overarching themes) for you to take a kick start in becoming a successful domain generalist and then a high-performing ultra generalist:

Technology
1. Artificial intelligence (AI)
2. Machine learning
3. Software development
4. Cloud computing
5. Cybersecurity
6. Internet of Things (IoT)
7. Robotics
8. Computer hardware
9. Virtual reality (VR) / augmented reality (AR)
10. E-commerce
11. EdTech (educational technology)
12. FinTech (financial technology)
13. Blockchain
14. Data science and analytics

Health Care and Life Sciences
15. Pharmaceuticals
16. Biotechnology
17. Health care providers (hospitals, clinics)
18. Health insurance
19. Medical research

Finance and Business
20. Banking
21. Investment management
22. Accounting and auditing
23. Consulting
24. Real estate
25. Insurance
26. Marketing and advertising
27. Human resources
28. Supply chain and logistics

Energy and Resources
29. Oil and gas
30. Renewable energy (solar, wind, hydropower)
31. Utilities (electricity, water)
32. Mining
33. Agriculture and food production
34. Forestry and conservation

Manufacturing and Construction
35. Automotive
36. Aerospace
37. Industrial machinery
38. Chemicals
39. Electronics
40. Consumer goods manufacturing
41. Construction (residential, commercial)

Creative and Media
42. Entertainment (film, TV, music)
43. Video games
44. Publishing (books, news)
45. Design (graphic, product)
46. Architecture
47. Arts and culture
48. Social media and influencing

Service and Hospitality
49. Retail
50. Travel and tourism
51. Restaurants and food service
52. Hotels and lodging
53. Event planning

Government and Public Sector
54. Defense and security
55. Education
56. Public administration

57. Infrastructure development
58. Resource management
59. Law enforcement
60. Nonprofit organizations

BONUS: EMERGING/NASCENT DOMAINS (FIT FOR AI ERA)

It's tricky to pinpoint what exactly qualifies as a future domain, as some are already emerging but will see even more dramatic growth, while others are truly nascent. Here is a list of domains that are likely to boom in the near future:

- Artificial general intelligence (AGI): AI systems matching or exceeding human intelligence across a wide breadth of tasks.
- Neurotechnology: Brain-computer interfaces, enhanced cognition, advanced mental health treatments.
- Personalized genomics and medicine: Tailored treatments, gene editing, and preventative health based on an individual's DNA.
- Human longevity and rejuvenation: Technologies significantly extending healthy lifespan and possibly reversing some aspects of aging.
- Space resources and commercialization: Asteroid mining, lunar outposts, space-based manufacturing, space tourism.
- Quantum computing: Unlocking next-level processing power for drug discovery, encryption, financial modeling, etc.
- Regenerative agriculture: Farming practices that improve soil health, capture carbon, and restore the ecosystems.
- Vertical farming: High-tech, indoor farming providing local food production on a massive scale.
- Climate engineering: Large-scale (sometimes controversial) technologies to manipulate the climate and counteract global warming.
- Decentralized social networks: Blockchain-based alternatives to today's social media giants, empowering user privacy and control.
- Synthetic biology: Engineering new organisms and biological systems for applications in medicine, materials, and beyond.

- Brain uploading/digital consciousness: Highly speculative; the theoretical transfer of a human mind into a digital form.
- Advanced nanotechnology: Molecular-level manufacturing for ultra-light materials, revolutionary medicine, etc.

On analysis, one can realize that there are several factors that are shaping future domains:

- Technology disruption: AI, automation, and emerging technologies transforming businesses across sectors.
- Societal needs: Rising concerns such as climate change, resource scarcity, and aging populations demand new solutions.
- Sustainability: Focus on responsible resource use, environmental protection, and green initiatives.
- Innovation: Research and development driving groundbreaking ideas and business models.
- Customer-centricity: Personalization, experience design, and the power of consumer choice.
- Globalization: Increasingly interconnected markets and competition on a global scale.

Ability to Acquire New Skills

Acquiring new skills can take the form of either upskilling or re-skilling. Enhancing existing skills and acquiring new skills to improve performance in a current role is called *upskilling*. The focus here is to stay current with industry advancements and evolving job requirements related to your existing role, mostly through complementary skills. For example, a marketing professional learns data analytics to better understand campaign performance and make more informed decisions.

Re-skilling, on the other hand, is about learning entirely new skills to transition into a different role, either within the company or in a new field. The focus here is on adapting to major workplace changes and opening new career pathways, mostly through contrasting skills. For example, a factory worker whose job is automated takes classes in coding to become a software developer.

Re-skilling is about lateral moves and opening new possibilities, while upskilling is about moving up within your current trajectory. However, both re-skilling and upskilling are vital in today's rapidly changing work environment as they help in technological disruption, career advancement, and organizational resilience. Generalists often thrive due to their impressive learning curve, which is essentially due to their attention to upskilling and re-skilling. Let's bring back the 2×2 *SDSU framework*, this time correlating ability to acquire new skills with success, establishing that:

I Shallow generalists have little to no success.

II Domain generalists have low success.

III Skill generalists have medium success.

IV Ultra generalists have high success.

Figure 5.3 illustrates the relationship between an individual's ability to acquire new skills (upskilling/re-skilling) and their likelihood of success. The quadrants define different scenarios. The four quadrants of the matrix correspond to different career paths too. Quadrant I represents individuals with limited upskilling/re-skilling capacity and minimal success. They have depth but lack the breadth of skills to succeed in a dynamic work environment. Quadrant II individuals have limited success and a stronger but still restricted ability in acquiring skills within specific domains. They often struggle

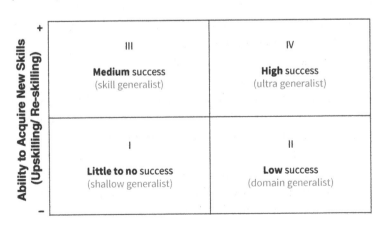

Figure 5.3 Skill merits and generalists.

to gain new skills but are confident in applying their existing skills to broader contexts and domains in adapting to new challenges.

Quadrant III represents individuals who achieve medium success due to their moderate upskilling and re-skilling ability. Individuals in quadrant III demonstrate high ability to acquire new skills but achieve medium success, possibly due to challenges in applying their new skills effectively in a variety of domains. Finally, quadrant IV depicts high success for those who actively acquire new skills, highlighting that adaptability and continuous learning are crucial for achieving greater success. Individuals in quadrant IV exhibit both high abilities to acquire new skills and high success, likely benefiting from their continuous learning and adaptability. These individuals are often highly sought after in the modern workforce.

WHY DOES ACQUIRING NEW SKILLS MATTER?

Acquiring new skills is crucial in today's fast-changing world, as it enables individuals to adapt to new challenges, leverage emerging opportunities, and remain relevant in their fields. As technology and industries evolve rapidly, skills that were once valuable can quickly become outdated, making continuous learning essential. Those who actively re-skill or upskill can fill gaps

❝Those who actively re-skill or upskill can fill gaps in the market, transition into new roles, or take on expanded responsibilities. ❞

in the market, transition into new roles, or take on expanded responsibilities within their organizations. In this way, the ability to acquire new skills directly affects employability, career growth, and resilience against automation or other market shifts.

Moreover, skill acquisition broadens a person's tool kit, allowing them to become more versatile and effective in problem-solving. For generalists, in particular, acquiring diverse skills enhances their adaptability across multiple domains, enabling them to connect ideas, innovate, and tackle complex problems from various perspectives. This adaptability not only increases their success in different roles but also positions them as valuable assets in interdisciplinary teams, where cross-functional knowledge is increasingly in demand.

Here are a few examples that highlight why this matters:

Career reinvention: Consider the story of J.K. Rowling, who started as a struggling writer and single mother before achieving massive success with the *Harry Potter* series. Before her success, Rowling took jobs as a researcher and teacher, each role requiring new skills. Later, her willingness to embrace screenwriting and work with new storytelling formats (such as the *Harry Potter* films) kept her creative output fresh and her work relevant. This reinvention demonstrates how learning new skills can open doors to unexpected and rewarding career paths.

Adapting to industry changes: Take the example of Kodak, the iconic photography company. When digital photography began to replace film, Kodak's failure to embrace new digital skills and technology led to its decline. In contrast, companies that proactively adapted to digital trends, such as Fujifilm, pivoted to different markets and survived. This shows how organizations that foster a culture of continuous skill acquisition can weather disruptions more effectively.

Responding to automation and AI: In fields such as accounting, routine tasks are increasingly automated. Accountants who learn data analysis, financial modeling, or coding gain a significant advantage—they can transition into roles that are less likely to be automated, such as financial strategy or analytics. By learning these new skills, they stay valuable in a landscape where technology is rapidly changing the nature of work.

Interdisciplinary innovation: Elon Musk, known for founding or leading companies in multiple industries (PayPal, SpaceX, Tesla, and Neuralink), is often cited as an example of a generalist who relentlessly acquires skills in new fields. Musk taught himself rocket science, electrical engineering, and software development. His ability to pull knowledge from different domains enables him to innovate across industries, addressing problems from angles that narrow specialists might miss.

Personal growth and confidence: On a personal level, learning a new skill—whether it's coding, a language, or public speaking—can boost confidence and open up new social or professional circles. For instance, many people who take up public speaking through organizations such as Toastmasters not only become better communicators but also gain the confidence to pursue leadership roles, start businesses, or network more effectively. The skill of speaking publicly becomes a launchpad for new opportunities.

In sum, acquiring new skills keeps individuals and companies resilient, enhances creativity, and makes success more likely across different circumstances.

HOW CAN ORGANIZATIONS ENCOURAGE A CULTURE OF UPSKILLING AND RE-SKILLING?

Creating a culture of upskilling and re-skilling is about creating an environment that is engaging, accessible, and aligned with organizational goals, allowing employees to upskill and re-skill in meaningful ways that benefit both them and the company. Here are practical techniques that organizations can use to promote re-skilling and upskilling:

Create clear skill pathways and certifications: Establishing defined pathways to develop specific skills, coupled with certifications or credentials, can motivate employees to upskill in a structured way. For example, *Google* offers certifications in fields such as project management and data analytics, and employees who complete these can transition to more specialized roles within the company. Certifications provide a sense of accomplishment and reinforce the value of newly acquired skills.

Encourage peer learning and mentorship: Building mentorship programs where senior employees mentor others in new skill areas can be highly effective. Additionally, hosting regular "lunch-and-learn" sessions, hackathons, or knowledge-sharing meetups encourages peer learning. Companies such as *Microsoft* and *IBM* use internal communities where employees share skills and collaborate on projects outside their day-to-day responsibilities, fostering an environment of continuous, cross-functional learning.

Align skill development with career advancement: Linking re-skilling and upskilling opportunities to promotions or lateral career moves encourages employees to take their development seriously. For example, Salesforce encourages employees to complete "Trailhead" learning modules and rewards them with badges that align with specific career pathways within the organization. Employees feel a sense of direction and purpose, knowing that skill development can open up new roles or higher positions.

Encourage cross-departmental collaborations and job rotations: Allow employees to gain new skills by working in different roles or departments temporarily. For example, Unilever's job rotation program helps employees develop a broader skill set by rotating through various roles, enabling them to learn about different functions and gain diverse perspectives. This type of hands-on experience helps employees build skills they might not acquire in their regular roles.

Hard vs Soft Skills of Generalists

Extending the discussion on upskilling and re-skilling, it is worth understanding the distinction between hard skills and soft skills, especially in the context of generalists: hard skills (also known as *technical skills*) represent specific know-how or training acquired through education, work experience, or specialized courses, whereas soft skills (also known as *leadership skills*) are traits that shape how we work with others and navigate work-place dynamics. Examples of hard skills include programming languages such as Python or Java, or statistical tools such as SPSS and SEM, whereas examples of soft skills include time management, problem-solving, decision-making, and other leadership skills.

Hard skills tend to be more specific to a job, role, or industry, such as coding in Python, using a statistical tool, or operating specialized machinery. While some hard skills, such as programming or data analysis, may be applicable across multiple fields, their utility often depends on the context, tools, or systems in place within a given role. In contrast, soft skills are universally relevant, shaping how we communicate, collaborate, and solve problems in any environment. For example, adaptability, critical thinking, and effective teamwork are valuable in virtually all professional settings, making them highly portable (transferable) across roles, industries, and even careers. This distinction underscores the adaptability and broad applicability of soft skills, even as certain hard skills may also transcend job boundaries when they align with common professional needs.

Soft skills are important as they contribute to teamwork, leadership, and workplace culture, and hard skills build strong understanding of technical acumen. Generalists often possess a combo of soft skills (leadership skills) and hard skills (technical skills), but are more inclined to develop and maintain soft skills as compared to hard skills. They get their real *general-ability* due to portable skills (transferable skills), which are essentially soft skills. Generalists possess a blend of hard and soft skills that enable them to excel in a variety of roles and contexts. Here's a breakdown of hard and soft skills commonly associated with generalists:

Soft skills for generalists

Explain It to Kids

Soft skills: are like invisible superpowers that help you get along with others and work well as a team!

Communication: Generalists possess strong communication skills, allowing them to convey ideas, collaborate with diverse teams, and influence stakeholders effectively.

Critical thinking: Generalists excel at critical thinking, analyzing complex problems, synthesizing information from different sources, and making informed decisions.

Creativity: Generalists demonstrate creativity and innovation, generating new ideas, approaches, and solutions to address emerging issues and opportunities.

Collaboration: Generalists thrive in collaborative environments, working essentially with cross-functional teams and wider stakeholders to achieve shared objectives and deliver results.

Emotional intelligence: Generalists possess high emotional intelligence, understanding their own emotions and those of others, managing interpersonal relationships, and navigating social dynamics effectively.

Problem-solving: Generalists are skilled problem solvers, capable of identifying root causes, brainstorming potential solutions, and implementing effective strategies to overcome obstacles.

Hard skills for generalists

Explain It to Kids

Hard skills: are like special tools and things that you can learn to use or do, such as riding a bike or playing an instrument!

Technology proficiency: Generalists possess a basic understanding of technology and digital tools, enabling them to adapt to digital workflows and leverage technology to enhance productivity and efficiency. However, specific technology skills can be related to SAP ERP, Microsoft Dynamics 365 ERP, Oracle ERP, etc. The advantage of learning this hard skill for generalists is to reduce tech intimidation and increase communication with tech teams.

Financial literacy: Generalists have a foundational knowledge of finance and accounting principles, enabling them to interpret financial statements, analyze budgets, and make informed financial decisions. However, specific financial literacy skills can be enhanced using accounting tools such as Xero, Sage, and Quickbooks. The advantage of learning this hard skill for generalists is to gain confidence in financial decision-making through data and numbers.

Project management: Generalists are proficient in project management, coordinating tasks, timelines, and resources to deliver projects on time and within budget. However, specific project management skills can be enhanced using tools such as Microsoft Project, Zoho, and Asana. The advantage of learning this hard skill for generalists is to drive project initiatives working with diverse specialists.

Research and analysis: Generalists are skilled in research and analysis, gathering data, conducting market research, and synthesizing insights to inform decision-making. Specific research analysis tools can be R, SAS, PowerBI, Rasch, etc. Here again, the advantage of learning this hard skill for generalists is to capture, analyze, and process technical data and information efficiently.

On an organizational level, extending the discussion of hard and soft skills, the diversity of skills is also important. Take these two workplace scenarios of product development and digital transformation:

- *Product development:* In many organizations, product development teams consist of individuals with diverse backgrounds, including engineers, marketers, designers, and finance professionals. Each team member brings their unique expertise to the table, contributing to the ideation, development, and launch of new products and services.
- *Digital transformation:* In today's digital age, businesses are undergoing digital transformation initiatives to stay competitive and meet evolving customer needs. Employees with cross-functional skills play a crucial role in driving digital innovation, whether it's implementing new technologies, redesigning business processes, or enhancing customer experiences across digital channels.

Overall, by possessing a combination of soft and hard skills, generalists are well equipped to navigate diverse roles, industries, and challenges, contributing to organizational success and driving innovation and growth. Here is another quite similar 2×2 *SDSU framework,* plotting soft and hard skills on the vertical axis, establishing that (in terms of skills indispensability):

I Shallow generalists are easy to replace.

II Domain generalists are somewhat easy to replace.

III Skill generalists are somewhat difficult to replace.

IV Ultra generalists are difficult to replace.

This diagram in Figure 5.4 divides individuals into four quadrants based on their skill set (technical or leadership) and the ease with which they can be replaced (skills indispensability). Quadrant I (shallow generalist) include individuals with specialized technical skills (hard skills) that are relatively easy to replace as the demand for niche skills is narrow, and they often lack leadership skills, which can help them join the management cadre. Quadrant II (domain generalist) includes those with technical skills (hard skills) that are somewhat harder to replace as they have the benefit of a few domains. They are skilled in a specific area and enjoy some domain versatility, but may again lack broader leadership abilities.

Moving up to quadrant III (skill generalist), we find individuals with leadership skills (soft skills) that are somewhat difficult to replace, as their combination of skills makes them a potential for promotion to management positions, or higher levels. Finally, quadrant IV (ultra generalist) contains individuals with leadership skills (soft skills) that are very difficult to replace, as their package of multiple skills in multiple domains gives them a sustainable competitive advantage. They have a greater ability to lead effectively, are highly sought after, and are often in high demand.

The arrows illustrate a suggested path for skill development, encouraging employees to move from technical roles to roles requiring more leadership skills. This pathway helps employees evolve

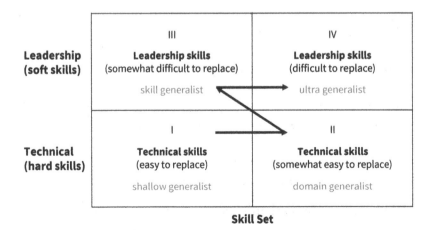

Skill Set

Figure 5.4 **Hard vs soft skills of generalists.**

from easily replaceable technical positions to more valuable and harder-to-replace leadership positions. It suggests that organizations should invest in helping technical specialists (quadrants I and II) develop soft skills, such as communication, decision-making, and team management, to move toward the more strategic and irreplaceable roles (quadrants III and IV).

Disciplinary Strokes of Generalists

The way we approach knowledge can be categorized by its level of disciplinary interaction or strokes. *Intra-disciplinary* work stays firmly within a single field, such as an engineer using established principles to design a bridge. *Cross-disciplinary* approaches borrow concepts from other fields, such as an architect considering the psychology of space when designing a building. *Multidisciplinary* approaches involve teams from different disciplines working on a shared problem, such as a team of engineers, marketers, and financial analysts launching a new product. Finally, *trans-disciplinary* approaches integrate knowledge to create entirely new frameworks.

The vested philosophy here is similar to that of *Socratic inquiry*— a form of inquiry and dialogue developed by the ancient Greek philosopher Socrates, often involving the use of probing questions to stimulate critical thinking and exploration of ideas.

To avoid confusion, here the word *discipline* means subject (which is an orientation of *skill* rather than domain). Imagine researchers combining subjects such as physics, biology, and philosophy to explore the nature of consciousness. Table 5.1 summarizes the differences between disciplines with some more examples.

Just like these four types of disciplinary interactions, generalists are unique in utilizing these approaches. Going to the 2×2 *SDSU framework*, plotting disciplines on the horizontal axis, we see that:

I Shallow generalists are intra-disciplinary.

II Domain generalists are cross-disciplinary.

III Skill generalists are multidisciplinary.

IV Ultra generalists are trans-disciplinary.

Table 5.1 Four strokes of a generalist

Generalist strokes	Key difference	Examples
Intra-disciplinary	Focuses entirely within a single discipline.	A literary critic analyzing a poem using established literary theory.
Cross-disciplinary	Views a topic from the perspective of another discipline(s).	An architect considering the psychological impact of building design on users.
Multi-disciplinary	Draws on multiple disciplines to address a topic.	A team of engineers, biologists, and sociologists collaborating on a sustainable city planning project.
Trans-disciplinary	Integrates different disciplines to create a new framework for understanding a topic.	Developing a field of study such as astrobiology, which combines astronomy, biology, geology, and chemistry to understand the possibility of life beyond our planet.

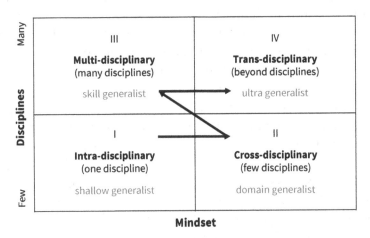

Figure 5.5 Disciplinary differences of generalists.

Figure 5.5 categorizes individuals based on the ascending number of disciplines/subjects. Quadrant I (shallow generalist) contains individuals with an intra-disciplinary focus, meaning they have limited knowledge beyond it. They lack a broad perspective and may struggle to adapt to new challenges. Quadrant II (domain generalist) describes those with a cross-disciplinary approach, where they incorporate knowledge from a few related disciplines. They are skilled in a specific subject and may not have a holistic understanding of complex problems.

Moving upwards, quadrant III (skill generalist) includes multidisciplinary individuals who engage with many disciplines, integrating knowledge from various fields or subjects. They possess a diverse range of skills. Finally, quadrant IV (ultra generalist) represents trans-disciplinary individuals who transcend traditional boundaries, creating new approaches by integrating diverse fields. They have a remarkable sense of connecting seemingly unrelated concepts and are often recognized as cherished innovative thinkers.

In an organizational setting, shallow generalists encouraging intra-disciplinary work strengthen core competencies within a specific subject. Domain generalists using cross-disciplinary thinking spark fresh ideas by looking at problems through new lenses. Skill generalists then using a multidisciplinary approach bring diverse subject expertise to complex challenges in a team. Ultra generalists supporting trans-disciplinary exploration lead to unconventional solutions that would not have been within traditional disciplinary boundaries. By understanding these approaches, managers and leaders can create an environment that fosters a richer and more innovative approach to work.

The arrows, here again, illustrate a recommended development path, guiding individuals from intra-disciplinary roles toward a trans-disciplinary mindset. This progression suggests that organizations should encourage employees to move beyond single-discipline expertise (quadrants I and II) and engage with multiple disciplines (quadrants III and IV) to foster innovation and adaptability. By encouraging employees to explore multiple fields and ultimately reach a trans-disciplinary mindset, organizations can cultivate professionals who bring unique, integrative insights and solutions, driving transformative growth and problem-solving abilities.

HOW CAN GENERALIST LEADERS TAKE ADVANTAGE OF THESE FOUR APPROACHES?

Here is how generalist leaders can leverage these four (intra-disciplinary, cross-disciplinary, multidisciplinary, and trans-disciplinary) approaches in their own unique way:

Intra-disciplinary: Foster Expertise

Shallow generalists deeply mastering their specific fields can create a backbone of strong core competencies within the organization.

Cross-disciplinary: Spark Innovation

Domain generalists can facilitate learning opportunities where disciplines overlap. Hosting cross-functional brainstorming sessions, they can encourage the exchange of ideas, potentially leading to novel solutions and approaches.

Multidisciplinary: Build Cohesive Teams

Skill generalists can leverage their understanding of various specializations to identify complementary skill sets. They can assemble effective multidisciplinary teams to address complex challenges, ensuring smooth communication and collaboration among diverse experts.

Trans-disciplinary: Drive Strategic Vision

Ultra generalists can encourage the development of shared language and frameworks across different fields. They have potential that can foster the kind of innovation that can transform multiple functions and industries.

POWER OF THE TRANS-DISCIPLINARY MINDSET

Cultivating a trans-disciplinary mindset is all about breaking out of disciplinary silos and embracing a systematic and connected way of thinking. In simple terms, it is about developing *intellectual curiosity*. Here are eight techniques you can employ to unlock the power of the trans-disciplinary mindset and become an ultra generalist:

1. *Read widely:* Step outside your usual disciplinary materials and explore books, articles, online courses, podcasts, or documentaries from different fields. This broadens your perspective and exposes you to new ways of thinking.
2. *Engage in interdisciplinary courses:* If available, take courses that bridge disciplines. This could be anything from a science course with a strong philosophical bent to a literature course that explores historical context.

3. *Practice identifying assumptions:* Recognize and challenge your own assumptions about how the world works. This opens you up to considering alternative viewpoints and integrating them into your thinking.

4. *Develop strong analytical skills:* Hone your ability to analyze information, identify relationships between seemingly disparate facts, and draw meaningful conclusions.

5. *Seek out diverse conversations:* Talk to people from different backgrounds and professions. Ask questions, listen actively, and try to understand their perspectives.

6. *Join or form trans-disciplinary teams:* Seek opportunities to work with people from different backgrounds. This fosters a collaborative environment where ideas can be exchanged and integrated.

7. *Learn to translate between disciplines:* Develop the ability to communicate complex ideas from your field in a way that is understandable to people outside your discipline. The same goes for understanding others' explanations.

8. *Reflect on your learning:* Process your experiences with trans-disciplinary thinking. Identify what worked well and what you can improve on.

Business leaders using a trans-disciplinary approach can design sustainable products and services, for example, a team of engineers, environmental scientists, and marketing specialists working together to develop eco-friendly products that are both functional and appealing to consumers. Leaders using a trans-disciplinary approach can enhance employee well-being too, for instance, a collaboration between HR professionals, psychologists, and data analysts to design a holistic employee wellness program that addresses physical, mental, and emotional well-being.

By embracing trans-disciplinary thinking and working, leaders can unlock the full potential of their teams, drive innovation, and tackle complex challenges in creative and effective ways. There can be some overlap between all these disciplinary interactions and generalist forms. However, the four types of generalists sketched in this book fall neatly within the four disciplinary approaches: intra-disciplinary, cross-disciplinary, multidisciplinary, and trans-disciplinary.

Top 40 Skills for Developing TGA

As a futurist, I enjoy reading, following, and analyzing fads, trends, and projections. I regularly share commentary and insights for *Fortune, Business Insider*, and *BBC*. In developing this list of skills, I have focused on what will be crucial for navigating the future workplace shaped by AI. Just like the list of top domains, here is a list of top 40 skills that can help managers and leaders best develop *the Generalist Advantage (TGA)*, in line with the demands and expectations from the AI revolution.

By no means is this an exhaustive list of skills. According to the *Future of Jobs Report and Global Skills Report*, there are over 400 skills that we commonly see in the workplace. Moreover, according to *LinkedIn*, there are around 50,000 skills globally.

As an ultra generalist, you are expected to invest in multiple skills. I have grouped the top skills in demand into themes enabling you to launch a successful skill generalist career and subsequently leading you to become a promising ultra generalist.

Core Cognitive Skills

1. Critical thinking: Analyzing information, identifying patterns and biases, making sound judgments.
2. Problem-solving: Breaking down complex issues, thinking creatively to develop viable solutions.
3. Decision-making: Analyzing information, considering alternatives, and taking decisive action.
4. Strategic thinking: Anticipating trends, understanding big-picture implications, making proactive decisions.
5. Metacognition: Awareness of your own thought processes, ability to change approaches when needed.
6. Systems thinking: Understanding how interconnected elements (social, technical, etc.) create larger outcomes.

Data Literacy and AI Interaction Skills

7. Data analysis: Gathering, structuring, interpreting, and making decisions based on data.
8. Statistical understanding: Knowledge of basic statistical concepts to critically evaluate information.

9. AI literacy: Understanding core AI concepts (without being a programmer), its strengths, and limitations.
10. Algorithmic thinking: Breaking down problems into steps AI systems can understand.
11. Prompt engineering: The art of effectively communicating tasks and requests to AI systems.
12. AI ethics: Using AI responsibly, understanding potential biases, and the impact on society.

Technology-Adjacent Skills
13. Basic programming: Enough to automate tasks, interact with existing codebases, and collaborate with developers.
14. Cybersecurity awareness: Protecting data and systems, recognizing common threats.
15. Digital fluency: Adapting to emerging technologies, staying ahead of the tech curve.
16. Computational thinking: Using computational concepts to solve problems across different fields.
17. Hardware understanding: Basic knowledge of computer components and networks.

Leadership Excellence Skills
18. Creativity: Generating new ideas, imaginative problem-solving, pushing beyond AI's limitations.
19. Emotional intelligence: Understanding and managing your own emotions and those of others.
20. Responsible leadership: Inspiring action, leading change, developing and mentoring others.
21. Cultural intelligence: Working effectively across diverse backgrounds and cultures.
22. People development: Recruiting, selecting, and onboarding diverse team members.
23. Influencing: Persuading, motivating, and negotiating effectively.
24. Delegation: Trusting and empowering team members.
25. Coaching and mentoring: Guiding and supporting others' development.

26. Diversity and inclusion: Fostering a culture of belonging and valuing diverse backgrounds.

Growth Acumen Skills
27. Agility: Being flexible, pivoting quickly when unexpected changes or errors occur.
28. Resilience: Bouncing back from setbacks, coping with ambiguity and the pressures of a fast-paced world.
29. Growth mindset: Viewing challenges as opportunities for learning, not as signs of failure.
30. Unlearning: Discarding obsolete knowledge and old assumptions as the environment shifts.

Execution Skills
31. Data-driven decision making: Applying data analysis to inform strategy.
32. Resource management: Managing project budgets, time, and people.
33. Performance management: Setting clear expectations, tracking progress, and development planning.
34. Process improvement: Finding efficiencies in workflows and systems.
35. Risk management: Identifying and mitigating potential challenges.

Impression Management Skills
36. Storytelling skills: Expressing ideas clearly, persuasion, storytelling (especially with technical topics).
37. Empathy: Understanding user needs, designing human-centered systems, advocating for users.
38. Interpersonal skills: Networking, building relationships, conflict resolution.
39. Feedback: Giving and receiving constructive feedback for growth.
40. Trust: Facilitating collaboration, trust, and a sense of shared purpose across disciplines and teams.

BONUS: EMERGING/NASCENT SKILLS (FIT FOR AI ERA)

This category will vary hugely depending on your field and domain. However, *AI-fication* is having a huge impact on the productivity, relevance, and displacement of jobs, roles, and careers in various concentrated industries. Here are some examples to illustrate the fusion of AI and these emerging skills:

- Health care: Understanding AI systems in medicine, medical ethics, patient data handling
- Finance: AI tools for trading, risk analysis, customer insights, fraud detection
- Law: AI's legal implications, copyright, privacy law, and understanding new regulations

Remember, the best leaders are those who are committed to lifelong learning and skill development. In the earlier chapters, we discussed some other classifications of skills too, such as *hard skills, soft skills*, and *portable skills*. These skills encompass various aspects of leadership and management, including interpersonal skills, problem-solving skills, planning and organization skills, relationship and team management skills, personal development and self-management skills, and technical and industry-specific skills.

Also remember that the significance of skill shifts depends on your leadership level, the industry, and company culture. These skills can be developed and honed over time, and they are crucial for effective management and leadership. Developing proficiency in these areas can help managers and leaders effectively navigate some of the contemporary business challenges of sustainability, responsible management, and resilience.

Chapter 5 Takeaways

- There is an increasing value of generalists, even in a world of specialists.
- There are limits to specialization! Study the Law of Specialist Saturation (LOSS), which illustrates the scenario of generalists thriving and specialists hitting the diminishing returns.
- Generalists excel in a variety of roles by balancing their hard skills (technical skills) with soft skills (nontechnical and interpersonal skills).
- You can cultivate your unique domain and skill palette—and leverage the Generalist Advantage—by exploring the top 60 domains and top 40 skills listed.

CHAPTER 6

The Generalist's Role in Innovation and Problem-Solving

Generalists Dealing with Uncertainty

Generalists thrive in uncertain environments by combining adaptability, critical thinking, and collaboration. Their practical insights empower them to make informed decisions and positively affect the team (and the organization) they serve.

Uncertain events have one key advantage: they empower us to think of organizational renewal. *Organizational renewal* is the process of revitalizing an organization by transforming its structure, culture, and processes to improve performance and adapt to changing environments.

Explain It to Kids

Uncertainty: is like when you're playing hide-and-seek, and you don't know where your friend is hiding—it makes the game exciting but a bit difficult!

In terms of adaptability, imagine a generalist working with a family facing financial instability. Rather than focusing solely on budgeting, they consider other factors: mental health, housing, employment, and community resources. This holistic approach helps them address underlying causes and create comprehensive solutions. Next in terms

131

of critical thinking, suppose a generalist encounters a client who suddenly lost their job. Instead of panicking, they assess the client's strengths, available support networks, and potential barriers. They collaboratively devise a plan that includes short-term assistance (such as emergency funds) and long-term strategies (such as skill development). Also, in terms of collaboration, suppose a generalist faces uncertainty while advocating for policy changes. They collaborate with other professionals, attend community meetings, and engage in dialogue. By networking, they gain insights, build alliances, and collectively address complex issues.

To do better in uncertain times, leaders need better *sight*. In this section, I would like to focus on four types of sights that leaders can center on.

Hindsight

Meaning: The ability to understand the nature of a situation clearly only after it has happened.

The "coulda, woulda, shoulda" feeling: It's that moment when you look back and think, "Ah, if only I'd known better!" Hindsight's like that annoying friend who always tells you what you should have done after the fact.

Where does it help? Hindsight isn't just about understanding what happened, but also about recognizing the factors that led to a particular outcome. It often involves a sense of "if only I knew then what I know now." So it is about expanding one's understanding. It is also about learning from the past as hindsight is essential for learning from our experiences and making better decisions in the future. The phrase "hindsight is 20/20" highlights the clarity we gain after the fact. Hindsight is also about learning the hard way. It is a good teacher, even if it's a bit harsh sometimes. The trick is to take what you learn and not make the same mistakes twice. It is like saying, "In hindsight, selling my shares in that company just before it took off was a poor financial decision."

Oversight

Meaning: The act of supervising or managing something.

The "another pair of eyes" feeling: Think of it like a positive, trusting relationship with the person providing oversight/supervision as it drastically changes the working experience. But it's all about whether that oversight feels like support or suffocating control. We want the good stuff, not the kind that makes us feel like we can't do anything without being judged. Frame oversight as a collaborative process of enhancing the work rather than nitpicking or finding flaws. It's like when proofreading your own work—you sometimes miss stuff because you're too close to it. That's why a second set of eyes is always helpful as oversight.

Where does it help? It helps in validation and confidence. Constructive oversight validates a generalist's ideas, especially when working in an unfamiliar territory. It acts as a quality control safeguard, giving them reassurance to execute more confidently. It also helps in building relationships as oversight creates opportunities to network and learn from experts in diverse fields, leading to a broader professional network for the generalist. For example, in terms of project management, a generalist project manager in health care might benefit from oversight by experienced project managers in construction or software development to learn risk mitigation tactics and agile methodologies. Likewise, in terms of marketing, a generalist marketer working for an educational platform might seek oversight from marketers in the entertainment or hospitality sectors, leading to out-of-the-box campaign ideas.

Insight

Meaning: A deep and accurate understanding of something, often a complex situation or concept.

The "light bulb" feeling: That feeling when things suddenly click and you understand something way better than before. It's like seeing the bigger picture, not just the individual pieces.

Where does it help? It helps go beyond surface-level knowledge as insight goes beyond mere facts or information. It involves grasping the underlying causes, connections, and implications within a situation. It also has an intuitive element as insights can sometimes have a sudden "aha!" quality to them, like putting together puzzle pieces. For example, imagine a team of managers sitting in a tense quarterly meeting. Picture that their revenue is steady, and innovation is stagnant. The CEO, after listening to fragmented updates, leans forward and says, "Everyone here is brilliant at what you do. But here's the problem—we're so focused on doing our jobs well that we have stopped seeing the bigger picture. What if marketing understood supply chain, and finance collaborated on customer experience? Let's stop asking, 'What's my job?' and start asking, 'What's our mission?' That's how we future-proof this business." The room falls silent and then buzzes with excitement as managers start brainstorming cross-functional ideas. The CEO's insights have created a sudden aha! moment.

Foresight

Meaning: The ability to anticipate or predict future events or developments and plan accordingly.

The "thinking ahead" feeling: It's like trying to read the future, but in a smart way. You look at what's happening now and figure out where things might be headed. It's like when someone says, "That company invested in green energy way before it was trendy—they had serious foresight."

Where does it help? It helps in being prepared. Foresight helps you avoid problems or grab opportunities before everyone else does. It's about making good guesses, not just blindly hoping for the best. For example, "The company's foresight in investing in renewable energy has paid off in the long run." It is not just about prediction. Foresight isn't about crystal-ball gazing, but informed anticipation based on trends, data analysis, and an understanding of potential scenarios. In terms of strategic advantage, foresight is incredibly valuable for businesses, organizations, and individuals as it aids in proactive planning and risk mitigation. In terms of different time horizons, foresight can focus on the immediate future, medium term, or very long-range outcomes. For example, "The investor's foresight in the tech sector led to significant returns."

Hindsight and foresight deal with timeline essentially, as hindsight looks at the past, but foresight looks to the future. However, oversight and insight deal with perception, as oversight is about surface-level understanding, and insight is about deep understanding. Table 6.1 summarizes the important distinction between these concepts:

Now that we understand the difference between these four types of sight, here is a 2×2 *SDSU framework*, sharing how different generalists deal with uncertainty. As sketched, *the Generalist Advantage* enables individuals to move from hindsight, through oversight and insight, to foresight.

I Shallow generalists are known for their hindsight

II Domain generalists are known for their oversight

III Skill generalists are known for their insight

IV Ultra generalists are known for their foresight

Figure 6.1 categorizes four types of generalists based on how each type of generalist approaches unknown or unpredictable situations. In the bottom left quadrant, we have hindsight associated with shallow generalists. This type of generalist focuses on learning from past mistakes and successes, using the knowledge and experience in a specialist

Table 6.1   Types of sights

	Hindsight	Oversight	Insight	Foresight
Focus	Past	Present	Present	Future
Nature	Understanding after the event	Surface-level comprehension	Deep-level comprehension	Anticipation before the event
Emotion involved	The "coulda, woulda, shoulda" feeling or feeling involving regret or self-criticism	The "another pair of eyes" feeling or feeling of "it makes sense now"	The "light bulb" feeling or feeling of "aha" or sharp understanding	The "thinking ahead" feeling or feeling of empowerment
Primary role	Learning from experience	Fixing issues, holistic thinking	Solving problems, gaining wisdom	Strategic planning, high-level decision-making

III **IN**sight (skill generalist)	IV **FORE**sight (ultra generalist)
I **HIND**sight (shallow generalist)	II **OVER**sight (domain generalist)

Dealing with Uncertainty

Figure 6.1   Uncertainty and generalists.

area to avoid repeating errors and capitalize on opportunities. Next, in the bottom right quadrant, we have oversight associated with domain generalists. This type of generalist has a wider domain understanding with experience of working in different industries/sectors, enabling them to benchmark their current domain with outside domains better.

In the top left quadrant, we have insight, which is associated with skill generalists. This type of generalist is skilled in a wide range of areas and uses that breadth to identify patterns and connections that others might miss, leading to innovative solutions. In the top right quadrant, we have foresight, associated with ultra generalists. This type of generalist possesses an even wider range of both skills and domains, allowing them to anticipate future trends and envision upcoming challenges better. Ultra generalists are assertive and composed following a proactive rather than reactive approach. This makes them particularly effective in *VUCA (volatile, uncertain, complex, and ambiguous)* environments.

Not every generalist is the same. Personality matters! Comfort with risk and ambiguity varies between shallow, domain, skill, and ultra generalists. Let's take an example of tolerance for ambiguity as it significantly varies between shallow generalists and ultra generalists. Generalists are accustomed to dealing with ambiguity and complexity, as they often work across multiple domains where clear-cut answers may not exist. They are comfortable operating in environments with incomplete information and are skilled at making decisions under uncertainty. However, shallow generalists are experts in a niche area, and they have little uncertainty as they continuously strive for answers in that focused space. Here, shallow generalists can benefit from hindsight, whereas ultra generalists can thrive on foresight.

Domain generalists are known for pattern recognition across fields. Their multidisciplinary experience allows them to draw on strategies employed in different domains to address current dilemmas. For them, oversight helps. Skill generalists, on other hand, are resourceful. Skill generalists instinctively leverage diverse skills and knowledge, crafting workarounds and makeshift solutions when the ideal path is blocked. For them, insights work best!

On a continuum, the more generalist you are, the more comfortable you are with the gray. You become less tied to rigid, predictable processes, and you develop a higher tolerance for navigating unknowns without getting overwhelmed by a lack of answers. Like-

❝the more generalist you are, the more comfortable you are with the gray. ❞

wise, the more generalist you are, the lower attachment you have to perfection. Ultra generalists quickly grasp the "good enough for now" approach, as they have to balance pace with productivity. This willingness to iterate over an extended period reduces paralysis in the face of the unknown. Overall, *the Generalist Advantage* is that they approach the unknown as a puzzle to be solved, not a crisis.

The idea then is to play to these strengths, like an ultra generalist. In fact, ultra generalists utilize different sorts of strategies to build organizational resilience to uncertainty by maximizing their generalist talent!

HOW DOES FORESIGHT HELP ULTRA GENERALIST LEADERS IN PREPARING FOR UNCERTAIN TIMES?

Here are some of the strategies and practical tips on how foresight can be a powerful tool for generalist leaders facing unpredictable circumstances:

Effective Strategies

♦ *Horizon scanning / Seeing around corners:* By recognizing emerging trends, potential disruptions, and weak signals, generalist leaders can anticipate challenges others might miss and adapt their approach before a crisis occurs.

- *Trend analysis/Spotting emerging markets:* Foresight allows generalists to see beyond current trends and into the needs of the future. This lets them be first movers in new sectors or develop innovative products and services before others recognize their potential.
- *Assessing potential threats:* Foresight helps leaders look beyond the immediate horizon to identify risks that might seem unlikely today but could become major issues down the road.
- *Minimizing vulnerability:* With a broader understanding of potential risks, leaders can take steps to proactively make their operations more resilient, whether it's diversifying supply chains, investing in cybersecurity, or building adaptable systems.
- *Discovering new partnerships:* Leaders with foresight can recognize areas where their skills and resources could intersect with untapped opportunities, fostering strategic collaborations that bring mutual benefit.

Practical Tips

- Embracing Scrappy Experiments
  - *Action > endless planning:* Start with basic hypotheses and small-scale testing rather than attempting extensive up-front analysis.
  - *Data-driven but not data-limited:* Collect data while acknowledging the unknown. Allow for real-time course correction without relying on complete information.
- Scenario-Based Thinking
  - *The what-ifs:* Leaders who cultivate foresight encourage themselves and their teams to constantly ask what-if questions, challenging assumptions and preparing them for a range of potential outcomes.
  - *Outside perspective:* Ask, "If someone from a radically different background faced this, how might they see it?" This keeps ideas flowing when your usual approaches hit a dead end.

“If someone from a radically different background faced this, how might they see it?”

◆ Building Resilience
  - *Failure as feedback:* Normalize that some paths won't pan out. Create a culture where missteps are reframed as opportunities for finding new routes.
  - *Celebrate wins along the way:* The very act of moving forward amid uncertainty is a success! Keep spirits up by acknowledging incremental progress.

GENERALIST-LED CASE STUDIES FOR UNCERTAIN EVENTS

Generalists, with their broad skill sets and holistic perspectives, are uniquely positioned to navigate the complexities of today's uncertain business landscape. Generalist leadership can be instrumental in guiding organizations through periods of uncertainty, from market disruptions to global crises. In this section, we explore three business scenarios where generalist leaders leverage their adaptability, broad knowledge base, and ability to connect disparate ideas to deal with uncertain events.

Scenario 1: Adapting to Market Disruption in Retail

◆ *Challenge:* A retail company faces a sudden disruption in its supply chain due to global shipping delays and rising material costs. As a result, inventory shortages threaten their ability to meet customer demand, especially during the holiday season.
◆ *Generalist Leadership Approach:*
  - A generalist leader would leverage their adaptability by quickly assessing alternative solutions across multiple domains—supply chain, logistics, marketing, and customer relations.
  - They might first coordinate with various teams to explore sourcing options from local suppliers or initiate partnerships with smaller vendors who can deliver on short notice.
  - Meanwhile, they could work with the marketing team to adjust messaging and manage customer expectations, offering promotions on available items while incentivizing preorders.
  - Their broad knowledge of different functions allows them to balance short-term tactical changes with long-term strategic adjustments, maintaining brand reputation and customer loyalty during an uncertain period.

Scenario 2: Navigating Rapid Technological Change in Health Care

◆ *Challenge:* A health care organization needs to implement a new digital platform for telehealth consultations after a sudden surge in patient demand for remote services. However, the organization is faced with low employee tech skills and patient privacy concerns, creating a barrier to fast implementation.

◆ *Generalist Leadership Approach:*

- The generalist leader approaches the challenge by forming a cross-functional team that includes IT, compliance, health care practitioners, and patient experience advocates.

- Drawing from diverse experiences in technology and human resources, they prioritize both technical and human elements. They propose a phased rollout, starting with a pilot program, ensuring that staff receive hands-on training and that patient data security protocols are rigorously tested.

- This phased approach balances technical requirements with employee adaptability, ultimately fostering confidence among staff and patients.

- By integrating insights from multiple areas, the generalist leader can effectively steer the organization through a complex technological shift without compromising service quality.

Scenario 3: Shifting Strategic Focus for a Software Company

◆ *Challenge:* A software company has invested heavily in a product feature based on market research that suddenly becomes obsolete due to a competitor's unexpected innovation. This leaves the company in a reactive position, and there's pressure from stakeholders to pivot quickly.

◆ *Generalist Leadership Approach:*

- A generalist leader would take an agile and holistic approach to pivot the strategy. Leveraging their broad business understanding, they facilitate brainstorming sessions with the product, marketing, and sales teams to identify emerging customer needs and potential new features.

- Drawing on their cross-industry insights, they guide the team toward a *minimal viable product (MVP)* approach—basic and light version of offering—allowing the company to test new features rapidly and gather user feedback.

- Additionally, they might advocate for a customer engagement strategy that openly communicates the pivot, building trust and buy-in from early adopters.
- By keeping a flexible perspective and balancing different business lenses, the generalist leader navigates the organization through the strategic shift while managing stakeholder expectations.

Generalists Tackling with Complexity

Generalists are often better equipped to deal with complexity due to their broad skill set and interdisciplinary work exposure. In terms of *skills*, a generalist leader in a technology company may draw on knowledge from engineering, marketing, finance, and psychology to develop a comprehensive strategy for launching a new product. In terms of *industry domain exposure*, a generalist leader in a health care organization may bring together clinicians, researchers, and administrators to develop a holistic approach to patient care.

One key advantage of complex events is that they encourage us to look for a *paradigm shift*. A paradigm shift is a fundamental change in how we perceive and understand the world, often resulting in a transformative shift in perspective.

Explain It to Kids

Complexity: is like a tricky puzzle with lots of pieces that fit together in many different ways!

Dealing with complexity is about the thought process, and there are four thinking styles that we often see in today's workplaces: silo thinking, divergent thinking, convergent thinking, and holistic thinking.

Silo Thinking

- *What it is:* Focusing only on your own department, team, or area of expertise, without considering the bigger picture.
- *Example:* A marketing head of department demanding marketing and promotion resources or funding without considering the overall strategy or benefits to the entire organization.

♦ *Workplace implications:* Lack of collaboration, misaligned goals, duplicated effort, and missed opportunities.

Divergent Thinking

♦ *What it is:* Generating as many ideas as possible, exploring all sorts of possibilities, and thinking outside the box.

♦ *Example:* A brand manager leading a brainstorming session where every idea, even the crazy ones, gets written on the board.

♦ *Workplace implications:* At the start of a project, when you're facing a new problem, or need a jolt of creativity.

Convergent Thinking

♦ *What it is:* Narrowing down ideas, evaluating options, and making logical decisions.

♦ *Example:* A human resource executive guiding his or her team through the brainstormed list and figuring out which ideas are actually feasible and fit the goal.

♦ *Workplace implications:* After you have explored possibilities, you will need to choose a direction and act.

Holistic Thinking

♦ *What it is:* Seeing the big picture, understanding interconnectedness, and considering the long-term impacts of decisions.

♦ *Example:* A CEO of an oil and gas company crafting a company strategy considering not only the financial impact but also the potential effects of gasoline emissions on employees, the community, and the environment.

♦ *Workplace implications:* For strategic planning, risk management, ethical decision-making, and overall leadership success.

Leaders may use these four types of thinking at different points. However, silo thinking is usually the discouraged approach as it limits innovation and collaboration, whereas holistic thinking is the goal as it enables generalist leaders to fit the different pieces of organization together. Table 6.2 outlines the key points of silo thinking, divergent thinking, convergent thinking, and holistic thinking.

Now that we understand the difference between these four types of thinking, Figure 6.2 shows a 2×2 *SDSU framework*, sharing how

Table 6.2   Four types of thinking

Thinking style	Focus	Key characteristics	Ideal use cases
Silo thinking	Narrowed	Disregards the big picture, limited to one's own area	Specialized tasks within a larger project
Divergent thinking	Expansive	Generates many ideas, open to unusual possibilities	Brainstorming, early stages of problem-solving, innovation
Convergent thinking	Analytical	Evaluates ideas, focuses on feasibility in decision-making	Choosing a path forward, refining solutions, turning ideas into action
Holistic thinking	Systems-focused	Sees the big picture, understands interconnectedness for long-term implications	Strategic decision-making, complex problem-solving, understanding environmental or social impact

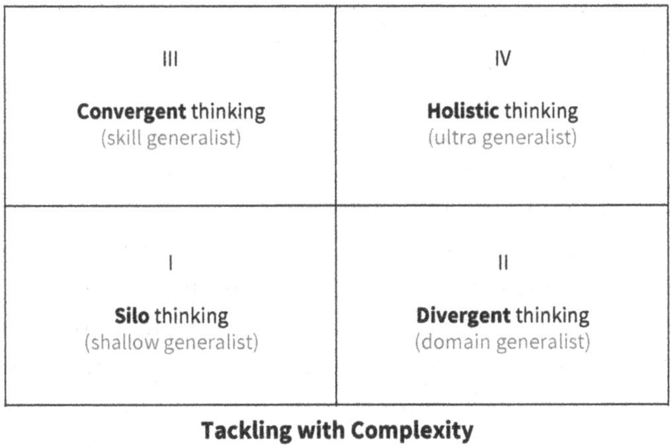

III	IV
Convergent thinking (skill generalist)	**Holistic** thinking (ultra generalist)
I	II
Silo thinking (shallow generalist)	**Divergent** thinking (domain generalist)

Tackling with Complexity

Figure 6.2 Complexity and generalists.

different generalists deal with complexity. As sketched, *the Generalist Advantage* here enables one to move from silo thinking, through divergent thinking and convergent thinking, to holistic thinking.

I Shallow generalists are known for their silo thinking

II Domain generalists are known for their divergent thinking

III Skill generalists are known for their convergent thinking

IV Ultra generalists are known for their holistic thinking

This figure illustrates different types of thinking patterns used by generalists, categorized by their approach to tackling with complexity. In the bottom left quadrant, we have silo thinking, associated with shallow generalists. This type of generalist focuses on a narrow range of information and may miss alternative perspectives. They may be more likely to make decisions based on expert information or preconceived ideas. Silo thinkers are practical and efficient in straightforward or routine tasks but may struggle to connect their work with larger organizational or interdisciplinary goals. Next, in the bottom right quadrant, we have divergent thinking, associated with domain generalists. This type of generalist has a wide understanding of domains, enabling them to generate a broad range of creative solutions. They are able to think outside the box and challenge conventional wisdom.

In the top left quadrant, we have convergent thinking, which is associated with skill generalists. This type of generalist excels at bringing together information and ideas to find a single, optimal solution. Their skill set enables them to critically analyze and synthesize information within a boundary. Convergent thinkers are particularly valuable in fields that excel at narrowing down options to the most effective solutions. They're often brought in to refine or perfect a solution. In the top right quadrant, we have holistic thinking, associated with ultra generalists. Holistic thinkers bring both breadth and depth, allowing them to approach complex systems with a comprehensive, interconnected perspective. This makes them invaluable in senior management or leadership roles, where a nuanced understanding and the ability to anticipate future implications are essential. Ultra generalists as holistic thinkers (like leaders with foresight earlier) excel in high-stakes settings, especially VUCA (volatile, uncertain, complex, and ambiguous) environments.

It won't be incorrect to state that the keys to successful generalist leadership include self-awareness and continuous evolution. Generalists holistically are more aware as they understand the risks of missing nuances from the big-picture perspective and seek input from specialists at crucial junctures. Moreover, generalists focus on continuous evolution as they accept their knowledge will naturally be broader than it is deep. They encourage a culture of constant learning, including learning from specialists for targeted expertise. A shallow generalist is essentially a specialist or expert.

Next, I would like to discuss complexity in terms of the other three types (domain, skill, and ultra generalist), which are closer to the notion of generalists. In terms of how generalists excel with complexity, here is how these three generalists are different:

1. *Bridge builders:* Domain generalists naturally translate complexities across industry teams. This smooths communication of critical information and fosters alignment among those who typically speak different languages.
2. *Skillful masters:* Skill generalists operate on the principle that skills help you take a large, complex problem and divide it into smaller, more understandable pieces. Moreover, the higher the skills, the easier it is to approach a complex problem.
3. *Big-picture thinkers:* Ultra generalists grasp how pieces of a complex system interact; spotting trends specialists focused on isolated parts might miss. This translates into holistic decision-making, minimizing unforeseen knock-on effects.

Practical examples of these three generalist leaders could be pictured like this:

♦ *The cross-discipline harmonizer:* When launching a multifaceted new product, a domain generalist leader takes advantage of industry exposure from unrelated industries and sectors. They create clear communication channels and focus on the interconnectedness of goals drawing from diverse industries, ultimately ensuring smoother adoption of the finished product.
♦ *The innovative strategist:* During a business disruption (such as a supply chain breakdown, tech shift, change in trends),

a skill generalist leader envisions multiple future scenarios based on the different skill sets he or she possesses. They take leverage of varied skills they have learnt and create a fusion that can give an unmatched benefit.

◆ *The ambiguity tamer:* Faced with regulations in flux, an ultra generalist leader doesn't demand detailed long-term plans. Instead, they create modular systems adaptable to shifting conditions, minimizing wasted effort when change happens mid-project.

HOW DOES HOLISTIC THINKING HELP ULTRA GENERALIST LEADERS IN SOLVING COMPLEX PROBLEMS?

Holistic thinking is like a *helicopter view*, and it enables you to see from a distance (from the top) to see the grand scheme of things. But keep in mind, great leaders don't just live in the helicopter! They also know how to zoom in, connect with teams, and execute the details. The key is having the flexibility to move between perspectives. Remember, you're not going to become a holistic guru overnight. Start small, but be consistent. Here are a few effective strategies and practical tips around holistic thinking that ultra generalists use in complex problem-solving:

Effective Strategies

◆ *Seeing the forest, not just the trees:* Leaders often get bogged down in the details of daily operations. An ultra generalist's helicopter view means rising above that to focus on the big picture: company vision, long-term goals, and the strategic direction.

◆ *Understanding interconnectedness:* Ultra generalist leaders take the helicopter view to see how different departments, teams, and even external factors affect each other. This helps avoid unintended consequences of decisions.

◆ *Prioritizing effectively:* It's easy to get caught up in the urgent but less important. Ultra generalists' helicopter view helps leaders distinguish between what's critical to overall success and what can be delegated or deprioritized.

Practical Tips

♦ *Break it down:* Divide large, complex tasks into smaller and more manageable chunks. This lessens cognitive overload and makes overengineering less tempting.

♦ *Schedule time for reflection:* Urge leaders to carve out dedicated time to step back from the day-to-day and think strategically.

♦ *Use visual tools:* Mind maps, flow charts, or visual dashboards help leaders see the bigger picture and identify connections.

♦ *Bust those biases:* We all have blind spots! Actively look for stuff that challenges what you think you know. Think like a spiderweb, not a checklist.

♦ *Imagine the ripple effect:* Your awesome idea over here might make waves you didn't expect over there. Think ahead to avoid future headaches.

♦ *Be a knowledge sponge:* Don't be afraid to geek out about stuff outside your usual zone. Read about different industries, pick up new skills, and stay curious.

♦ *Find your sparring partner:* Have that go-to person who pokes holes in your plans before you roll them out.

Caution: Don't overengineer! In managing complex tasks, a lot of leaders fall into the trap of overengineering. *Overengineering* largely happens because of perfectionism. The desire for flawless solutions can lead to endless tinkering. Second, there is a fear of failure, a temptation to pile on features or safeguards to mitigate all possible risks. The third reason is scope creep—projects slowly becoming more elaborate without careful evaluation of what's essential.

In this situation, there are a few ways you can prevent overengineering. First, start with the *why*. Constantly refocusing the team on the fundamental problem they're solving and the core value they're delivering to the user/customer helps. Remember, everything else is secondary. Next, embrace the *minimum viable product (MVP)*. MVP is about launching a functional (basic) version initially. This allows you to get real-world feedback, learn, improve, and avoid wasted effort on features that don't matter. Third, *timebox decisions* and iterations. Setting clear deadlines and limits on how many rounds of refinement a project gets is of good value. Fourth, celebrate *progress over perfection*. Encourage a culture where shipping something good is more valuable than endlessly pursuing an unattainable ideal. Finally, empower teams to say *no*. Foster an environment where team members feel comfortable pushing back if they believe a feature or plan is becoming unnecessarily complex. These practical insights often help ultra generalists in avoiding the trap of overengineering.

GENERALIST-LED CASE STUDIES FOR COMPLEX PROBLEMS

There are various leadership challenges with very complex projects. This may include specific leadership hurdles such as managing time and scope with shifting goals and fostering team adaptability. In terms of risk assessment, generalists identify broad areas of potential failure points by seeking expert input into multiple areas, enabling more effective contingency planning. In terms of failure as feedback, they leverage a wider set of experiences to make the most of setbacks. This reduces defensiveness and creates a team focused on finding what works now, not simply proving their original plan was *right*. Let's dive into examples highlighting generalist leadership strengths when faced with the tangled beast of complex projects.

Scenario 1: The Legacy System Revamp
- *Challenge:* A company must modernize an essential, decades-old, and poorly documented software system developed in-house. Specialists understand the current state but lack the bigger picture for future evolution.
- *Generalist Leader Approach:*
  - Assembles a team combining deep technical understanding of the old system with expertise in emerging tech trends. Ensures a translator/facilitator role exists to bridge understanding gaps.
  - Drives constant feedback loops to avoid veering too far into theoretical improvements without factoring in the current system's limitations.
  - Identifies zones for innovation—areas where modernization benefits outweigh risks, allowing the project to advance in digestible segments.

Scenario 2: Launching a High-Stake, Cross-Functional Initiative

◆ *Challenge:* Multiple departments must collaborate on a new offering involving significant changes to customer workflows, software interactions, and internal processes. Specialists get mired in the granular issues of their area.

◆ *Generalist Leader Approach:*

- Establishes a shared central project vision with metrics that prioritize progress toward that outcome over minor wins within isolated work units.
- Proactively identifies friction points between department goals. Drives constant negotiation and compromises based on how adjustments contribute to the larger project outcome.
- Anticipates resistance to change. Employs skills in persuasion and uses cross-industry examples to show the necessity of disrupting internal norms for long-term benefits.

Scenario 3: The Moving Target Client Project

◆ *Challenge:* Client specifications shift significantly mid-project. Specialists may resist reworking already finished aspects, losing sight of the client's core needs.

◆ *Generalist Leader Approach:*

- Prioritizes regular client check-ins to uncover major goal changes as early as possible, minimizing wasted effort for downstream teams.
- Revisits original problem statements, reminding teams the solutions serve those broader issues, not simply what was requested months ago.
- Creates a culture of flexible iteration—work is seen as stepping stones for improvement, not set in stone the first time round.

Innovation Ins and Outs of Generalists

Innovation is about creating value, as much as it is about uniqueness. Moreover, it is about introducing new ideas, methods, processes, products, or services that can enhance the productivity of an organization. It is not a surprise that generalists fuel innovation. In terms of connecting the unconnected, their multidisciplinary knowledge helps them spot overlooked links between ideas, technologies, or processes. For example: a software company utilizes its user interface (UI) designer's expertise in psychology to revamp a sales portal, increasing ease of use and ultimately driving up conversion rates.

Explain It to Kids

Innovation: is like using your imagination to create new toys, games, or ideas, which calls for fun!

Likewise, generalists often adapt outside inspiration, as they draw ideas from unconventional sources, transferring solutions from outside their original context. For example, an e-commerce start-up borrows gamification concepts from educational apps to make their customer loyalty program more engaging, significantly boosting retention. Also, generalists drive innovation by challenging industry defaults. They bring a fresh perspective, questioning outdated practices and assumptions that experts take for granted. For example, a health care provider with a marketing background suggests moving a portion of consultations online, a radical idea then, but now commonplace after the pandemic.

In terms of resourcefulness and experimentation, generalists are less tied to deep specialization, and they invest in *rapid prototyping*—exploring ideas by actively experimenting—and low-cost testing of concepts. For example, before embarking on expensive app development, they utilize simple online tools to create a mock-up of their new service, gathering valuable customer feedback early on. Moreover, generalists are translators for innovation. They make complex ideas understandable to different teams, ensuring buy-in from decision-makers as they are less focused on technical aspects. For example, when pitching a new AI-driven analytics platform, the focus isn't on algorithms, but on the real-world business benefits such as time saved and more precise forecasting.

There are two main approaches to innovation: inside-out innovation and outside-in innovation. *Inside-out innovation* begins with the company's internal strengths, expertise, and existing technologies.

The question is: "What can we create with what we have?" *Outside-in innovation*, on the other hand, begins by deeply understanding customers' needs, pain points, and desires. The question is: "What does the market truly want?" Products or services are developed and then pushed to the market when working on inside-out, whereas in outside-in, product or service development is tailored to address those specific needs. Table 6.3 presents key distinction points between inside-out and outside-in innovation.

- *Example of inside-out innovation:* A technology company develops a new, highly efficient microprocessor and then seeks out applications based on that processor's capabilities.
- *Example of outside-in innovation:* A software company realizes customers are struggling with a complicated data management task. They develop a user-friendly tool specifically to streamline that process.

Similar to this, there are two other aspects of innovation: explorative innovation and exploitative innovation. *Explorative innovation* focuses on creating entirely new products, services, or business models (often it involves moving into uncharted territories, such as a blue ocean strategy). On the other hand, *exploitative innovation* focuses on refining and improving existing products, services, or processes (often it is about building on what already works). We often call environments where both aspects are covered *ambidextrous organizations*—organizations that excel at both exploiting existing capabilities for efficiency and exploring new opportunities for innovation.

Table 6.3   Inside-out vs outside-in innovation

	Inside-out innovation	Outside-in innovation
Focus	Company's strengths and expertise	Market needs and customer desires
Process	Leverages existing assets and R&D	Leverages market research to develop solutions
Example	Develop new tech and find applications	Identify customer pain point to create solution
Pros	Builds on core competencies	High potential for market success
Cons	May not address market needs	Requires significant market research

Table 6.4 Explorative vs exploitative innovation

	Explorative innovation	Exploitative innovation
Focus	Radically new	Refinement of existing
Risk	High-risk, high-reward	Lower-risk, predictable returns
Approach	Experimentation, venturing into new domains	Optimization, leveraging current knowledge
Examples	Breakthrough invention	Enhancing an existing offering (product or service line)

Table 6.4 presents key distinction points between explorative and exploitative innovation.

♦ *Examples of explorative innovation:* Introduction of the original smartphones, development of gene therapy treatments, pioneering virtual reality in the gaming industry.
♦ *Examples of exploitative innovation:* Iterations of smartphones with better cameras, new varieties of an existing soft drink, streamlining a manufacturing process for cost reduction.

Now that we understand the difference between inside-out and outside-in innovation, and likewise the difference between explorative and exploitative innovation, here is a 2×2 *SDSU framework*, plotting organizational excellence on the y-axis and innovation on the x-axis, sharing how generalists can drive their innovation:

I Shallow generalists are best cut out for inside-out innovation.

II Domain generalists are best cut out for outside-in innovation.

III Skill generalists are best cut out for inside-out innovation.

IV Ultra generalists are best cut out for outside-in innovation.

Figure 6.3 divides the concept of innovation into four quadrants, each representing a different type of generalist with a distinct approach to innovation.

Quadrant I: Inside-out innovation (shallow generalist) focuses on operational excellence, and typically relies on the organization's existing resources, structures, and expertise, using these internal

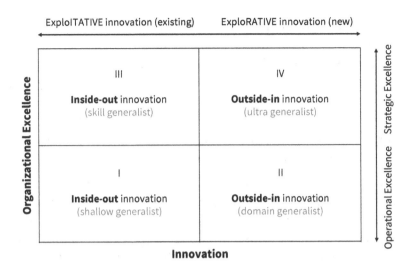

Figure 6.3 Innovation types and generalists.

strengths to drive incremental improvements. Inside-out innovation here is largely focused on efficiency and minor process enhancements. Shallow generalists in this quadrant may make small-scale, short-term changes that optimize specific processes without challenging the broader strategic direction of the organization. Their familiarity with internal routines makes them adept at spotting areas for improvement in current operations, though they may lack the perspective for more groundbreaking changes.

Quadrant II: Outside-in innovation (domain generalist) also focuses on operational excellence, but leverages external ideas and trends. Domain generalists bring in new perspectives from outside the organization, applying lessons from other industries or emerging trends to improve day-to-day processes. By bringing external insights to bear on existing operations, these individuals drive innovation that aligns with industry benchmarks and evolving best practices. Domain generalists in this role are adept at adapting external innovations to the company's context, making them valuable for organizations aiming to modernize or adapt quickly without altering their overarching strategy.

Quadrant III: Inside-out innovation (skill generalist) focuses on leveraging varied knowledge within the organization to achieve strategic excellence. Skill generalists excel at drawing on established internal strengths to create more substantial, long-term improvements aligned with the company's vision and goals. Their innovation is more strategic than operational, as they seek to transform core competencies or existing expertise into competitive advantages. This type of inside-out innovation is ideal for organizations looking to double down on their unique strengths, refining and scaling them to drive sustainable growth and differentiation.

Quadrant IV: Outside-in innovation (ultra generalist) engages in innovating with a strategic focus. They combine a deep understanding of external trends and market shifts with an ability to integrate those insights into a transformative vision for the organization. Ultra generalists in this quadrant look beyond the company's current strengths, seeking to incorporate entirely new capabilities, technologies, or business models. This type of innovation is exploratory and high impact, often redefining the organization's position and image in the market. Ultra generalists drive breakthrough innovations that align with future-oriented strategies, making them highly valuable for companies aiming to stay at the forefront of industry shifts or disrupt their markets.

INNOVATION MANAGEMENT PRACTICES FOR GENERALISTS

Pragmatically speaking, let's break down how you can tailor your innovation management practices to empower different kinds of generalists:

Managing Innovation for Shallow Generalists
- Partner shallow generalists (also known as hyper specialists) with wider generalists who can help quickly assess the feasibility of ideas and refine their focus.
- Support swift knowledge acquisition in domains relevant to their innovation. Encourage the *minimum viable knowledge (MVK)* approach to prioritize rapid gains. MVK is the amount of information that you need to know about a subject to operate effectively in that domain.

- Being process obsessed, these generalists often innovate through process optimization. Task them with analyzing bottlenecks and devising creative solutions.

Managing Innovation for Domain Generalists

- Use them as industry trend scouts. Allow them to guide longer-term visioning sessions as they grasp how various puzzle pieces of their industry could potentially change.
- Push them to think beyond existing industry practices. Ask *what-if questions* that provoke them to look outside the usual approaches.
- Facilitate networking and knowledge exchange with peers in the industry. Outside voices can prevent stagnant internal echo chambers.

Managing Innovation for Skill Generalists

- Let them tackle cross-departmental problems where their general skill set brings a fresh approach others would miss.
- Provide access and experimentation time with new technology and tools that could lead to skills enhancement.
- Skill generalists often excel at driving ideation sessions, so let them guide their teams toward novel problem-solving.

Managing Innovation for Ultra Generalists

- Create freedom for unconstrained exploration of ideas, even if seemingly unrelated to immediate business goals. A percentage of innovation time must be *blue sky thinking* (brainstorming without limitations).
- Connect them with thought leaders in disparate fields to fuel fresh thinking and potential crossover connections.
- Challenge their biases by pushing back on their overconfidence. Even ultra generalists can fall into patterns; they need constructive critics to keep evolving.

Organizations can maximize innovation from generalists by creating "sandbox spaces," which is allowing dedicated time, resources, and the freedom to explore, separate from daily responsibilities. Also, providing mentorship opportunities for the different types of generalists can guide them, creating a culture of constructive challenges that can further spur innovation for generalists.

GENERALIST-LED INNOVATION CASE STUDIES

The Generalist Advantage has worked for a lot of companies in driving their innovation. *WhatsApp*, for instance, disrupted expensive SMS services by offering free messaging across borders. *Airbnb* introduced a new business model by connecting travelers with unique accommodations. In the music industry, *Spotify* pioneered music streaming, changing how people access and enjoy music. Here are some more examples of generalist-led innovation:

3M: The innovation giant specifically encourages interdisciplinary teams and knowledge sharing, developing generalist leadership acumen. This is how a "slightly sticky" adhesive evolved into the now ubiquitous Post-it notes.

Dyson: Combining a background in both design and engineering, James Dyson as outside-in generalist revolutionized the vacuum cleaner. His outside perspective led to an entirely new and improved system.

Tesla: Elon Musk, a classic ultra generalist, unafraid to dive into drastically different fields (space exploration, EVs, and neurotechnology), sees patterns across industries and drives a radical level of innovation. Elon—a generalist with expertise in engineering, entrepreneurship, and technology—has led Tesla to develop cutting-edge electric vehicles, solar energy products, and energy storage solutions.

Apple: Steve Jobs, as a generalist with a background in design, engineering, and business, played key roles in driving innovation at Apple by combining his diverse expertise to create groundbreaking products like the iPhone and iPad.

Amazon: Amazon is a good example of innovation driven by a generalist approach. Founder Jeff Bezos, with a background in computer science and finance, applied his diverse skills to disrupt traditional retail models and revolutionize e-commerce, live streaming, and cloud computing.

Google: Google's culture of innovation is fueled by generalists who embrace experimentation, collaboration, and creativity. Cofounders Larry Page and Sergey Brin, with backgrounds in computer science and mathematics, fostered a culture of innovation that has led to the extension of transformative products and services such as Google Search, Gmail, and Google Maps.

Problem-Solving Modes of Generalists

Generalists employ various problem-solving modes to tackle challenges and drive solutions across different domains, including experimental, pragmatic, ethical, and iterative problem-solving modes. They are generally better at *lateral thinking*—a problem-solving approach that involves looking at issues from unconventional angles.

Explain It to Kids

Problem-solving is like being a detective: you look for clues to figure out how to fix a puzzle or make something work better!

In terms of experimental problem-solving, generalists embrace experimentation as a means of exploring potential solutions and learning from failure. They prototype ideas, test hypotheses, and gather feedback to refine their approach and improve outcomes over time. In terms of pragmatic problem-solving, generalists prioritize practicality and feasibility when developing solutions to real-world problems. They consider resource constraints, time limitations, and other practical considerations to ensure that their solutions are viable and actionable.

Next, generalists also adopt an ethical problem-solving approach, as they work on the ethical implications of their decisions and actions when solving problems. They adhere to ethical principles and values, strive to do no harm, and prioritize the well-being of all stakeholders involved. Oftentimes, they make use of an *iterative problem-solving mode*, through which generalists approach problem-solving as an iterative process, continuously refining their solutions based on feedback and results. They monitor progress, evaluate outcomes, and adjust as needed to achieve desired goals and objectives. These problem-solving modes enable generalists to navigate diverse challenges, innovate, and drive solutions across various domains and contexts.

However, in talking about generalists and the problem-solving conundrum, I would like to discuss the approach of zooming in and zooming out first. Zooming in and zooming out are powerful metaphors for how we shift our focus to tackle problems effectively. Here's how they work:

- *Zooming-in approach to problem-solving:* This approach focuses on the nitty-gritty of a problem. It analyzes specific components, data points, or individual steps in a process. It is helpful in analyzing root causes (drilling down to the core reason behind an issue), understanding a mechanism (how does a specific piece of the problem function?), and spotting errors or inconsistencies (where exactly are things breaking down?).

- *Zooming-out approach to problem-solving:* This approach, conversely, takes a big-picture view of the problem, its context, and potential solutions. It helps in seeing wider patterns (are there related issues or trends contributing to the problem?), prioritization (where does this problem fit within your overall goals?) and exploring broader solutions (are there alternative frameworks or approaches you haven't considered?).

Both approaches complement each other. You can't truly understand a problem without both perspectives. Zooming in too much leads to tunnel vision, while only zooming out could mean missing crucial details. So, effective problem-solving often involves switching between zooming in and out multiple times. You might start big picture, zoom in to analyze, then zoom out to consider broader solutions. Example: let's say your car ignition is not working. Zooming in suggests checking the battery, fuel levels, specific fuses, examining for signs of mechanical failure. Zooming out suggests asking: When did this problem start? Are there other symptoms? Is it a user error issue (like leaving the lights on)? Is there a bigger trend (such as this happening periodically)? So are you zooming in or out right now? This is the question I want you to start with.

Taking the zoom perspective further, let's talk about focus. There are four types of focus. Here's a breakdown of the differences between deep focus, micro focus, macro focus, and meta focus. Think of these less like strict categories and more as different lenses through which you can view your tasks and goals.

Deep Focus

◆ Deep focus is intense, sustained concentration on a single task for an extended period, minimizing distractions. It allows you to dive into the complexities of a task, problem, or piece of information.

◆ *Examples:*
  ● A programmer coding without interruption for hours.
  ● A writer deeply immersed in drafting a chapter.
  ● A scientist analyzing complex data.

Micro Focus

◆ Micro focus is on the smallest, most immediate actions within a task or project. It involves breaking things down into small, concrete steps. This manages emotional overload and makes progress feel achievable, especially with large tasks.

◆ *Examples:*
  ● Focusing on writing a single paragraph instead of an entire essay.
  ● Completing one item on a project to-do list.
  ● Solving one part of a math equation.

Macro Focus

◆ Macro focus is the big-picture view of your goals, projects, and priorities. It keeps you connected to the overall direction you want to move in. It also prevents getting lost in the details and ensures actions align with the larger purpose.

◆ *Examples:*
  ● A start-up owner considering their overall business strategy.
  ● A student keeping their final year goals in mind while planning each week.
  ● Someone reviewing their budget in the context of their long-term financial aspirations.

Meta Focus

◆ Meta Focus is built on the why behind what you're doing. It connects to your core values, motivations, and the real impact you want to make. It drives motivation, meaning, and resilience—especially for challenging or long-term goals.

◆ *Examples:*

- A doctor remembering their patient-driven values amid difficult tasks.
- An entrepreneur being motivated by their vision of improving people's lives.
- A student focused on the long-term impact of their education on their future.

These focus types are *not mutually exclusive*—you can often utilize them in combination. For instance:

Deep focus + Micro focus: Breaking a complex task into small pieces helps you apply deep focus to each component individually.

Macro focus + Meta focus: Your big-picture goals should ideally align with your core values.

Table 6.5 presents a summary of the four types of focus.

But how does focus support problem-solving? Focus and problem-solving are deeply intertwined. Focus builds mental muscle! Your

Table 6.5   Types of focus needed for problem-solving

	What is it?	What's the purpose?	Any examples?
Deep focus	Intense concentration on a single task	Complex problem-solving	Coding, writing, data analysis
Micro focus	Focus on the smallest steps	Manages emotional overload, makes progress achievable	Writing a paragraph, completing a to-do list item
Macro focus	Big-picture view of goals and priorities	Maintains direction, avoids getting lost in details	Business strategy, student planning, financial budgeting
Meta focus	Focus on the why behind your actions	Motivation, meaning, resilience	Patient-centered care, purpose-driven entrepreneurship

focus strengthens solving problems. Each problem acts as a form of mental training. It is rewarding! The sense of accomplishment from solving a problem reinforces the benefits of concentration, promoting positive cycles. It identifies distractions. The problem-solving process helps you become more aware of the things that break your focus in the process, allowing you to manage them better. Different focus types are for different problem-solving stages. For example, you might use deep focus to analyze the core of the problem and micro focus to ascertain the steps of the problem.

Here's a breakdown of the key connections between focus and problem-solving: *Deep focus* facilitates the exploration of multiple solutions. You have the mental space to consider unconventional approaches. *Micro focus* makes progress tangible, fueling motivation to continue tackling the problem. *Macro focus* helps prioritize and allocate resources effectively, maximizing problem-solving efforts. *Meta focus* facilitates creative thinking and seeking out-of-the-box solutions when directly connected to the purpose of solving the problem.

Now that we understand the difference between these four types of focus, here is a 2×2 *SDSU framework* sharing how different generalists use different focus approaches to problem-solving. As sketched, *the Generalist Advantage* enables individuals to move from deep focus, through macro focus and micro focus, to meta focus.

I Shallow generalists are known for deep focus.

II Domain generalists are known for macro focus.

III Skill generalists are known for micro focus.

IV Ultra generalists are known for meta focus.

Figure 6.4 divides the concept of problem-solving modes into four quadrants. Each quadrant offers a distinct way of engaging with problems, depending on the individual's skill set and domain experience breadth, making them suited for different types of challenges and organizational roles. The deep and micro focus quadrants are more execution oriented, while the macro and meta focus quadrants are strategic, making this framework useful for identifying the right generalist approach for specific problem-solving scenarios.

III **Micro** focus (skill generalist)	IV **Meta** focus (ultra generalist)
I **Deep** focus (shallow generalist)	II **Macro** focus (domain generalist)

Problem-Solving Modes

Figure 6.4 Problem–solving modes and generalists.

Quadrant I (shallow generalist) is about deep focus. This approach allows individuals to develop a nuanced understanding of a specific area. They can identify subtle patterns and make incremental improvements due to their deep engagement with one area. Quadrant II (domain generalist) is about macro focus. This approach is ideal for solving complex problems from a fresh outsider perspective. These individuals are adept at creating broad strategies and drawing connections between different parts of their domain.

Quadrant III (skill generalist) is about micro focus. This approach excels at breaking down complex problems into smaller, more manageable tasks, and they are able to identify the most efficient and effective way to solve them. This style is often associated with systems thinking, where the focus is on understanding how different parts of a system interact with each other. Quadrant IV (ultra generalist) finally is about meta focus. It is a high-level, overarching approach to problem-solving. Ultra generalists have wide-ranging knowledge and focus on connecting ideas across multiple fields, which allows them to view problems through a meta-lens. This mode is ideal for strategic and visionary thinking. They are often suited for leadership roles or roles that require orchestrating multiple perspectives. This style is often associated with a creative mindset, where the focus is on generating new ideas and approaches.

PROBLEM-SOLVING APPROACHES OF GENERALISTS

Let's explore the unique problem-solving approaches that only generalists can offer:

The Detailed Prototyper: Shallow Generalist

- *Strength:* Bias toward action and swift testing of rough concepts over endless theorizing.
- *Approach:* Breaks down large problems into smaller, testable chunks, quickly getting feedback that drives iterations toward functional (even if scrappy) solutions.
- *Example:* Launches a basic landing page to gauge interest for a new service rather than wasting months on complex development without market validation.

The Pattern Seeker: Domain Generalist

- *Strength:* Spots connections across fields, seeing similarities between seemingly unrelated problems.
- *Approach:* Leverages knowledge from one domain to propose solutions inspired by another context. He or she will ask, "Has anyone solved something similar to this, even if it was in a completely different industry?"
- *Example:* Notices customer service bottlenecks resemble traffic flow issues, prompting the use of queueing theory concepts to revamp the intake process.

The Bricoleur: Skill Generalist

- *Strength:* Resourcefulness and recombination of existing elements into new configurations.
- *Approach:* Starts with an inventory of what's readily available (skills, tools, knowledge) and recombines those in nonstandard ways to achieve a workable solution.
- *Example:* Lacks coding expertise but utilizes a combination of online automation tools, basic scripts, and team member resources to create a makeshift data analysis workflow.

The Translator: Ultra Generalist

- *Strength:* Synthesizes ideas across disciplines, explaining complex concepts in simple terms. Unburdened by ingrained assumptions, asks seemingly "naive questions" that cut to the core of the issue.

- *Approach:* Bridges divides between specialists, facilitates communication, and focuses on solutions through shared understanding of the overall problem. Also, this challenges the "we've always done it this way" mentality, often revealing underlying factors others have become blind to.
- *Example:* Distills an engineer's technical jargon about a product flaw, framing it in terms of customer impact for the sales and marketing teams, ensuring cross-functional alignment.

Generalists aren't limited to just one mode. They fluidly shift between and combine these approaches. Also, mode choice depends on the problem's nature and available resources. Nevertheless, these modes complement, not replace, problem-solving.

GENERALIST-LED PROBLEM-SOLVING CASE STUDIES

In complex and unpredictable business environments, problem-solving demands more than just deep expertise. *The Generalist Advantage* has worked for a lot of companies in this respect to solve their problems. This section highlights real-world examples where leaders with generalist skills, spanning multiple disciplines, drive transformative solutions to tackle business challenges. These leaders leverage their versatility to address issues that don't fit neatly into any single field, from rapid market pivots to technological disruptions and evolving consumer demands.

Starbucks, for instance, under the leadership of Howard Schultz, a generalist with a background in marketing and management, adapted to the 2008 recession by focusing on quality and the in-store experience rather than cost-cutting. His multifaceted approach preserved brand loyalty and set the company up for sustained growth. In the FMCG industry, *Unilever* CEO Paul Polman, with experience spanning finance, consumer goods, and sustainability, steered Unilever toward a purpose-driven model by integrating environmental and social goals into the business strategy. His broad perspective led to the successful implementation of the Sustainable Living Plan, boosting brand reputation and long-term growth. At *Slack*, founder Stewart Butterfield, with experience in design, gaming, and entrepreneurship, originally created the platform as a pivot from a failed gaming project. His generalist approach helped transform Slack into a groundbreaking team communication tool, widely adopted across industries for its user-friendly design and functionality. Here are some more examples of generalist-led problem-solving:

Netflix: As streaming competition intensified, Netflix CEO Reed Hastings, who has experience across software engineering, education, and media, led a pivot from DVD rentals to a streaming service and then into original content. This generalist perspective helped Hastings make bold, future-oriented decisions that disrupted traditional media, transforming Netflix into a global entertainment powerhouse.

Procter & Gamble: Faced with a rapidly changing consumer goods market, Procter & Gamble's CEO A.G. Lafley championed an "open innovation" model. With a generalist background in brand management and strategic leadership, Lafley encouraged collaboration across different teams and with external partners, accelerating innovation and strengthening P&G's product lineup, which led to increased market share.

Virgin Group: Richard Branson's entrepreneurial spirit and diverse interests have enabled him to build a successful conglomerate across various industries. His generalist mindset allows him to identify opportunities and take calculated risks.

IDEO: This design and innovation consultancy firm fosters a culture of generalist thinking. By bringing together diverse teams with different expertise, IDEO generates creative solutions to complex problems.

Microsoft: When Satya Nadella became CEO of Microsoft, he used his background in engineering, cloud services, and management to pivot the company toward cloud computing and open-source collaboration. Nadella's generalist mindset drove cultural and strategic shifts, helping Microsoft regain relevance (corporate resurgence) in the tech industry and grow significantly in value.

IKEA: IKEA faced supply chain disruptions and shifting consumer demands but adapted through the guidance of CEO Jesper

Brodin, who leveraged his experience across manufacturing, logistics, and retail strategy. His generalist approach enabled IKEA to innovate in areas such as sustainable sourcing and e-commerce, ensuring resilience and alignment with evolving consumer values.

Chapter 6 Takeaways

- ◆ Generalists see patterns that specialists often overlook. They thrive in ambiguity and use it as an opportunity for innovation.
- ◆ Generalists encourage a culture of experimentation, risk-taking, and heterogeneous collaboration when solving problems.
- ◆ Generalists can harness insights from multiple domains to fuel breakthrough ideas, which is a powerful leadership attribute in the face of disruption, adversity, or calamity.

CHAPTER 7

The Generalist Advantage in Action—Case Studies

Explain It to Kids

Case study: is like a story that helps us learn by looking closely at what happened in a real-life situation, like how a superhero got stuck or solved a problem!

Case Study 1: Shallow Generalist as a Leader | Analysis till Paralysis

THE CASE OF BEN BENNETT: ANALYSIS PARALYSIS IN THE FACE OF DISRUPTION

Ben Bennett, the former CEO of Reliable Systems, embodied the image of a meticulous leader. With a PhD in electrical engineering and an MBA from a top business school, his credentials suggested infallible decision-making ability. Yet, Reliable Systems, once a pioneer in enterprise software, faltered during his tenure, ultimately leading to an acquisition at a fraction of its potential value.

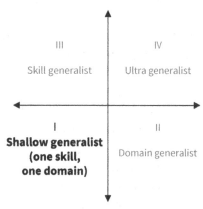

Bennett's leadership style, characterized by excessive analysis, a relentless focus on perfection, and a fear of failure, offers a classic case study on the dangers of "analysis paralysis" and the need for decisive action in a rapidly changing business environment.

EARLY SUCCESS: THE RISE OF A METICULOUS LEADER

Ben Bennett joined Reliable Systems as a software engineer during its initial growth phase. His technical expertise and attention to detail propelled him through the ranks, eventually positioning him as the company's chief technology officer (CTO). In this role, Bennett earned his reputation as a strategic thinker and meticulous planner. His decisions were deliberate, calculated, and data driven.

This approach served Bennett well for a substantial part of his career. In the early 2000s, the enterprise software industry favored stability and robust, albeit complex, solutions. Reliable Systems' flagship product was recognized for its reliability, even as it demanded a considerable implementation investment from clients.

When the company's long-time CEO retired, Ben Bennett appeared the natural successor. His extensive experience, deep understanding of the company's technology, and proven analytical abilities made him a logical choice for the board of directors.

CHANGING TIDES: EMERGING DISRUPTION

As Bennett assumed the role of CEO in 2010, the technological landscape was subtly but significantly shifting. The emergence of cloud computing began to challenge the traditional, on-premises enterprise software model. Software-as-a-Service (SaaS) competitors began to appear, offering lower costs and ease of implementation. These newcomers often lacked the breadth of Reliable Systems' solutions, but they catered to a growing need for faster deployment and agile features.

Bennett acknowledged the changing market, but his response was measured and cautious. He tasked internal teams with analyzing cloud technology and its potential implications. Endless discussions and reports were generated, meticulously dissecting the pros and cons of a transition toward a cloud-based model.

THE PERILS OF PERFECTIONISM

Ben Bennett's demand for perfection delayed any significant shift in Reliable Systems' business model. Market research and competitor analysis reports piled up, as did projections and risk assessments. The need for more data, more analysis, and more refined plans stalled crucial decisions and the implementation of a much-needed pivot in strategy.

As competitors gained market share with their nimble cloud offerings, Bennett doubled down on analysis and planning. His belief that a perfectly designed strategy would allow Reliable to leapfrog the competition obscured the danger of inaction. Internally, the culture became increasingly risk averse and bogged down by bureaucracy. Frustrated with delays, talented engineers and product managers began to leave the company.

THE COST OF INDECISION

By 2015, it became clear that Reliable Systems was losing ground rapidly. Revenue started to decline, and the stock price fell. Bennett's focus shifted from growth to survival. He initiated rounds of layoffs and drastic cost-cutting measures that further demoralized the remaining employees and hampered innovation.

Desperately, Bennett authorized a rushed attempt to launch Reliable's own cloud-based solution. However, by now the product lagged the competitors' offerings, both in features and user-friendliness. Its reception in the market was lukewarm at best.

RESULTS

In 2018, with dwindling cash reserves and few prospects, Reliable Systems became an acquisition target. A larger competitor, sensing an opportunity to acquire valuable intellectual property and a beleaguered customer base, bought the company at a significantly undervalued price. Ben Bennett was asked to resign shortly after. The case of Ben Bennett and Reliable Systems offers several potent lessons:

- ◆ *Analysis paralysis:* In a time of rapid technological shifts, the need for analysis must be balanced with decisive action. Too much emphasis on planning and data can lead to a state of paralysis, where opportunities are lost, and competitors gain insurmountable leads.

- *Iteration over perfection:* In a dynamic market, it's often more effective to adopt an iterative approach; get products in the hands of users quickly, gather feedback, and refine them along the way, rather than aiming for the perfect solution on a theoretical drawing board.
- *The perils of fear:* Leaders driven primarily by a fear of failure tend to avoid risks essential for adaptation and innovation. This can lead to a risk-averse culture within a company, stalling necessary change.
- *Opportunity cost:* The true cost of indecision is not always immediately tangible but is reflected in opportunities missed and markets lost to bolder competitors.

DISCUSSION QUESTIONS

1. Could Ben Bennett have changed his leadership style? Were there measures he could have taken to foster a more agile and decisive culture at Reliable Systems?
2. Is a meticulous, data-driven approach fundamentally wrong? How can leaders balance the need for analysis with the need for action?
3. What role could the board of directors have played in either guiding or pressuring Bennett toward a more adaptive strategy?
4. Are there industries or situations where a meticulous approach similar to Bennett's is more likely to succeed?

Case Study 2: Domain Generalist as a Leader | Cross-Industry Adaptability

THE CASE OF REBECCA MARTINEZ: LEVERAGING CROSS-INDUSTRY INSIGHTS FOR TRANSFORMATIONAL GROWTH

Rebecca Martinez, the recently appointed CEO of DB Transportation Corp, had an unexpected career trajectory. Starting in the nonprofit sector, she later transitioned to technology start-ups and eventually found herself in the logistics and transportation industry. Her success in revitalizing DB Transportation Corp, a century-old company facing declining profits, hinged on her unique ability to draw insights from her diverse professional experiences, fueling innovation and driving transformational growth amid economic headwinds.

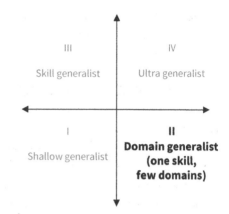

EARLY INFLUENCES: FOUNDATIONS IN THE NONPROFIT SECTOR

Martinez's initial career path focused on social impact. Fresh out of college, she joined a nonprofit organization dedicated to educational equity in underprivileged areas. Her time in the nonprofit sector taught her several critical lessons:

- *Resourcefulness:* The need to achieve ambitious goals with limited budgets instilled a creative approach to problem-solving.
- *Stakeholder management:* Successfully navigating grant applications, donor relationships, and community partnerships honed her communication and collaboration skills.
- *Mission-driven focus:* Working in the nonprofit sector instilled in Martinez a strong sense of purpose, fostering a belief that businesses could generate profits while driving positive change.

PIVOT TO TECH: EMBRACING A CULTURE OF AGILITY

Driven by a desire to gain a broader understanding of business operations, Martinez made a seemingly unconventional leap into the world of early-stage tech start-ups. This fast-paced environment demanded a marked shift in her approach. She learned:

- *Speed over perfection:* Start-ups taught her the value of rapid prototyping, iterating based on market feedback, and embracing a fail-fast mentality for learning.
- *Customer obsession:* Working closely with early adopters emphasized the relentless focus on understanding and solving acute customer pain points.

+ *Data as a guide:* Metrics and analytics became central to her decision-making process, providing a counterbalance to intuition and a language for objective evaluation.

THE TEST: REVITALIZING A LEGACY BUSINESS

Rebecca Martinez's diverse background caught the eye of the board of directors at DB Transportation Corp, a well-established logistics company in need of fresh perspectives. The company had become complacent, struggling with shrinking margins, outdated technology, and operational inefficiencies. Martinez's outsider status and blend of experiences seemed to be an unconventional yet intriguing prospect.

TRANSFERRING LEARNINGS: DRIVING CHANGE AT DB TRANSPORTATION CORP

Taking the helm of DB Transportation Corp, Martinez strategically applied the lessons she gathered from her previous roles:

+ *Redefining the mission:* She inspired employees by reconnecting the company's core purpose of facilitating global connections with a broader vision linked to sustainability and community support, reminiscent of her nonprofit experience.
+ *Embracing agile principles:* Martinez implemented agile methodologies borrowed from the start-up world. These focused on cross-functional teams, fast iterations, and continuous process improvements throughout the organization.
+ *Customer-centricity:* Using her tech-sector experience, she mandated customer journey mapping and created initiatives for direct customer feedback loops to inform product development.
+ *Data-informed decision-making:* Martinez prioritized the modernization of data infrastructure at DB Transportation Corp. This enabled informed decision-making at all levels, aligning company actions with real-time market conditions.

RESULTS

Rebecca Martinez's cross-industry approach yielded measurable results within a remarkably short period:

♦ *Profitability:* Within two years, DB Transportation Corp saw a reversal of its declining margins as operational inefficiencies were eliminated, and innovative service offerings targeted untapped customer segments.

♦ *Innovation:* The company launched a successful sustainability initiative that improved fuel efficiency while also positioning DB Transportation Corp as an environmentally responsible partner, attracting a new clientele segment.

♦ *Employee morale:* The revitalized sense of purpose, combined with the agile and empowering work environment, led to improved employee retention and greater talent acquisition.

DISCUSSION QUESTIONS

1. How common are executives with cross-industry experience? What are the benefits and potential challenges of such untraditional career paths?
2. Is Rebecca Martinez's success replicable, or is it a combination of personal skills and specific circumstances?
3. What are the industries most likely to benefit from leaders with diverse professional backgrounds?
4. How can organizations foster a culture that welcomes and values the insights gained from cross-sector experience?

Case Study 3: Skill Generalist as a Leader | Applying Unrelated Skills

THE CASE OF ALI SHAIKH: THE POWER OF UNRELATED SKILLS IN A DYNAMIC ENVIRONMENT

Ali Shaikh, the VP of Product Development at Miro Electronics, a mid-sized technology firm, rose through the ranks due to his unusual mix of skills and an ability to creatively synthesize his knowledge for success within the company. Starting as a software developer, Ali's unconventional hobbies and side interests, ranging from improv theater to furniture restoration, have proven surprisingly influential in driving groundbreaking product innovation and building cross-functional teams.

EARLY INFLUENCES: A DEVELOPER AND A HOBBYIST

Ali Shaikh's path was not linear. Initially drawn to technology, he earned a bachelor's degree in computer science and began his career as a developer at Miro Electronics. However, outside of work, Shaikh was an avid hobbyist. He had a passion for improv theater, attended weekend workshops on furniture restoration, and even tinkered with vintage electronics. These seemingly unconnected interests would later prove instrumental in his success.

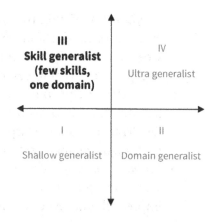

THE BENEFITS OF UNRELATED SKILLS

Shaikh's diverse pursuits cultivated several key skills that gave him an edge in his professional life:

- *Creative problem-solving:* Improvization demanded on-the-spot thinking and the ability to adapt to unexpected scenarios. This translated into a unique capacity for solving unique engineering problems elegantly.
- *Empathy and communication:* Participating in improv troupes fostered deep empathy for others' emotional states and excellent communication skills. These proved invaluable in managing stakeholders, bridging the gap between technical teams and customers.
- *Hands-on approach:* Restoring old furniture encouraged hands-on experimentation and an understanding of how different components come together in a functional system— a perspective he applied to product design.

APPLYING THE UNEXPECTED: INNOVATION AT MIRO ELECTRONICS

Miro Electronics initially thrived thanks to its core line of data analytics software. However, as the market matured, competitors began to catch up, and innovation slowed down. Ali Shaikh, by now leading a product development team, recognized the need for transformational growth. He leveraged his unconventional skill set to catalyze a series of influential changes:

- *Human-centered design:* Inspired by his improv experience, Shaikh introduced user-experience workshops focused on understanding the emotions and pain points of Miro Electronics' customers. This led to the development of more intuitive interfaces and features that significantly differentiated their products.
- *Hack days and cross-team collaboration:* Shaikh instituted company-wide hack days where teams from different departments (engineering, marketing, customer support) worked together on short-term projects. These sessions broke down silos and generated out-of-the-box solutions, fueled by the diverse perspectives and skills of participants.
- *From refinement to experimentation:* Shaikh encouraged a shift from perfecting existing products to a culture of rapid prototyping. His hands-on restoration experience informed this focus on building minimal viable products, testing them on the market, and iterating based on feedback.

RESULTS

Ali Shaikh's approach resulted in significant, measurable impacts for Miro Electronics:

- *Product differentiation:* New features inspired by user-experience insights earned high customer acclaim and propelled the company ahead of its competitors.
- *Market expansion:* The intuitive design and focus on core user needs helped Miro Electronics penetrate previously untapped market segments, expanding their customer base.
- *Cross-functional agility:* Hack days and improved communication led to a more integrated company culture, resulting in a faster pace of innovation and a better response to emerging market trends.

This case study demonstrates that innovation and success in business don't always come from deeply specialized knowledge.

Sometimes, the greatest competitive advantage lies in the ability to bridge the unexpected, leveraging a diverse set of skills (especially unrelated skills), experiences, and perspectives.

DISCUSSION QUESTIONS

1. Are leaders like Ali Shaikh exceptionally rare, or can organizations encourage employees to develop unrelated skills that might translate into unexpected benefits?
2. Could Shaikh's approach work in more traditional or highly regulated industries? What challenges might it face?
3. How can companies balance the need for specialization with encouraging broader skill development in their employees?
4. How can a leader identify seemingly unrelated skills within a team and unlock their combinatorial potential for problem-solving and innovation?

Case Study 4: Ultra Generalist as a Leader | Thriving in Uncertain Times

THE CASE OF ADELE ORTIZ: LEADING WITH RESILIENCE AND ADAPTABILITY IN A WORLD OF DISRUPTION

Adele Ortiz is the CEO of FusionTech, a rapidly growing technology firm specializing in supply chain optimization software. What sets Ortiz apart is her diverse background: having started her career in health care management, she transitioned to finance before landing in the technology sector. Her unique path, marked by seemingly divergent skills and industry expertise, has been instrumental in FusionTech's ability to navigate the unpredictable business landscape of recent years.

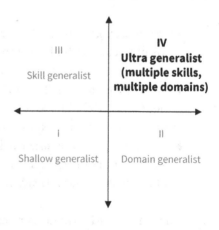

III
Skill generalist

IV
**Ultra generalist
(multiple skills,
multiple domains)**

I
Shallow generalist

II
Domain generalist

THE VALUE OF MULTI-DOMAIN EXPERTISE

Ortiz's success highlights the importance of leaders who possess knowledge and skill sets across various sectors, especially in an era of disruption and uncertainty:

- *Broader perspective:* Experience in multiple industries allows leaders like Ortiz to identify trends, patterns, and potential solutions that those with a narrower focus might miss. For example, her insight into health care logistics contributed to groundbreaking innovations in FusionTech's supply chain software.
- *Cross-pollination of ideas:* Leaders with a multi-domain background often bring practices, methodologies, and problem-solving techniques from one industry to another. Ortiz's background in finance infused her approach with an emphasis on data-driven decision-making and risk management— vital in navigating supply chain shocks.
- *Empathy and understanding:* Working in contrasting sectors can cultivate deep empathy for different stakeholders and their unique challenges. Ortiz's background in health care fostered a focus on the ultimate human impact of supply chain technology on factors such as access to medicine and critical supplies.

RESILIENCE IN UNCERTAIN TIMES

In recent years, businesses have faced unprecedented challenges: the global pandemic, economic instability, and rapid technological change. Adele Ortiz's leadership exemplifies how individuals with versatile skill sets and experience are particularly adept at weathering these storms:

- *Anticipating disruption:* Ortiz's multi-industry knowledge allowed her to anticipate vulnerabilities within her own sector. Informed by experience in other fields, she proactively diversified suppliers and developed contingency plans that made FusionTech more resilient to supply chain disruptions.
- *Agile strategy:* With uncertainty as a constant, multi-skilled leaders understand that rigid long-term plans become obsolete

quickly. Ortiz adopted an agile approach, emphasizing frequent reassessment of market needs and a willingness to shift the company's direction when necessary.

♦ *Building adaptable teams:* Recognizing that company-wide resilience depended on adaptability at all levels, Ortiz prioritized upskilling initiatives and cross-functional collaboration. This fostered a more adaptable workforce, able to handle unexpected challenges as they arose.

RESULTS

Adele Ortiz's leadership, guided by her multifaceted experiences, has yielded impressive results for FusionTech:

♦ *Market growth:* FusionTech experienced sustained growth through economic downturns, in part due to its ability to rapidly pivot offerings in response to emerging needs—an agility linked to Ortiz's leadership.

♦ *Industry recognition:* Ortiz is widely respected as a thought leader. Her insights, drawing from cross-domain expertise, are regularly sought at conferences and within her industry.

♦ *Organizational culture:* FusionTech has built a reputation as a workplace that values diverse perspectives and continuous learning, attracting top talent and fostering innovation.

The case of Adele Ortiz underscores the growing importance of versatile and adaptable leaders. In an uncertain world, those possessing diverse skills and a broader understanding of interconnected systems are particularly well-equipped to lead organizations not just to survival, but to continued growth and innovation.

DISCUSSION QUESTIONS

1. How prevalent are multi-skilled leaders like Adele Ortiz? Are they becoming more common in today's volatile business climate?

2. Can organizations deliberately foster cross-industry experience and diverse skill sets in their employees, or is it best to rely on accidental career paths that lead to unexpected combinations?

3. What are the specific challenges that leaders coming from multiple industries might face in gaining acceptance and trust within a new company or sector?

4. Are there any industries where specialized knowledge is paramount and multi-industry experience might be less beneficial?

Chapter 7 Takeaways

- ◆ Learn from the shallow generalist: Avoid analysis paralysis and take decisive action, even with limited information.
- ◆ Emulate the domain generalist: Leverage your domain expertise to adapt to new industries and roles.
- ◆ Apply the skill generalist approach: Utilize your core skills to tackle diverse challenges and opportunities.
- ◆ Embrace the ultra generalist mindset: Thrive in uncertainty by embracing change and continuous learning.

PART III

Self-Assessment

CHAPTER 8

The Generalist Quotient (GQ)™

What Is a Generalist Quotient?

GQ is the measure of an individual's ability to apply a wide range of *skills* across various *domains*. It highlights their versatility, adaptability, and capacity to integrate diverse perspectives.

Where Can I Check My Generalist Quotient?

Scan here:

www.mansoorsoomro.com/generalist-quotient/

How Can the Generalist Quotient Self-Assessment Help Me?

You can use this free online GQ self-assessment:

a) to ascertain your generalist type (based on the *shallow, domain, skill,* or *ultra generalist [SDSU] framework*), and

b) to develop a road map for self-development (in order to capitalize on *the Generalist Advantage [TGA]*).

Afterword

The word "afterword" has always made me laugh a little. It seems to signal closure, and finality, like a neat bow placed on top of a carefully wrapped package. But here's the thing about embracing the generalist mindset: the journey doesn't have a tidy destination. It's a thrilling, often winding road trip, one where the best discoveries happen when you ditch the *Global Positioning System (GPS)* and embrace a few scenic detours.

When I started writing this book, I won't lie, there was a part of me that felt a little cynical and intimidated. Who was I to offer advice and encouragement on the potential of generalists? What helped me then was my love of research and a big-picture understanding of the human potential to tackle a topic I have been passionately curious about at primary school, college, university, and later during my corporate life. Being a generalist is a mindset that unlocks possibilities at every turn. You may have reached the end of these chapters, but in some ways your adventure truly begins now!

Here's hoping this book didn't just provide answers, but rather stirred up a whole lot of confusion and uncomfortable questions—questions about how to embrace your passions, leverage your existing skill set, find communities that ignite your enthusiasm, and, perhaps most importantly, define your own rules for success.

Throughout this book, we have explored the myriad ways in which breadth of knowledge, versatility of skills, and openness to new experiences can provide a distinct advantage in navigating the complexities of the modern landscape. *The Generalist Advantage* empowers us to approach problems from multiple angles, drawing upon insights from diverse domains to arrive at creative and innovative solutions. It fosters a spirit of collaboration and empathy, recognizing the value of diverse perspectives in addressing complex issues and driving positive change.

But embracing the generalist mindset is not without its challenges. It requires us to confront our own limitations, to step outside of our areas of expertise, and to embrace the discomfort of the unknown. It demands patience, perseverance, and a willingness to embrace failure as an essential part of the learning process. Yet, for those who dare to embrace the generalist mindset, the rewards are abundant. It

> **" for those who dare to embrace the generalist mindset, the rewards are abundant. "**

empowers us to make meaningful contributions to the world around us, whether through our work, our relationships, or our creative endeavors.

At its core, I wrote this book to challenge conventional wisdom and invite readers to reconsider their notions of success and fulfillment. The book aims to explore the myriad ways in which a generalist approach can offer a distinct advantage in navigating the complexities of the modern world. And by no means is *The Generalist Advantage* a solitary pursuit. It thrives in dialogue, in the fertile soil of collective wisdom.

Also, this book is not merely an intellectual exercise; *it is a call to action*. It is a rallying cry for those who refuse to be confined by the labels and limitations imposed by society. It is a manifesto for the restless spirits who yearn to explore the uncharted territories of knowledge and experience. It is a road map for those who seek to forge their own path—a generalist path—in a world that too often demands conformity.

You should be confident to wear and bold enough to carry *The Generalist Advantage* with grace. Be the alchemist who turns knowledge into insight, who transforms curiosity into wisdom. It is important to invest in the generalist's toolbox. Consider the tools you've acquired— the chisel of curiosity, the compass of empathy, and the lens of synthesis. These are not mere metaphors; they are instruments of transformation. The generalist's toolbox is portable and adaptable. It fits in the pocket of your mind, ready to be deployed when challenges arise.

In today's era of rapid change where AI influence and impact is fundamentally rewriting the why and how we work, a generalist is bound to thrive. They adapt when paradigms shift, for their toolbox is not rigid—it expands. When art merges with science, when education blends with gamification, when innovation challenges tradition, when creativity meets constraints, and when passion collides with practicality, the generalist steps forward, unafraid.

Acknowledgments

I was told that writing a book is rewarding as it gives you a chance to share your voice, distill your knowledge, and create something that can impact others. But I was not informed enough that it has its own set of challenges, especially that of *imposter syndrome*. One day you feel like a genius as words and ideas flow by; the next day you seem to be lost as you have run out of new concepts and practical examples. Self-doubt creeps in, but nothing beats the satisfaction of crafting a compelling chapter, and then completing a book.

Striking the right balance between theoretical concepts and practical advice can be difficult. Too much theory can be dry, while too much practicality can oversimplify complex issues. As I reflect on the completion of *The Generalist Advantage*, I am overwhelmed with gratitude for the support, guidance, and blessings of countless people who helped me in this expedition.

Starting with the *Wiley* team, whose professionalism and meticulousness have brought this book to life, *Annie Knight*, executive editor, thank you for believing in this project, even when it was barely a collection of rambling notes. Thank you for seeing the promise in my very scattered pitch and the potential amid the mess of notes disguised as a book proposal. *Vithusha Rameshan* and *Venkat Sankar*, managing editors, you helped me remain on track with the deadlines and navigated my over-enthusiasm with tact. *Alice Hadaway*, editorial assistant, your support was instrumental in consolidating the book and giving it a final finish. To Wiley's editorial team—you transformed chaos into coherence.

I would also like to thank *Des Dearlove*, Thinkers50 cofounder. Des, you were the first one to cherish my book proposal, and you stood like a strong support pillar in highlighting the novelty of this book. My academic discourse on the topic of generalist and specialist initially started with *Prof. Mohd Hizam Hanafiah*, who was my PhD supervisor. I enjoyed our chat and informal discussions while stepping out of the research cubicle (carrel room). Thank you for being a guiding star!

My wife, *Sara*—you gave me wings to fly in pursuing the dream of writing this book. Carving out dedicated writing time is tough, especially while juggling work and other commitments, but with your incredible support, see what we have accomplished today. Cheers, darling!

You all will agree that *staying* motivated is always challenging. In those times especially, my two sons, *Khizr* and *Hamdan*, gave me just the right doses of energy and courage I needed to pick up the pace. And how can I forget that all this success has a promising foundation that was built (years and years ago) for me by my parents, *Abdul Razzak* (Abu) and *Rukhsana* (Ami)—love you both so much! To my siblings, *Huda, Muneeb, Sanah*, and *Arham*—you all have inspired me on so many occasions (I have lost count now!)

I am immensely grateful to various organizations, firms, and institutions who provided a testing bed for my ideas, models, and philosophies. Published authors, peer academic faculty members, thought leaders, and media journalists—all those advance notes of praise, blurbs, and testimonials that you have provided for my book mean a lot to me. Your words have strengthened my resolve.

I would like to express my gratitude to the participants and respondents of my research studies, interviews, and surveys as your perspectives and experiences have enriched the content of this book. Your willingness to share your insights, challenges, and successes has provided valuable firsthand knowledge of the topics and themes explored in *The Generalist Advantage*.

To the brilliant generalists I interviewed—your stories made this book come alive! Thank you for sharing your wins, your struggles, and that undeniable spark that defines you. Whether it was a long Zoom/Teams call, an epic email exchange, or a whirlwind interview session filled with tangents and excitement, each of you inspired me beyond measure.

As the ink dries on the final pages of *The Generalist Advantage*, I am humbled by the collective effort that birthed this book. It takes a village—a symphony of minds—to create something of substance.

And finally, to you, dear reader, who turned these pages with anticipation, who pondered the intersections, who embraced *The Generalist Advantage*—I raise my pen in salute. May your journey continue beyond these words, across disciplines, toward excellence.

About the Author

Mansoor Soomro, PhD

Dr. Mansoor Soomro is a management scholar, researcher, thought leader, and futurist. He leads the Future of Work (FOW) research unit at the *Teesside University International Business School, United Kingdom*. Before that, he was the MBA Program Director for Senior Leader Apprenticeship. He has designed and facilitated various leadership development programs for *Fortune 500 companies*. Mansoor is known for his powerful and influential keynote sessions.

He holds a strong international corporate background of working with Siemens in more than 10 countries and managing a diverse multicultural team of more than 500 executives for over seven years. He served on the Siemens Middle East I&C Managing Board and enjoyed his senior-level appointments as the Regional Head of Performance Management with Siemens Asia Pacific and Head of Commercial Operations with Siemens Middle East.

Dr. Mansoor's multifaceted career, encompassing academia and industry, positions him as a prominent figure in the realms of leadership and management. He holds a PhD in management, and his educational journey reflects a commitment to understanding and addressing complex global challenges through interdisciplinary approaches.

He writes business articles for *Fortune* magazine. His research, commentary, insights, and contributions have been featured on the *BBC, CNN, The Wall Street Journal, Business Insider, Fortune, Newsweek, Financial Times, The Telegraph, Bloomberg, The Independent, The Times, New Statesman, Dow Jones, Financial News London, Harvard Business Publishing, Mirror UK, ITV News, Euronews, TalkTV, Dubai Eye, The Sun, HR Brew, The Japan Times, Human Resources Director Magazine, iNews, Mail Online, Daily Express UK,*

Daily Mail, Daily Star, Raconteur, WorkLife News, AACSB, CABS, CMI, EEUK, Yahoo, HRD America, iNEWS, North East Chamber of Commerce, PR in HR, Teesside University, Cambridge University, and multiple other prominent international media and publication outlets. He has received speaker invitations from the United Nations, World Bank, and Cambridge University.

As a futurist and thought leader, he stays ahead of the curve, continuously exploring emerging trends, and identifying opportunities that unlock new possibilities for businesses and their talent. By championing a human-centric approach to work, his power-packed keynote sessions, executive education products, leadership development training sessions, and consulting assignments empower individuals, teams, and organizations to thrive amid rapid change.

The Generalist Advantage is Dr. Mansoor's magnum opus—a celebration of the curious mind, the polymath spirit, and the beauty of embracing versatility. His hope is that readers through this book will discover their own unique advantage in this ever-evolving world. He is the host of the *In Conversation* podcast, whereby he interviews speakers from the worlds of business, culture, and sports.

Dr. Mansoor is also a member of the Harvard Business Review Advisory Council (an opt-in research community of business professionals), the Academy of Management (US), and the Strategic Management Society (US). He is a certified Abilitie Simulation Facilitator (US), certified HRDF Trainer (Malaysia), certified REACH Practitioner (US), certified LDP Trainer (Australia), and certified Business Edge IFC Trainer (World Bank). He is a Fellow of the Higher Education Academy (FHEA), accredited by the AdvanceHE.

www.mansoorsoomro.com

Glossary

ambidextrous organization   Organizations that excel at both exploiting existing capabilities for efficiency and exploring new opportunities for innovation. The term was first coined by Robert Duncan.

cognitive flexibility   The mental ability to switch between different thoughts, ideas, or tasks while adapting to new situations.

complementary skills   The abilities that enhance and support each other when combined, leading to a more effective and well-rounded team or individual performance.

contrasting skills   The different or opposing abilities that, when utilized together, can provide diverse perspectives and approaches to problem-solving and innovation.

convergent thinking   A cognitive process characterized by focusing on a single solution or idea to a problem, often associated with analytical reasoning and problem-solving.

divergent thinking   A cognitive process characterized by creating compound ideas, possibilities, or solutions in response to a single problem or question, often associated with creativity and innovation.

domain generalist (also known as industry generalist)   An individual who has one major skill but exposure to a few different domains/industries.

epiphany   A sudden and profound realization or insight, often resulting from a combination of reflection, intuition, and new information.

generalist (also known as multi-potentialite or polymath)   An individual who possesses a wide range of interests, knowledge, abilities, or experiences.

generalist quotient (GQ)   The measure of an individual's ability to apply a wide range of skills across various domains. It highlights their versatility, adaptability, and capacity to integrate diverse perspectives.

hard skills   Specific, teachable abilities or technical knowledge that can be quantitatively measured, such as proficiency in a programming language or operating machinery.

imposter syndrome   The term was first coined by psychologists Pauline Clance and Suzanne Imes as the persistent feeling of inadequacy and self-doubt experienced by many high achievers. For generalists, imposter syndrome can arise from fear that their wide-ranging interests represent a lack of focused expertise.

intellectual curiosity   A strong desire to learn, explore, and understand the world.

intellectual humility The awareness of one's limitations in knowledge and the openness to new ideas and perspectives.

jack-of-all-trades, master of none A phrase often used to describe generalists. While it acknowledges their versatility, it also implies that they lack deep expertise. However, some argue that being a "master of none" is an asset in today's complex world.

lateral thinking A problem-solving approach, first used by the psychologist Edward de Bono, that involves looking at issues from unconventional angles.

Law of Specialist Saturation (LOSS) While the initial introduction of specialists yields significant improvements in specific areas, beyond a certain point, the marginal benefits of additional specialization decrease. Staying an expert in a single area for too long can actually become counterproductive.

meta-learning The process of learning how to learn. Mastering meta-learning gives generalists an edge, allowing them to quickly absorb new information from a variety of domains.

Near Future Readiness Index (NFRI) An index that measures an individual's or organization's preparedness to adapt to and thrive in the imminent future, focusing on agility, innovation, and forward-thinking capabilities. It assesses readiness for upcoming changes and challenges in the near-term landscape.

organizational renewal The process of revitalizing an organization by transforming its structure, culture, and processes to improve performance and adapt to changing environments.

paradigm shift A fundamental change in how we perceive and understand the world, often resulting in a transformative shift in perspective.

portable skills (also known as transferable skills or universal skills) Abilities that are not confined to a single job, role, or industry.

portfolio career An approach to employment prioritizing multiple income streams and skill sets. Many generalists adopt this model, working freelance, juggling smaller passion projects, or combining positions.

prototyping Exploring ideas by actively experimenting, building iterations, and getting quick feedback before fully investing time and resources into a project. Prototyping encourages the generalist's desire to learn by doing and helps avoid being paralyzed by perfectionism.

serendipity The occurrence of unexpected discoveries or accidental insights while seeking something else, often resulting from a combination of curiosity, openness, and chance. This plays into the generalist's capacity to glean insights from a wide array of encounters. The term was coined by Horace Walpole.

shallow generalist (also known as hyper-specialist) An individual who has one major skill predominately in one domain/industry.

skill generalist An individual who has a few different skills predominately in one domain/industry.

Socratic inquiry   A form of inquiry and dialogue developed by the ancient Greek philosopher Socrates, often involving the use of probing questions to stimulate critical thinking and exploration of ideas.

soft skills   Interpersonal and emotional intelligence traits that enable someone to work well with others and navigate complex social dynamics, such as communication and leadership skills.

specialist (also known as an expert or a master)   An individual who possesses a deep focus on a specific interest, knowledge, ability, or experience.

systems thinking   A holistic method to recognize complexities within an organization, considering the interconnection between different parts of a system. The concept was coined by the biologist Ludwig von Bertalanffy when introducing Systems Theory.

T-shaped professional   A concept popularized by Tim Brown, the CEO of IDEO, which suggests that T-shaped professionals combine deep expertise in one area (the vertical line of the T) with a broad understanding of multiple areas (the horizontal line of the T).

the 10,000-hour rule   A concept popularized by Malcolm Gladwell, arguing that extensive practice is essential for mastering any field.

the generalist advantage (TGA)   It refers to the benefits gained from having a broad skill set and diverse domain exposure, allowing individuals or organizations to adapt to various roles, think creatively, solve problems, and build resilience in dynamic environments.

the Medici effect   A concept popularized by Frans Johansson, highlighting an effect that describes how groundbreaking innovations often arise at the intersection of different fields or unrelated disciplines.

ultra generalist   An individual who has multiple skills in multiple domains/industries. It is the top-most level one can achieve in the journey of becoming a generalist.

wicked problems   Complex, dynamic issues defying classification within a single discipline and lacking easy solutions. The design theorists Horst Rittel and Melvin Webber originated this concept when studying the notion of complexity.

Further Reading

Abdaal, A. (2023). *Feel-Good Productivity: How to Do More of What Matters to You.* Cornerstone Press.

Abhishek, K. (2021). "Generalists versus Specialists: The Winner Doesn't Take It All," *Forbes.*

Agnihotri, A., and Bhattacharya, S. (2021). "Generalist versus Specialist CEO and R&D Commitment: Evidence from an Emerging Market," *Journal of Management & Organization*, pp. 1–17. doi: 10.1017/jmo.2021.7.

Ahmed, W. (2019). *The Polymath: Unlocking the Power of Human Versatility.* Wiley.

Aivazian, V. A., Lai, T.-k., and Rahaman, M. M. (2013). "The Market for CEOs: An Empirical Analysis," *Journal of Economics and Business.* Elsevier Inc., 67, pp. 24–54. doi: 10.1016/j.jeconbus. 2013.02.001.

Arthur, Y., and Dave, U. (2019). *Reinventing the Organization: How Companies Can Deliver Radically Greater Value in Fast-Changing Markets.* Harvard Business Review Press.

Austin, M. J., et al. (2013). "Becoming a Manager in Nonprofit Human Service Organizations: Making the Transition from Specialist to Generalist," *Administration in Social Work*, 37(4), pp. 372–385. doi: 10.1080/03643107.2012.715116.

Balsmeier, B., and Buchwald, A. (2014). "Who Promotes More Innovations? Inside versus Outside Hired CEOs," *Industrial and Corporate Change*, 24(5), pp. 1013–1045. doi: 10.1093/icc/dtu020.

Bao, X., Mirchandani, P., and Shang, J. (2022). "Specialist or Generalist VC? Financing a Techstar Supply Chain with a Milestone Option," *SSRN Electronic Journal*, pp. 1–35. doi: 10.2139/ssrn. 4203554.

Barroso, M. M. (2023). "Many Roads Lead to Rome: Educational and Work Trajectories of Middle Managers in Sweden and Portugal," *Nordic Journal of Transitions, Careers and Guidance*, 4(1), pp. 1–14. doi: 10.16993/njtcg.55.

Bartlett, S. (2023). *The Diary of a CEO: The 33 Laws of Business and Life*. Ebury Edge.

Baruch, Y., Bell, M. P., and Gray, D. (2005). "Generalist and Specialist Graduate Business Degrees: Tangible and Intangible Value," *Journal of Vocational Behavior*, 67(1 SPEC. ISS.), pp. 51–68. doi: 10.1016/j.jvb.2003.06.002.

Berman, S. J., et al. (2016). "How Successful Firms Guide Innovation: Insights and Strategies of Leading CEOs," *Emerald Strategy & Leadership*, 44(5), pp. 21–28. doi: 10.1108/SL-07-2016-0062.

Bono, E. de (2016). *Lateral Thinking: A Textbook of Creativity*. Penguin Life.

Boom, I. H., and Pennink, B. W. (2012). "The Relationship between Humanness and Knowledge Sharing in Malaysia," *Gadjah Mada International Journal of Business*, Vol. 1(2), pp. 99–122.

Botha, F. (2018). "Why Your Company's Survival Depends on Your Becoming a Generalist," *Forbes*.

Bradt, G. (2012). "When to Hire Generalists vs. Specialists: Lessons from the Fab Five," *Forbes*.

Braunerhjelm, P., and Thulin, P. (2023). "Does Innovation Lead to Firm Growth? Explorative versus Exploitative Innovations," *Applied Economics Letters*, 30(9), pp. 1179–1182. doi: 10.1080/13504851.2022.2041166.

Brockman, P., Lee, H. S. G., and Salas, J. M. (2016). "Determinants of CEO compensation: Generalist-Specialist versus Insider-Outsider Attributes," *Journal of Corporate Finance*. Elsevier B.V., 39, pp. 53–77. doi: 10.1016/j.jcorpfin.2016.04.007.

Brown, B. (2021). *Atlas of the Heart: Mapping Meaningful Connection and the Language of Human Experience*. Vermilion.

Buckingham, M. (2015). *StandOut 2.0: Assess Your Strengths, Find Your Edge, Win at Work*. Harvard Business Review Press.

Buyl, T., et al. (2011). "Top Management Team Functional Diversity and Firm Performance: The Moderating Role of CEO Characteristics," *Journal of Management Studies*, 48(1), pp. 151–177. doi: 10.1111/j.1467-6486.2010.00932.x.

Byun, H., and Raffiee, J. (2023). "Career Specialization, Involuntary Worker–Firm Separations, and Employment Outcomes: Why Generalists Outperform Specialists When Their Jobs Are

Displaced," *Administrative Science Quarterly*, 68(1), pp. 270–316. doi: 10.1177/00018392221143762.

Cain, M. D., and McKeon, S. B. (2016). "CEO Personal Risk-Taking and Corporate Policies," *Journal of Financial and Quantitative Analysis*, 51(1), pp. 139–164. doi: 10.1017/S0022109016000041.

Cain, S. (2013). *Quiet: The Power of Introverts in a World That Can't Stop Talking*. Penguin.

Campbell, D. (2014). "Why Hospitals Need More Generalist Doctors and Specialist Nurses," *The Conversation*.

Canfield, J. (2005). *The Success Principles: How to Get from Where You Are to Where You Want to Be*. Harper Non Fiction.

Cannella, A. A., et al. (2008). "Top Management Team Functional Background Diversity and Firm Performance: Examining the Roles of Team Member Colocation and Environmental Uncertainty," *Academy of Management*, 51(4), pp. 768–784.

Carnegie, D. (2006). *How to Win Friends and Influence People*. Vermilion.

Casserly, M. (2012). "The Secret Power of the Generalist—And How They'll Rule the Future," *Forbes*.

Ceniza-Levine, C. (2018). "To Advance in Your Career, Is It Better to Be a Specialist or Generalist?," *Forbes*.

Chan, K., and Renée, M. (2015). *Blue Ocean Strategy: How to Create Uncontested Market Space and Make the Competition Irrelevant*. Harvard Business Review Press.

Chang, Y. Y., Dasgupta, S., and Hilary, G. (2010). "CEO Ability, Pay, and Firm Performance," *Management Science*, 56(10), pp. 1633–1652. doi: 10.1287/mnsc.1100.1205.

Chatjuthamard, P., et al. (2022). "Corporate Governance and Generalist CEOs: Evidence from Board Size," *Corporate Governance*, 22(1), pp. 148–158. doi: 10.1108/CG-02-2021-0058.

Chen, G., et al. (2021). "Generalist versus Specialist CEOs and Acquisitions: Two-Sided Matching and the Impact of CEO Characteristics on Firm Outcomes," *Strategic Management Journal*, 42(6), pp. 1184–1214. doi: 10.1002/smj.3258.

Chen, G., and Huang, S. (2017). "Generalist vs. Specialist CEOs: How CEO Human Capital Shapes the Firm's Acquisition Behaviour and Performance," *Academy of Management*.

Cheng, T. Y., et al. (2020). "Does the Fit of Managerial Ability with Firm Strategy Matters on Firm Performance," *Journal of Asian Finance, Economics and Business*, 7(4), pp. 9–19. doi: 10.13106/JAFEB.2020.VOL7.NO4.9.

Chesbrough, H. (2003). *Open Innovation: The New Imperative for Creating and Profiting from Technology*. Harvard Business Review Press.

Chollet, B., et al. (2015). "Market Knowledge as a Function of CEOs' Personality: A Fuzzy Set Approach," *Journal of Business Research*. Elsevier Inc., 69(7), pp. 2567–2573. doi: 10.1016/j.jbusres.2015.10.137.

Christensen, C. (2013). *The Innovator's Dilemma: When New Technologies Cause Great Firms to Fail (Management of Innovation and Change)*. Harvard Business Review Press.

Clear, J. (2018). *Atomic Habits*. Random House Business.

Clifton, D. (2017). *Strengths Finder 2.0*. Gallup Press.

Collins, J. (2001). *Good to Great: Why Some Companies Make the Leap. and Others Don't*. Random House Business.

Colson, E. (2019). "Why Data Science Teams Need Generalists, Not Specialists," *Harvard Business Review*.

Covey, S. (2004). *7 Habits Of Highly Effective People*. Simon & Schuster UK.

Crossland, C., et al. (2014). "CEO Career Variety: Effects on Firm-Level Strategic and Social Novelty," *Academy of Management*, 57(3), pp. 652–674. doi: 10.5465/amj.2012.0469.

Curcillo, J. (2024). *The Generalist's Advantage: How to Harness the Raw Power of Cross-Disciplinary Thinking*. Synergy Thinkers Press.

Custódio, C., Ferreira, M. A., and Matos, P. (2013). "Generalists versus Specialists: Lifetime Work Experience and Chief Executive Officer Pay," *Journal of Financial Economics*, 108(2), pp. 471–492. doi: 10.1016/j.jfineco.2013.01.001.

Custódio, C., and Metzger, D. (2013). "Financial Expert CEOs: CEO's Work Experience and Firm's Financial Policies," *Journal of Financial Economics*. Elsevier, 114(1), pp. 125–154. doi: 10.1016/j.jfineco.2014.06.002.

Datta, S. D., and Datta M. I. (2014). "Upper-Echelon Executive Human Capital and Compensation: Generalist vs Specialist

Skills," *Strategic Management Journal*, 51(2), pp. 315–334. doi: 10.1002/smj.

Donald, M. (2017). *Building a StoryBrand: Clarify Your Message So Customers Will Listen*. HarperCollins Leadership.

Driesch, T., et al. (2015). "How CEO Experience, Personality, and Network Affect Firms' Dynamic Capabilities," *European Management Journal*. Elsevier Ltd, 33(4), pp. 245–256. doi: 10.1016/j.emj.2015.01.003.

Duckworth, A. (2016). *Grit: The Power of Passion and Perseverance*. Scribner Book Company.

Duhigg, C. (2016). *Smarter Faster Better: The Secrets of Being Productive in Life and Business*. Random House.

Duhigg, C. (2024). *Supercommunicators: How to Unlock the Secret Language of Connection*. Random House.

Dweck, C. (2017). *Mindset: Changing the Way You Think to Fulfill Your Potential*. Robinson.

Edmondson, A. (2018). *The Fearless Organization: Creating Psychological Safety in the Workplace for Learning, Innovation, and Growth*. Wiley.

Edmondson, A. (2024). *Right Kind of Wrong: How the Best Teams Use Failure to Succeed*. Penguin.

Elena, L., et al. (2018). "The Fastest Path to the CEO Job, According to a 10-Year Study," *Harvard Business Review*.

Ellingrud, K. (2023). "Generative AI and the Future of Work in America," McKinsey.

Epstein, D. (2019). "Don't Underestimate Generalists: They Bring Value to Your Team," Knowledge at Wharton.

Epstein, D. (2020). *Range: How Generalists Triumph in a Specialized World*. Macmillan.

Erikson, T. (2019). *Surrounded by Idiots: The Four Types of Human Behaviour (or, How to Understand Those Who Cannot Be Understood)*. Vermilion.

Evdokimov, E., Hanlon, D., and Lim, E. K. Y. (2022). "Do Generalist CEOs Magnify Boardroom Backscratching?," *Journal of Business Ethics*. Springer Netherlands, 181(1), pp. 221–247. doi: 10.1007/s10551-021-04895-0.

Evdokimov, E., and Yusoff, I. (2024). "CEO Succession and Auditor Going Concern Decisions: An Analysis of Outsider CEOs and Generalist Skills," *Journal of Accounting and Public Policy*. Elsevier Inc., 43 (December 2023), p. 107159. doi: 10.1016/ j.jaccpubpol.2023.107159.

Evergreen, B. (2023). *Autonomous Transformation: Creating a More Human Future in the Era of Artificial Intelligence*. Wiley.

Fahrenkopf, E., Guo, J., and Argote, L. (2020). "Personnel Mobility and Organizational Performance: The Effects of Specialist vs. Generalist Experience and Organizational Work Structure," *Organization Science*, 31(6), pp. 1601–1620. doi: 10.1287/ORSC. 2020.1373.

Fatt, J. P. T. (2004). "'Leadership Styles between Technical and Non-Technical Superiors: Guess Who Will Give Subordinates More Freedom on the Job?," *Journal of Technical Writing and Communication*, 34(1), pp. 91–111. doi: 10.2190/Y1QW-4BQU-R1 78-L3GT.

Fernandez, R. (2016). "5 Ways to Boost Your Resilience at Work," *Harvard Business Review*.

Ferreira, D., et al. (2012). "Who Gets to the Top? Generalists versus Specialists in Managerial Organizations," *The RAND Journal of Economics*, 43(4), pp. 577–601.

Fleischmann, K. (2015). "Generalist Designers, Specialist Projects: Forming Multidisciplinary Teams That Work," *International Journal of Learning, Teaching and Educational Research*, 13(3), pp. 26–40.

Frances, F., and Anne, M. (2023). *Move Fast and Fix Things: The Trusted Leader's Guide to Solving Hard Problems*. Harvard Business Review Press.

Frank, N., and Florenta, T. (2020). "In R&D, Generalists Are More Valuable Than You Think," *Harvard Business Review*.

Fricke, D., and Roukny, T. (2020). "Generalists and Specialists in the Credit Market," *Journal of Banking and Finance*. Elsevier B.V., 112, p. 105335. doi: 10.1016/j.jbankfin.2018.04.014.

Furr, N. R., Cavarretta, F., and Garg, S. (2012). "Who Changes Course? The Role of Domain Knowledge and Novel Framing In Making Technology Changes. *Strategic Entrepreneurship Journal*, 6(3), pp. 236–256.

Gabaix, X., and Landier, A. (2008). "Why Has CEO Pay Increased So Much?," *Quarterly Journal of Economics*, 123(1), pp. 49–100. doi: 10.1162/qjec.2008.123.1.49.

Gelb, M. (2000). *How to Think Like Leonardo Da Vinci: Seven Steps to Genius Every Day*. Dell Publishing Company.

Ghosh, B., and Balachander, S. (2007). "Competitive Bundling and Counterbundling with Generalist and Specialist Firms," *Management Science*, 53(1), pp. 159–168. doi: 10.1287/mnsc.1060.0601.

Gilbert, E. (2015). *Big Magic: How to Live a Creative Life, and Let Go of Your Fear*. Bloomsbury Publishing.

Gladwell, M. (2009). *Outliers: The Story of Success*. Penguin.

Goel, A. M., and Thakor, A. V. (2008). "Overconfidence, CEO Selection, and Corporate Governance," *Journal of Finance*, 63(6), pp. 2737–2784. doi: 10.1111/j.1540-6261.2008.01412.x.

Goertzel, B. (2014). "Artificial General Intelligence: Concept, State of the Art, and Future Prospects," *Journal of Artificial General Intelligence*, 5(1), pp. 1–48. doi: 10.2478/jagi-2014-0001.

Goleman, D. (2007). *Social Intelligence: The New Science of Human Relationships*. Arrow Publishing.

Goodall, A. H. (2012). "A Theory of Expert Leadership," *EconStor*.

Gore, A. K., Matsunaga, S., and Eric Yeung, P. (2011). "The Role of Technical Expertise in Firm Governance Structure: Evidence from Chief Financial Officer Contractual Incentives," *Strategic Management Journal*, 32(7), pp. 771–786. doi: 10.1002/smj.907.

Gounopoulos, D. and Pham, H. (2018). "Specialist CEOs and IPO Survival," *Journal of Corporate Finance*. Elsevier B.V., 48, pp. 217–243. doi: 10.1016/j.jcorpfin.2017.10.012.

Graham, D. (2018). *Switchers: How Smart Professionals Change Careers—and Seize Success*. Amacom.

Grant, A. (2021). *Think Again: The Power of Knowing What You Don't Know*. WH Allen.

Grant, A. (2023). *Hidden Potential: The Science of Achieving Greater Things*. Penguin.

Greene, R. (2014). *The Concise Mastery*. Profile Books.

Guay, W., Taylor, D. J., and Xiao, J. J. (2014). "Adapt or Perish: Evidence of CEO Adaptability to Industry Shocks," The Wharton School.

Guy, K., and Madisun, N. (2024). *Think Remarkable: 9 Paths to Transform Your Life and Make a Difference*. Wiley.

Hakim, M. S., and Liu, C. L. (2021). "Generalist or Specialist? The Skills of CEO and Director That Really Matter to Firm Performance," *Modern Economy*, 12(12), pp. 1768–1781. doi: 10.4236/me.2021.1212090.

Hamel, G., and Zanini, M. (2020). *Humanocracy: Creating Organizations as Amazing as the People Inside Them*. Harvard Business Review Press.

He, Z. (2014). "Are CEOs with a PhD More Innovative?," University of New Orleans.

Helen, T., and Sarah, E. (2020). *The Squiggly Career*. Portfolio Penguin.

Herrmann, P., and Datta, D. K. (2005). "Relationships between Top Management Team Characteristics and International Diversification: An Empirical Investigation," *British Journal of Management*, 16(1), pp. 69–78. doi: 10.1111/j.1467-8551.2005.00429.x.

Hoozée, S., Maussen, S., and Vangronsveld, P. (2019). "The Impact of Readability of Corporate Social Responsibility Information on Credibility as Perceived by Generalist versus Specialist Readers," *Sustainability Accounting, Management and Policy Journal*, 10(3), pp. 570–591. doi: 10.1108/SAMPJ-03-2018-0056.

Hossain, A., et al. (2023). "Generalist CEO and Carbon Emissions," *Journal of Economic Behavior and Organization*. Elsevier B.V., 213 (January), pp. 68–86. doi: 10.1016/j.jebo.2023.07.016.

Hrazdil, K., et al. (2023). "Generalist CEOs and Conditional Accounting Conservatism," *Journal of Business Finance and Accounting*. doi: 10.1111/jbfa.12761.

Ichiro, K., and Fumitake, K. (2019). *The Courage to Be Disliked: A Single Book Can Change Your Life*. Allen & Unwin.

Ishak, R., Ismail, K. N. I. K., and Abdullah, S. N. (2012). "Corporate Performance, CEO Power and CEO Turnover: Evidence from Malaysian Public Listed Companies," *Jurnal Pengurusan*, 35, pp. 33–41.

Ivanova, N., Klimova, A., and Thorngate, W. (2023). "Generalists' Career in Modern Organizations and Education: Theoretical Review," *Organizational Psychology*, 13(2), pp. 158–173. doi: 10.17323/2312-5942-2023-13-2-158-173.

Iyengar, S. (2023). *Think Bigger: How to Innovate*. Columbia University Press.

Jill, C. (2020). "Adaptability Should Be Your New Hire's Top Soft Skill. Here's How to Test for It," *Fast Company*.

John, M. (2009). *How Successful People Think: Change Your Thinking, Change Your Life*. Center Street.

Juma, A. (2022). *The Master Generalist: How to Pursue Mastery, Chase Curiosity, and Cultivate Your Career in an Age of Uncertainty*. High Friday Publishing.

Kabir, M., and Rashid, H. (2023). "Do Generalist CEOs Engage in More Tax Avoidance Than Specialist CEOs?," *Accounting and Business Research*, pp. 1–27. doi: 10.1080/00014788.2023.2183486.

Kahneman, D. (2012). *Thinking Fast and Slow*. Penguin.

Kalelkar, R., et al. (2023). "Generalist CEOs and the Readability of the 10-K Report," *Advances in Accounting*. Elsevier Ltd, (December 2021), p. 100680. doi: 10.1016/j.adiac.2023.100680.

Kallias, A., et al. (2023). "One Size Does Not Fit All: The Conditional Role of CEO Education on IPO Performance," *Journal of Business Research*. Elsevier Inc., 157(December 2021), p. 113560. doi: 10. 1016/j.jbusres.2022.113560.

Kaplan, S. N., Klebanov, M. M., and Sorensen, M. (2012). "Which CEO Characteristics and Abilities Matter?," *Journal of Finance*, 67(3), pp. 973–1007. doi: 10.1111/j.1540-6261.2012.01739.x.

Ken, B., and Randy, C. (2022). *Simple Truths of Leadership: 52 Ways to Be a Servant Leader and Build Trust*. Berrett-Koehler Publishers.

Ketterer, M. (2023). "Knowledge Workers' Self-Directed Learning Framework for Future of Work Era," Laurea University of Applied Sciences.

Kim, K. H., et al. (2009). "CEO Duality Leadership and Corporate Diversification Behavior," *Journal of Business Research*, 62(11), pp. 1173–1180. doi: 10.1016/j.jbusres.2008.10.017.

Kim, S. (2019). *Radical Candor: How to Get What You Want by Saying What You Mean*. Pan Macmillan UK.

King, T., Srivastav, A., and Williams, J. (2016). "What's in an Education? Implications of CEO Education for Bank Performance," *Journal of Corporate Finance*, 37, pp. 287–308. doi: 10.1016/ j.jcorpfin.2016.01.003.

Koo, K. (2013). "Human Capital between Generalists and Specialists: How Does It Impact Innovation?" Available at SSRN:

https://ssrn.com/abstract=2312896 or http://dx.doi.org/10.2139/ssrn.2312896.

Lakshman, C. (2007). "Top Executive Knowledge Leadership: Managing Knowledge to Lead Change at General Electric," *Journal of Change Management*, 5(4), pp. 429–446. doi: 10.1080/14697010 500401540.

Lee, L. (2010). "Don't Be Too Specialized If You Want a Top Level Management Job," Insights by Stanford Business, Stanford Business School.

Lee, S.-H. (2005). "Generalists and Specialists, Ability and Earnings," University of Hawaii.

Lei, L., and Wu, X. (2022). *Thinking Like a Specialist or a Generalist? Evidence from Hidden Champions in China, Asian Business and Management*. Palgrave Macmillan UK. doi: 10.1057/s41291-020-00114-2.

Lencioni, P. M. (2012). *The Advantage: Why Organizational Health Trumps Everything Else In Business*. Wiley.

Li, P.-Y. (2016). "The Impact of the Top Management Teams' Knowledge and Experience on Strategic Decisions and Performance," *Journal of Management & Organization*, 23(04), pp. 504–523. doi: 10.1017/jmo.2016.24.

Lin, Y. C., et al. (2014). "CEO Characteristics and Internal Control Quality," *Corporate Governance (Oxford)*, 22(1), pp. 24–42. doi: 10.1111/corg.12042.

Liu, C., Shi, W., and Wei, K. C. J. (2016). "CEO Expertise and the Design of Compensation Contracts: Evidence from Generalist versus Specialist CEOs," NHH Brage.

Liu, C.-L. (2017). "Skill Specialist or Generalist? Does CEO Substitute or Complement Directors?," Yuntech.

Liu, X. (2022). "Generalist vs Specialist CEOs and Inter Region Mergers and Acquisitions: Evidence from China," *NNSFC*.

Liz, W., and Greg, M. (2015). *Multipliers: How the Best Leaders Make Everyone Smarter*. Harper Business.

Lu, A., et al. (2020). "After Bubble Busts: The Generalist-Specialist Tradeoff in IT Career Mobility Post Dotcom," *International Conference on Information Systems, ICIS*, pp. 0–16.

Lurie, J. D., Goodman, D. C., and Wennberg, J. E. (2002). "Benchmarking the Future Generalist Workforce," *Effective Clinical Practice*, 5(2), pp. 58–66.

Ma, Z., et al. (2021). "Generalist CEOs and Credit Ratings," *Contemporary Accounting Research*, 38(2), pp. 1009–1036. doi: 10.1111/1911-3846.12662.

Makarevich, A. (2018). "Ties of Survival: Specialization, Inter-Firm Ties, and Firm Failure in the U.S. Venture Capital Industry," *Journal of Business Research*. Elsevier, 86(April 2017), pp. 153–165. doi: 10.1016/j.jbusres.2018.02.001.

Malmendier, U., and Tate, G. (2005). "Does Overconfidence Affect Corporate Investment? CEO Overconfidence Measures Revisited," *European Financial Management*, 11(5), pp. 649–659. doi: 10. 1111/j.1354-7798.2005.00302.x.

Mansharamani, V. (2012). "All Hail the Generalist," *Harvard Business Review*.

Mansharamani, V. (2020). *Think for Yourself: Restoring Common Sense in an Age of Experts and Artificial Intelligence.* Harvard Business Review Press.

Mansharamani, V. (2024). *The Making of a Generalist: An Independent Thinker Finds Unconventional Success in an Uncertain World.* Outfox Publishing.

Manson, M. (2016). *The Subtle Art of Not Giving a F*ck: A Counterintuitive Approach to Living a Good Life.* Harper.

Marco, I., and Karim, L. (2020). *Competing in the Age of AI: Strategy and Leadership When Algorithms and Networks Run the World.* Harvard Business Review Press.

Marcus, B., and Ashley, G. (2019). *Nine Lies About Work: A Freethinking Leader's Guide to the Real World.* Harvard Business Review Press.

Margerison, C. (2007). "Chief Executives' Perceptions of Managerial Success Factors," *Journal of Management Development*, pp. 47–60.

Martin, G., and Joshua, Y. (2024). *The Bonfire Moment: Bring Your Team Together to Solve the Hardest Problems Startups Face.* Harper Business.

Meijenfeldt, F. A. B., Hogeweg, P., and Dutilh, B. E. (2023). "A Social Niche Breadth Score Reveals Niche Range Strategies of Generalists and Specialists," *Nature Ecology and Evolution*. Springer US, 7(5), pp. 768–781. doi: 10.1038/s41559-023-02027-7.

Meyer, E. (2014). *The Culture Map: Breaking Through the Invisible Boundaries of Global Business.* PublicAffairs.

Mishra, D. R. (2014). "The Dark Side of CEO Ability: CEO General Managerial Skills and Cost of Equity Capital," *Journal of Corporate Finance*. Elsevier B.V., 29, pp. 390–409. doi: 10.1016/j.jcorpfin.2014.10.003.

Mueller, P., Georgakakis, D., and Winfried Ruigrok, W. (2017). "Jack of All Trades or Master of None? CEO Experience Variety and Firm Performance." In *Academy of Management Proceedings*, vol. 2017, no. 1, p. 17662. Briarcliff Manor, NY 10510: Academy of Management.

Mumford, M. D., et al. (2002). "Leading Creative People: Orchestrating Expertise and Relationships, *Leadership Quarterly*, 13(6), pp. 705–750. doi: 10.1016/S1048-9843(02).00158-3.

Mumford, T. V., Campion, M. A., and Morgeson, F. P. (2007). "The Leadership Skills Strataplex: Leadership Skill Requirements across Organizational Levels," *Leadership Quarterly*, 18(2), pp. 154–166. doi: 10.1016/j.leaqua.2007.01.005.

Murmann, S. (2014). "Who Matters More? The Impact of Functional Background and Top Executive Mobility on Firm Survival," *Strategic Management Journal*, 51(2), pp. 315–334. doi: 10.1002/smj.

Nadkarni, S., and Herrmann, P. O. L. (2010). "CEO Personality, Strategic Flexibility, and Firm Performance: the Case of the Indian Business Process Outsourcing Industry," *Academy of Management*, 53(5), pp. 1050–1073.

Nasirov, S., Li, Q. C., and Kor, Y. Y. (2021). "Converting Technological Inventions into New Products: The Role of CEO Human Capital," *Journal of Product Innovation Management*, 38(5), pp. 522–547. doi: 10.1111/jpim.12601.

Naveen, L. (2006). "Organizational Complexity and Succession Planning," *The Journal of Financial and Quantitative Analysis*, 41(3), pp. 661–683.

Pellegrino, E. D. (2000). "Can the Generalist Survive the 21st Century?," *The Journal of the American Board of Family Practice*, 13(4), pp. 312–314. doi: 10.3122/15572625-13-4-312.

Philip, T. (2006). *Expert Political Judgment—How Good Is It? How Can We Know?* Princeton University Press.

Pink, D. (2018). *Drive: The Surprising Truth About What Motivates Us.* Canongate Books.

Pitcher, P., and Smith, A. D. (2001). "Top Management Team Heterogeneity: Personality, Power, and Proxies," *Organization Science*, 12(1), pp. 1–18. doi: 10.1287/orsc.12.1.1.10120.

Polman, P., and Winston, A. (2021). "6 Types of Resilience Companies Need Today," *Harvard Business Review*.

Pothier, W. G., Howard, H., and Campbell, P. (2019). "Pathways to Becoming an Academic Subject Specialist: Insights from Three Librarians," *Partnership Journal*, 14(1), pp. 1–9. doi: 10.21083/partnership.v14i1.5172.

Prasad, S. (2009). "Task Assignments and Incentives: Generalists versus Specialists," *RAND Journal of Economics*, 40(2), pp. 380–403. doi: 10.1111/j.1756-2171.2009.00070.x.

Rathnayaka, P., et al. (2022). "Specialist vs Generalist: A Transformer Architecture for Global Forecasting Energy Time Series," *International Conference on Human System Interaction, HSI*. IEEE, 2022-July, pp. 1–5. doi: 10.1109/HSI55341.2022.9869463.

Ravin, J., and John, B. (2022). *Work without Jobs: How to Reboot Your Organization's Work Operating System*. MIT Press.

Reavey, B., Zahay, D., and Rosenbloom, A. (2021). "Updating the Marketing Research Course to Prepare the Marketing Generalist," *Journal of Marketing Education*, 43(3), pp. 333–353. doi: 10.1177/02734753211043925.

Riani, A. (2022a). "Are Generalists Or Specialists Better Startup Founders?," *Forbes*.

Riani, A. (2022b). "Generalist Vs. Specialist Teams: How To Build A Highly Creative Startup," *Forbes*.

Rob, C., and Karen, D. (2023). *The Microstress Effect: How Little Things Pile Up and Create Big Problems—and What to Do about It*. Harvard Business Review Press.

Sabel, C. A., and Sasson, A. (2023). "Different People, Different Pathways: Human Capital Redeployment in Multi-business Firms," *Strategic Management Journal*, 44(13), pp. 3185–3216. doi: 10.1002/smj.3533.

Samir, S. (2022). "Artificial Intelligence: The Generalist-Specialist Division is a Dangerous Cognitive Bias, *The Times of India*.

Sarah, G. (2023). "Are We Entering the Age of the Workplace Generalist?," *People Management Magazine*.

Scarnati, J. T. (2015). "Beyond Technical Competence: Nine Rules for Administrators," *NASSP Bulletin*, 78(561), pp. 76–83. doi: 10.1177/019263659407856113.

Schelfhaudt, K., and Crittenden, V. L. (2005). "Specialist or Generalist: Views from Academia and Industry," *Journal of Business Research*, 58(7), pp. 946–954. doi: 10.1016/j.jbusres.2003.12.003.

Schwab, K. (2017). *The Fourth Industrial Revolution*. Crown Currency.

Senge, P. (2006). *The Fifth Discipline: The Art and Practice of the Learning Organization*. Random House Business.

Serfling, M. (2014). "CEO Age and the Riskiness of Corporate Policies," *Journal of Corporate Finance*, 25, pp. 251–273. doi: 10.1016/j.jcorpfin.2013.12.013.

Serres, N. (2019). "Move Over, Specialists: The Rise of the Generalist Is Here," *Forbes*.

Sharma, R. (2006). *Who Will Cry When You Die?* Jaico Publishing House.

Sher, B. (2007). *Refuse To Choose! Use All of Your Interests, Passions, and Hobbies to Create the Life and Career of Your Dreams*. Rodale Press.

Shroff, R. (2023). "Specialist Or Generalist? Why GIC Leaders Should Try a Little of Both," *Forbes*.

Sinek, S. (2019). *The Infinite Game: How Great Businesses Achieve Long-lasting Success*. Penguin.

Sinniah, S., et al. (2022). "Post-COVID-19 Organizational Resilience in the Manufacturing and Service Industries," *Journal Pengurusan*, 66 (December). doi: 10.17576/pengurusan-2022-66-02.

Smith, V., et al. (2017). "The Changing Nature of Diplomacy in the 21st Century: From Diplomatic Generalists to Four Types of Specialists," *Journal of Materials Processing Technology*, 1(1), pp. 1–8.

Soomro, M. (2022a). "Five 'Don'ts' After Two Years of Covid-19," Teesside University.

Soomro, M. (2022b). "Is the 6-Hour Workday the Answer to a Better Work-Life Balance?", *Euronews*.

Soomro, M. (2022d). "Leading Your Business After the Pandemic—Five Key Considerations," Chartered Association of Business Schools. Available at: https://smallbusinesscharter.org/news-and-insights/insights/leading-your-business-after-the-pandemic-five-key-considerations.

Soomro, M. (2023a). "15 Big Ideas That Will Shape 2024," LinkedIn News UK. Available at: https://www.linkedin.com/pulse/15-big-ideas-shape-2024-linkedin-news-uk-adpsc/?trackingId=uCmjUcS UQTyRqZ9zrjbipA%3D%3D.

Soomro, M. (2023b). "5 Big Ideas That Will Change Finance in 2024, According to Experts on LinkedIn," LinkedIn News UK. Available at: https://www.linkedin.com/pulse/5-big-ideas-change-finance-2024-according-experts-linkedin-wawae/?trackingId=myRjXLzB Qym7BjfK4T0TLw%3D%3D.

Soomro, M. (2023c). "AI Is 'Absolutely' Coming After Your Job If You Work in Customer Service. But It's Not All Bad," *Euronews*. Available at: https://www.euronews.com/next/2023/07/19/ai-is-absolutely-coming-after-your-job-if-you-work-in-customer-service-but-its-not-all-bad.

Soomro, M. (2023d). "America Is Ready for the 4-Day Workweek," *Newsweek*. Available at: https://www.newsweek.com/america-ready-4-day-workweek-1788204.

Soomro, M. (2023e). "Banks' Strict Return-to-Office Mandates Risk Sparking Talent Exodus," *Financial News London (DowJones)*. Available at: https://www.fnlondon.com/articles/banks-strict-return-to-office-mandates-risk-sparking-talent-exodus-20230810.

Soomro, M. (2023f). "Changing the Business Model of Business Schools," AACSB. Available at: https://www.aacsb.edu/insights/articles/2023/05/changing-the-business-model-of-business-schools.

Soomro, M. (2023g). "Four-Day Work Week: The Revolutionary New Way of Working Explained," *The Independent*. Available at: https://www.indy100.com/news/four-day-work-week-uk.

Soomro, M. (2023h). "Four Day Work Week vs. Six Hour Work Days. Which Would You Prefer?," PR in HR.

Soomro, M. (2023i). "From Burnout to Bliss: How the 4-Day Work Week Impacts Wellbeing," North East Chamber of Commerce. Available at: https://www.necc.co.uk/from-burnout-to-bliss-how-the-4-day-work-week-impacts-wellbeing/.

Soomro, M. (2023j). "Gen Z Is lonLly. Going Back to the Office May Be the Cure for Some," *Business Insider*. Available at: https://www.businessinsider.com/cure-for-gen-z-loneliness-heading-returning-to-office-2023-10.

Soomro, M. (2023k). "Global Heating and the Future of work," *The New Statesman*. Available at: https://www.newstatesman.com/spotlight/sustainability/climate/2023/08/heatwaves-global-warming-future-work.

Soomro, M. (2023l). "How Banking Tech Is Serving Customers Better," *Raconteur*. Available at: https://www.raconteur.net/insights/innovation-and-transformation-in-banking.

Soomro, M. (2023m). "How HR Can Tailor Workplace Policies to Address Heat Waves," *HR Brew*.

Soomro, M. (2023n). "How Will Extreme Temperatures and Heatwaves Change How We Work?," *BBC WorkLife*. Available at: https://www.bbc.com/worklife/article/20230719-how-will-extreme-temperatures-and-heat-waves-change-how-we-work.

Soomro, M. (2023o). "Remote Work: Is It Time for Workers to Go Back to the Office?," *Euronews*.

Soomro, M. (2023p). "Should Those Who Work from Home Be Paid Less?," *The Times*. Available at: https://www.thetimes.com/business-money/money/article/should-those-who-work-from-home-be-paid-less-8xszr30zb.

Soomro, M. (2023q). "The 4-Day Workweek Could Be the Best Way to Bridge the Gender Pay Gap—and the Companies That Have Tried It Are Living Proof," *Fortune*. Available at: https://fortune.com/2023/10/24/4-day-workweek-best-way-bridge-gender-pay-gap-companies-living-proof-mansoor-soomro/.

Soomro, M. (2023r). "UK Employers Warm to the Idea of a Four-Day Working Week," *Raconteur*. Available at: https://www.raconteur.net/future-of-work/employers-warm-to-four-day-week.

Soomro, M. (2023s). "What Microsoft's Earnings Tell Us about AI and Cloud Trends," *Fortune CFO Daily*. Available at: https://fortune.com/2023/10/25/microsoft-earnings-ai-cloud-trends/.

Soomro, M. (2023t). "Why Shorter Days, Not Weeks, Could Be the Answer to Work-Life Balance," *WorkLife*. Available at: https://www.worklife.news/leadership/six-hour-workday/.

Soomro, M. (2023u). "Why Taking a Mental Health Day Could Be Bad… for Your Mental Health," *The Independent*. Available at: https://www.independent.co.uk/life-style/health-and-families/features/mental-health-days-work-disadvantages-b2415758.html.

Soomro, M. (2024a). "AI and HR: A Breakdown of HR Today, Tomorrow and in the Months to Come," *Human Resources Director Magazine*.

Soomro, M. (2024b). "British Workers Are Working 19 Million Days of Unpaid Overtime a Month," *Daily Mail*.

Soomro, M. (2024c). "By 2040, Salaries Won't Exist—and Four Other Ways Work Will Be Unrecognisable," *iNews*. Available at: https://inews.co.uk/inews-lifestyle/by-2040-salaries-wont-exist-ways-work-will-be-unrecognisable-2863046.

Soomro, M. (2024d). "Gen Alpha and AI Set to Disrupt Wealth Management Industry, Argue Futurists," *Financial Times*. Available at: https://www.pwmnet.com/gen-alpha-and-ai-set-to-disrupt-wealth-management-industry-argue-futurists.

Soomro, M. (2024e). "How Gen Z Is Using Tech," LinkedIn News. Available at: https://www.linkedin.com/news/story/how-gen-z-is-using-tech-5800116/.

Soomro, M. (2024f). "How to Leverage AI While Preserving Human Skills," Chartered Management Institute. Available at: https://www.managers.org.uk/knowledge-and-insights/article/how-to-leverage-ai-while-preserving-human-skills/.

Soomro, M. (2024g). "Modern Household Appliances Hit the Scrapheap Sooner Than Older Models," *The Telegraph*.

Soomro, M. (2024h). "More Than Three-Quarters of Brits Are Working an Extra 19 Million Days of Unpaid Overtime Each Month," *The Sun*. Available at: https://www.thesun.co.uk/money/28092335/brits-working-millions-days-unpaid-overtime-each-month/.

Soomro, M. (2024i). "The Human Touch AI Virtual Assistants Can't Replace," *BBC WorkLife*. Available at: https://www.bbc.com/worklife/article/20240109-the-human-touch-ai-virtual-assistants-cant-replace.

Soomro, M. (2024j). The Lifespan of Large Appliances Is Shrinking," *Wall Street Journal*. Available at: https://www.wsj.com/personal-finance/the-lifespan-of-large-appliances-is-shrinking-e5fb205b.

Soomro, M. (2024k). "UK Employees Are Doing an Extra 5.5 Hours of Unpaid Work Every Month," Yahoo Life.

Soomro, M. (2024l). "UK Workers Clock in 19 Million Unpaid Overtime Days Monthly, Study Found," *Mirror UK*. Available at: https://www.mirror.co.uk/lifestyle/unpaid-overtime-time-management-well-32870725.

Soomro, M. (2024m). "Unpaid Overtime Crisis: British Employees Work Millions of Extra Hours," *Daily Express UK*. Available at: https://www.express.co.uk/life-style/life/1902405/Unpaid-overtime-Work-life-balance-Time-management-Well-being? trk=public_post_comment-text.

Soomro, M. (2024n). "Unpaid Overtime Hits 153 Million Hours a Month among UK Workers, Study Finds," *Daily Star*. Available at: https://www.dailystar.co.uk/news/uk-news/unpaid-overtime-time-management-well-32870992.

Soomro, M. (2024o). "Vindication for the Cheap White Refrigerator! Those Fancy Appliances Break—and Are So Expensive to Fix," *Business Insider*. Available at: https://www.businessinsider.com/white-fridge-refrigerator-gets-vindication-appliances-nene-leakes-2024-2?amp.

Soomro, M. (2024q). "When Hot Weather Arrives, Worker Productivity Is at Risk," *Bloomberg*.

Soomro, M. (2024r). "Working 9 to 9! British Workers Are Doing the Equivalent of 19 Million Extra Days of Unpaid Overtime Every Month," *Mail Online*. Available at: https://www.dailymail.co.uk/news/article-13451443/British-workers-19-million-days-unpaid-overtime.html.

Soomro, M. A., et al. (2022). "Workforce Resilience in the Post-COVID-19 Era: Differences Based on Manufacturing–Service Orientation and Firm Size," *Production Planning and Control*. Taylor & Francis, pp. 1–13. doi: 10.1080/09537287.2022.2106446.

Sperber, S., and Linder, C. (2016). "The Impact of Top Management Teams on Firm Innovativeness: A Configurational Analysis of Demographic Characteristics, Leadership Style and Team Power Distribution," *Review of Managerial Science*.

Ståhle, P., Ståhle, S. and Aho, S. (2011). 'Value Added Intellectual Coefficient (VAIC): A Critical Analysis', *Journal of Intellectual Capital*, 12(4), pp. 531–551. doi: 10.1108/14691931111181715.

Stretton, A. (2020). "Specialist PM and More Generalist Project-Related Contributors to Organisational Strategic Management," *PM World Journal*, IX(I), pp. 1–24.

Suzuki, N. (2007). "The Executive Profile of Engineering and Non-Engineering CEOs: US and Japan," *Emerald*, 4(12), p. 80.

Teodoridis, F. (2021). "Don't Underestimate the Role of Generalists in Innovation," *Fortune.*

Teodoridis, F., Bikard, M. and Vakili, K. (2018). "When Generalists Are Better Than Specialists, and Vice Versa," *Harvard Business Review.*

Torres, N. (2016). "Generalists Get Better Job Offers Than Specialists," *Harvard Business Review.*

Tseng, Y. W., Rowe, F., and Lin, E. S. (2023). "An Elon Musk Generalist or a Specialist? The Impacts of Interdisciplinary Learning on Post-Graduation Outcomes," *Studies in Higher Education,* pp. 1–26. doi: 10.1080/03075079.2023.2252889.

Vallone, T., Elia, S., and Greve, P. (2023). "International Environmental Complexity and the Demand for Generalists and Specialists in Executive Selection," *Global Strategy Journal,* 13(3), pp. 581–619. doi: 10.1002/gsj.1463.

Wang, S., Macy, M., and Nee, V. (2023). "Specialization in the Marketplace for Ideas," *PLoS ONE,* 18(10 October), pp. 1–18. doi: 10.1371/journal.pone.0293355.

Wapnick, E. (2018). *How to Be Everything: A Guide for Those Who (Still) Don't Know What They Want to Be When They Grow Up.* HarperOne.

Warren, B., and Burt, N. (2004). *Leaders: Strategies for Taking Charge.* Collins Business Essentials.

Watkins, M. (2013). *The First 90 Days: Proven Strategies for Getting Up to Speed Faster and Smarter.* Harvard Business Review Press.

Watts, D. (2001). "CEO's Role in IT-Driven Organizational Change," *Journal of Information Technology Theory and Application,* 3(3), pp. 44–55.

Weerasinghe, T., Liyanage, B. K., and Lakmali, M. A. D. (2021). "Are Human Resource Management Professionals Generalists or Specialists—A Critique," *Academia Letters* (April), pp. 0–5. doi: 10.20935/al549.

Wendy, S., Marianne, L., and Amy, E. (2022). *Both/And Thinking: Embracing Creative Tensions to Solve Your Toughest Problems.* Harvard Business Review Press.

Williams, C., Chen, P.-A., and Agarwal, R. (2016). "Rookies and Seasoned Recruits: How Experience in Different Levels, Firms and

Industries Shapes Strategic Renewal in Top Management," *Strategic Management Journal.*

Wood, J., and Vilkinas, T. (2005). "Characteristics Associated with Success: CEOs' Perspectives," *Leadership & Organization Development Journal,* 26(3), pp. 186–196. doi: 10.1108/0143773051 0591743.

Wortman, J., and Wood, D. (2011). "The Personality Traits of Liked People," *Journal of Research in Personality,* 45(6), pp. 519–528. doi: 10.1016/j.jrp.2011.06.006.

Xu, X. (2023). "Generalist CEOs, Management Risk and Internal Control Weaknesses," *Journal of Business Finance and Accounting* (August 2019), pp. 1–31. doi: 10.1111/jbfa.12691.

Xu, Y., et al. (2021). "Generalists vs. Specialists: Who Are Better Acquirers?," *Journal of Corporate Finance.* Elsevier B.V., 67 (February), p. 101915. doi: 10.1016/j.jcorpfin.2021.101915.

Yeoh, G. (2021). "Forget Picking a Career Specialisation. Being a Generalist Is a Lot More Fulfilling," CNA Singapore.

Zambrana, R., and Zapatero, F. (2021). "A Tale of Two Types: Generalists vs. Specialists in Asset Management," *Journal of Financial Economics.* Elsevier B.V., 142(2), pp. 844–861. doi: 10.1016/j.jfineco.2021.04.027.

Zandi, G., et al. (2015). "Is a MBA Degree Necessary to Be a CEO of Large Corporation: The Case of Fortune Magazine Global Top 100 Corporations," *International Business Research,* 8(12), p. 96. doi: 10.5539/ibr.v8n12p96.

Zbib, L., and Asare, K. (2023). "The Generalist CEO Pay Premium and CEO Risk Version," *Journal of Corporate Accounting and Finance,* 34(4), pp. 89–107. doi: 10.1002/jcaf.22638.

Zimmerman, R. D. (2008). "Understanding the Impact of Personality Traits on Individuals' Turnover Decisions: A Meta-analytic Path Model," *Personnel Psychology,* 61(2), pp. 309–348. doi: 10.1111/j.1744-6570.2008.00115.x.

Index

Please note that page numbers referring to Figures are followed by the letter '*f*', while references to Tables are followed by the letter '*t*'.

Accenture, 72
accounting tools, 117
adaptability of generalists, 14, 71
  ability to work outside domain, 101, 103
  boosting, 96
  building adaptable teams, 178
  case study, 176
  change/industry change, adapting to, 104, 113
  cross-industry *see* cross-industry adaptability, SDSU framework
  difficulties with, 96
  domain generalists, 71
  leadership, 74, 178
  market disruption in retail, 139
  tactical, 21
  to uncertainty, 131
  to the unexpected, 46
  see also flexibility
agility of thinking, 21, 25, 31
  case studies, 171–2, 175, 177–8
agriculture, regenerative, 109
AI *see* artificial intelligence (AI)
Airbnb, 14, 156
Amazon, 156
ambidextrous organizations, 151
ambiguity, 75, 84, 88, 127, 146
  tolerance for, 136
analysis till paralysis, 21
  case study, 167–8, 169
analytical skills, developing, 124

"another pair of eyes" feeling *see* oversight
anticipation, 20–1
Apple, 4, 14, 156
appliance design, 13
artificial intelligence (AI), xxii, xxv, 46–8, 69
  artificial general intelligence (AGI), 109
  complementary and contrasting skills, 36, 37
  developing portable skills, 42–5
  disciplinary blind spots, 48–52
  displacement of jobs, 19, 41, 47
  emerging domains fit for, 109–10
  emerging skills fit for, 128
  growth, 41, 42, 46, 47
  interaction skills, 125–6
  portable skills essential for professional resilience, 39–45
  predictive analytics, AI-powered, 45
  responding to, 113
  strengths of, 46
  and unique value of humans (versatility), 46–8
assumptions, identifying, 124
automation, 46, 113
  see also artificial intelligence (AI)

Bain & Company, 72
balance, generalist bringing, 96

beginner's mind, 50
Bennett, Ben (case study) *see under* shallow generalists (S)
Bezos, Jeff, 156
big-picture thinking, 14, 31, 56
  cognitive skills, 125
  complex problems, generalists tackling, 145, 158
  future-focused and visionary industries, 89
  holistic approach, 146
  macro focus, 159, 160
  shallow generalists, 68, 69*t*
  strategists, 25, 27*t*, 30*t*, 31, 57
black swan (major surprise) events, 23
blind spots, disciplinary
  seeing beyond, 51–2
  strategies to overcome, 49–50
  see also artificial intelligence (AI); disciplinary interaction, approaches
blue sky thinking, 155
Boston Consulting Group, 72
boundary spanning leadership, 49
brain uploading, 110
brainstorming
  cross-functional sessions, 123, 134
  divergent thinking, 142
  generalist leadership approach, 140
  outsider-perspective, 85
  problem-solving, 117
  without limitations, 155
Branson, Richard, 165
bridge building, 13–14, 145
Brin, Sergey, 156
Brodin, Jesper, 165–6
Brown, Tim, 4–5
burnout trap, 21–2
business focus, 23
business problems, 9, 46–48
Butterfield, Stewart, 164

careers
  aligning skill development with advancement, 114
  opportunities, 18–19
  portfolio, 57–8
  productivity and career lifespan, 96–7
  reinventing, 112–13
  resilience, 42
  switching companies early, 64–5
  switching companies later, 65–6
  transitions, 42
  unconventional paths, 84
case studies
  complex problems, tackling, 148–9
  innovation, generalist-led, 156–7
  problem-solving modes, 164–6
  skill generalist as leader, 173–6
  uncertain events, preparing for, 139–41
  see also under domain generalists (D); shallow generalists (S); skill generalists (S); ultra generalists (U)
change, adapting to, 104
change management, 32
climate engineering, 109
cognitive adaptability, 76–7
cognitive ease, 48
cognitive flexibility, 25, 26*t*, 29*t*, 31
cognitive skills, 125
collaboration, 13, 61, 72, 75, 124, 131, 132
  actionable points, 56
  case study, 175
  and communication, 78, 123, 171
  cross-departmental, 115
  cross-functional, 32, 74, 98
  cross-team, 175
  effective, 38
  enhancing, 13
  facilitating, 49
  fostering, 13, 96, 104

interdisciplinary, 31, 49, 51
multidisciplinary, 86
and networking, 69
problem-solving, 77
skill generalists, 78
soft skills, 116
stifling, 7
strategic, 50
uncertainty, 132
collective brain trust, 15
comfort zone clinger, specialist as, 7
communication, 22, 36, 46, 78, 85,
    117, 123
barriers to, 98
bridge building, 75, 145, 164
case study, 174
clear channels of, 145
and collaboration, 78, 123, 171
conflict management, 44
crisis management, 101
diverse conversations, seeking
    out, 124
effective, 30, 104
and empathy, 174
improved, 175
and influence, 40
interdisciplinary, 30
and miscommunication, 67
soft skills, 116
specialists, communication gap
    between, 56
strong skills, 36, 43, 81, 116
teamwork, 165
company mindset, 15
complementary skills, 36, 38
complex problems, generalists
    tackling, 5, 58, 98, 103, 112,
    116, 121, 141–9
being a knowledge sponge, 147
biases, dealing with, 147
big-picture thinking, 146
breaking down of tasks, 147
case studies, generalist-led, 148–9
convergent thinking, 142, 144
defining complexity, 141

divergent thinking, 142, 144
downplaying complexity,
    challenge of, 21
effective prioritizing, 146
high-stake, cross-functional
    initiative, 149
holistic thinking, 142, 146–8
interconnectedness, 146
legacy system revamp, 148
moving target client project, 149
progress versus perfection, 148
reflection, scheduling time for, 147
ripple effect, 147
scenarios, 148–9
silo thinking, 141–2, 144
TGA, possible paths of, 68, 69,
    71, 78, 86, 89
ultra generalists leaders, holistic
    thinking useful for, 146–8
visual tools, using, 147
confidence, 113
construction, 10, 90, 108
consultants, 75
contextual analysis, 46
contextual intelligence, 25, 31
contextual relativity, 7–8
contrasting skills, 35–9
controlling, principles of, 49
convergent thinking, 142, 144
COVID-19 pandemic, 14–15, 25
craftsmanship, 6, 13
creativity, 3, 4, 21, 35, 37, 96, 113,
    114, 124, 156, 186
campaigns, 55
coaching techniques, 82
communication skills, 22
creative connections, 46
creative thinking, 29, 67–8,
    125, 161
development of TGA, 108
generalists, 5, 57
industries, 81
leadership excellence skills, 126
mindset, 162
problem-solving, 31, 42, 72, 85

creativity, (*Cont.*)
  case studies, 171, 174
  skill generalists, 78
  skills, 36
  soft skills, 116
  solutions, 144, 155, 165, 185
  strategic skill development, 80
  video editing skills, 81
crisis management, 101
critical thinking, 25, 31, 41, 116
cross-disciplinary approaches, 30,
    120, 123
  defining, 120
  domain generalists, 122
  harmonizers, 145
  innovation, 11, 30, 51, 123
  scientists, xxv
  SDSU framework, 121, 122
  skills and experiences, 97
  ultra generalists, 83
cross-functional liaison, 5
cross-industry adaptability, SDSU
    framework, 58–60
  case study, 170–3
cross-pollination, 50
cultural context and myths about
    generalists, 13
curiosity, 4, 15, 22, 51, 55
  curiosity-driven exploration, 79
  generalists thriving on, 17
  insatiable, 86
  intellectual, 123
  transforming into wisdom, 186
  working outside domain, 102
customer services, 36, 40, 75, 78,
    81, 90, 163
customer-centricity, 110

da Vinci, Leonardo, 56, 84
data literacy, 125–6
DB Transportation Corp (case
    study) *see under* domain
    generalists (D)
decision-making myth regarding
    generalists, 10

deep focus, 159, 160, 161, 162
departmental silos, removing, 105
detail, attention to, 68, 168
digital consciousness, 110
digital transformation, 118
disciplinary interaction, approaches
  ascending number of disciplines/
      subjects, 121
  cross-disciplinary *see* cross-
      disciplinary approaches
  differences between disciplines,
      120, 121*t*
  how leaders can benefit
      from, 122–3
  interdisciplinary *see* interdiscipli-
      nary approaches
  intra-disciplinary, 120–2, 124
  learning to translate between
      disciplines, 124
  meaning of discipline, 120
  multidisciplinary *see* multidiscipli-
      nary approaches
  SDSU framework, 120–2
  trans-disciplinary, 120, 122, 123–4
  see also blind spots, disciplinary
discomfort learning, seeking, 50
disruptions, 145–6, 177
  analysis till paralysis, 167–8
  anticipating, 177
  envisioning disruptive
      events, 23–4
  industry, 57
  market, 139
  potential, 14, 30, 46, 137
  retail sector, adapting to, 139
  scanning for, 20
  supply chain, 165, 177
  technical/technological, 5, 9, 14,
      110, 111, 164
  transformative, 23
  weather, 46, 113
  workplace environments, 89
divergent thinking, 142, 144
diversity, xxiii
  and balance, 37, 38

of collective knowledge, 57
and decision-making, 10
domain, 89
of generalists, 55–8
and hiring, 22
and inclusion, 127
industries, connections
    between, 56
of knowledge, 9, 57
making a tool, 80
skills, 103, 118
topics, exploring, 69
domain and skill variation among
    generalists, 95–129
ability to work outside domain
    see outside-the-domain skills
domain-flexibility, 102, 103
emerging domains, 109–10
encouraging a culture of upskilling
    and re-skilling, 114–15
increased innovation, 104
industry domain exposure, 141
Law of Specialist Saturation
    see Law of Specialist
    Saturation (LOSS)
new skills, ability to acquire,
    110–15
significance of acquiring new
    skills, 112–14
top 60 domains for developing
    TGA, 106–10
domain generalists (D)
adaptability, 71
"anticipating disruptors," 72
beneficial environments, 74–6
bridge building, 145
case study (Rebecca Martinez of
    DB Transportation Corp)
agility, 171–2
cross-industry adaptability,
    170–3
    customer-centricity, 171, 172
    data-informed
      decision-making, 172
    discussion questions, 173

driving of change, 172
early influences in nonprofit
    sector, 171
employee morale, 173
innovation, 173
legacy business, revitalizing, 172
mission-driven focus, 171, 172
profitability, 173
resourcefulness, 171
results, evaluating, 172–3
speed taking precedence over
    perfection, 171
stakeholder management
    skills, 171
transferring of learning, 172
transformational growth, 170–1
characteristics, 60, 72–3
complex problems, tackling, 144
consultants, 75
cross-functional collaboration, 74
cross-industry expertise, 72, 74–5
defining, 71–2
diversification of projects, 74
emerging industries, 75
external opportunities,
    identifying, 72
fast-paced and dynamic
    environments, 75
flexibility of, 75
how to become, 73–4
industry conferences, 74
industry generalists, as, 63
industry knowledge, 72
industry sectors suited to, 74–5
innovation catalysts, 72
innovation management
    practices, 155
macro focus, 162
mergers and acquisitions, 76
micro-niches, identifying, 73
multidisciplinary approaches, 137
networking, 73
pattern seeker, 163
problem-solving, 75, 122
pros and cons, 73

domain generalists (D) (*Cont.*)
  quadrant of, 62
  relationship-building, 73
  side gigs, 74
  start ups and small businesses, 75
  strategic learning plans, 74
  uncertainty, 136, 137
  workplace environments suited
    to, 75–6
domains (industry bases)
  defining, 61
  emerging (fit for AI), 109–10
  multi-domain expertise, value
    of, 177
  top 60, for developing TGA,
    106–10
  working outside *see* outside-
    the-domain skills
Dyson, 13, 156
easily replaceable myth concerning
    generalists, 12
Economic and Social Research
    Council (ESRC), 64
ecosystem thinking, 21
educational technology, teacher
    with skills in, 36
Einstein, Albert, xxvii
emotional intelligence, 46, 116
empathy, 174, 177
energy and resources, 108
entrepreneurship, xxv, 6, 89–90
entry-level positions, myth that
    generalists are only good
    at, 11–12
epiphany, 49
errors, learning from, 105
established paradigms favorer,
    specialist as, 7
ethical guidance, 46
evolution, embracing, 22
execution skills, 127
executive coaching, 82
experimentation, 23, 175
expert brick wall point, 97, 98

expert saturation point, 97, 98
expertise, 7, 12, 15, 25, 50, 52, 58,
    152, 156
  and adapting to change, 104
  coding, 163
  and competitive advantage, 154
  complementary skills, 36
  creative industries, 81
  cross-domain, 178
  cross-industry, 72, 73
  culture shift, 105
  deep, 5, 18, 19, 61, 68, 70, 97, 99,
    102, 164
  domain, 103
  industry, 176
  multidisciplinary, 86
  multi-domain, 177
  multi-domain, value of, 177
  Near Future Readiness, 19–20
  product development, 118
  in psychology, 150
  SDSU framework based on, 60,
    61, 72, 73, 75, 79
  silo thinking, 141
  single-discipline, 122
  of specialists, 101
  specialized, 9
  subject, 10, 122
  targeted, 145
  technical, 6, 75, 90, 100, 148, 168
  top-level, 79
  unreliable, 67
  wide, 61
  working outside domain, 101, 186
  see also expert brick wall point;
    expert saturation point;
    specialists
"explain to a child" exercise, 50
exploitative innovation, 151, 152
exploration guides, generalists seen
    as, 10
explorative innovation, 151, 152
extroversion myth regarding
    generalists, 11

finance and business, 107
financial literacy, as hard skill, 117
flexibility, 3, 10, 56, 58, 72
    cognitive, 25, 26*t*, 29*t*, 31
    of domain generalists, 75
    domain-flexibility, 102, 103
    flexible working, 19
    generalist leadership approach,
        140, 149
    growth acumen skills, 127
    movement between perspec-
        tives, 146
    of skill generalists, 78
    technical adaptability, 21
    of ultra generalists, 86
    see also adaptability of generalists
focus
    deep, 159, 160, 161, 162
    issues of, 56–7
    macro, 159, 160, 161, 162
    meta, 160, 161, 162
    micro, 159, 160, 161, 162
    mission-driven (case study), 171
    myth that generalists lack, 9–10
    narrowing of, 96
    problem-solving, 158–9, 160*t*
    shallow generalists, 68
    strategic, 140–1
foresight
    benefits of, 134
    data-driven, 138
    defining, 134
    effective strategies, 137–8
    emerging markets, spotting, 138
    and hindsight, 134
    holistic thinking, 144
    horizon scanning, 137
    and insight, 134–5
    new partnerships, discover-
        ing, 138
    outside perspective, 138
    and oversight, 134–5
    potential threats, assessing, 138
    practical tips, 138–9
    resilience, building, 139

scenario-based thinking, 138
scrappy experiments, embracing,
    138
strategic, 21, 24
as thinking ahead, 134
threat assessment, 138
trend analysis, 138
ultra generalists leaders, helping,
    137–9
valued by generalists, 14
what-ifs, 138
freelance work, 82
Fujifilm, 113
FusionTech (case study) *see under*
    ultra generalists (U)
Future of Jobs Report and Global
    Skills Report, 125
future-focused industries, 89

Generalist Advantage, the *see* TGA
    (the Generalist Advantage)
generalist mindset, 3, 10, 13, 32,
    45, 165
Generalist Quotient (GQ)
    checking, 183–4
    defining, 183
    self-assessment, xxv, 43, 184
generalists
    chance of becoming top
        management, xxiv
    defining who is, 3–6, 55–6
    defining who is not, 6–8
    degrees of generalist-ness, 7
    disciplinary strokes of *see*
        disciplinary interaction,
        approaches
    distinguished from specialists,
        17–19
    diversity of, 55–8
    generalist thinking, 61
    generalist-type profiles, 37
    hard and soft skills, 115–20
    innovation and problem-solving
        see innovation;
        problem-solving

generalists (*Cont.*)
as multi-potentialities, 4, 56
myths about, 9–13
and NFR, 23–4
power of, xxiii
productivity, 97, 98
skill merits, 111
skills pyramid, 44–5
strengths, risks and organizational aspects, 90–1, 92*t*
see also Near Future Readiness
(NFR); SDSU (shallow,
domain, skill, ultra)
framework (2x2); skills;
TGA (the Generalist
Advantage)
generalist-specialist debate,
7–8, 17–19
breadth versus depth, 17–18
career opportunities, 18–19
conceptual differences, 17, 18*t*
individual preferences, 19
learning approach, 18
transition between generalists
and specialists, 33
versatility versus specialization, 18
workplace application
differences, 19*t*
genomics, personalized, 109
Gladwell, Malcolm, 8
globalization, 110
Gmail, 157
Google, 114, 156–7
Google Maps, 157
Google Search, 157
government and public sector, 108–9
GQ *see* Generalist Quotient (GQ)
grit personality, 25, 31
growth acumen skills, 127
hack days, 175
hard skills, 76, 115–20, 128
Hastings, Reed, 165
HCI *see* human-computer
interaction (HCI)

health care
development of TGA, 107
management, 176
rapid technological change
in, 140
shallow generalists (S), 70
helicopter view, 99, 146
hindsight, 132, 135
holistic thinking, 142, 144,
145, 148–9
horizon scanning, 137
hospitality industry, 108
human-computer interaction
(HCI), 41
hyper-specialists *see* shallow
generalists (S)

IBM, 114
idea adaptors, 24
IKEA, 165–6
impression management skills, 127
industry domain exposure, 141
industry generalists *see* domain
generalists (D)
industry recognition, 178
information silo seeker,
specialist as, 7
innovation
building innovation spaces, 22
case studies, generalist-led,
156–7, 173, 174–5
contribution of generalists to, 13,
131–66
domain generalists, 72, 155
as innovators, 56
ins and outs of generalists,
149–57
skill generalists, 155
sparking innovation, 96
ultra generalists, 155
cross-disciplinary approaches, 11,
30, 51, 123
defining, 150
exploitative, 151, 152

explorative, 151, 152
future domains, 110
groundbreaking, 101
innovation management
    practices, 154–7
inside-out, 150, 151, 152, 153–4
interdisciplinary, 113
outside-in, 151, 152, 153, 154
outside-the-domain skills, 104
stagnation of, 96
strategists, 145–6
translators for, 150
see also problem-solving
inside-out innovation, 150, 151,
    152, 153–4
insight, 133–4
intellectual curiosity, 123
intellectual humility, 50
interdisciplinary approaches, 6,
    11, 144
breakthroughs, 49
collaboration, 31, 49, 51
communication, 30
courses, taking, 123
fit, 42
innovation, 113
problem-solving, 32
teamwork, 42, 112, 156
work exposure, 141
interests, multiple, 56
interviews, 25
intra-disciplinary approaches,
    120–2, 124
intrapreneur, generalist as, 5
intrepid change maker, 25, 31
iPad/iPhone, 156

jack-of-all-trades, master of none,
    8–9, 67
jargon, 49, 56, 164
job rotations, 106, 115
job searches, 38
Jobs, Steve, 4, 84, 156
Johansson, Frans, 101

know-it-all freaks, 15
knowledge, xxv, 3, 4, 18, 36, 49, 72,
    82, 120, 135–6, 141, 173, 186
absorbing, xxiv
acquiring, 17, 22, 42, 154
    rapid acquisition, 85, 87
base, 69
breadth of, 17, 57, 72, 139,
    145, 185
collective, 57
complex problems, generalists
    tackling, 147
cross-domain, 31
cross-functional, 112
in-depth, 18, 68, 69, 70
diversity of, in generalists, 9, 14,
    24, 137
domain, 106, 163
embracing pursuit of, 86–7
exchange of, 14, 155
external, 106
foundational, 117
hardware understanding, 126
industry, 5, 72
integrating, 12, 120, 122
limitations of, 50
limited, 121
minimum viable knowledge
    (MVK), 154
multidisciplinary, 150
multi-industry, 177
obsolete, 127
peer-to-peer coaching, 106
prioritizing flow of, 22
self-knowledge, 10
sharing, 21, 114, 156
and skill sets, 177
solidifying, 77
specialized, 6, 12, 175–6, 179
statistical, 125
surface-level, 67, 133
technical, 6, 56, 98
thirst for, xxvi
transferring, 9, 79

knowledge (*Cont.*)
  translation of, 13, 30–1
  unfamiliar, 77
  varied, 153
  well-rounded, 89
  wide-ranging, 9, 162
  see also skills
Kodak, 113
KSBs (knowledge, skills and
    behaviours), 58

Lafley, A.G., 165
language barriers, 49
lateral thinking, 157
Law of Specialist Saturation (LOSS),
    xxvi, 95–101
  difficulties with relying totally on
    specialists, 100
  generalist optimization, 98, 99
  over time, 96–7
  reasons for, 99–100
  resource management, 100
  scenarios, 100–1
  specialist saturation, 98
  why seen as a loss, 99–100
leadership, 20, 24, 36, 38, 51–2, 65,
    85, 101, 104, 116, 120,
    148, 173
  actions, 106
  adaptive, 74, 178
  boundary spanning, 49
  fear of failure, 170
  future-minded leaders, 21–2
  generalist leaders, 11–15, 23, 32,
    45, 48, 122–3, 140, 142,
    145–6, 156
    ultra generalists, 137–9, 146–8
    see also TGA (the Generalist
      Advantage)
  leadership excellence skills, 126–7
  and management, 89, 100, 107,
    122, 125, 128
  multi-domain background, 177
  multi-skilled leaders, 177–8
  niche leaders, 6

operating outside domain, 102
parameters, 26
potential, 78
roles, 15, 32, 85, 113, 144, 162
skills, 78, 115, 119, 126–7, 164, 177
specialist, 95
strategic, 89, 165
strong, 46, 148
style, xxiv, 168, 170
successful leaders, 13, 142
succession, 90
thought leaders, 155
training, 95
trans-disciplinary approach, 124
versatile leaders, 45, 47
learning culture, fostered by
    generalists, 15
lifelong craftsmanship, 13
"light bulb" feeling *see* insight
LinkedIn, 125
longevity and rejuvenation, 109
LOSS *see* Law of Specialist
    Saturation (LOSS)

McKinsey & Company, 72
macro focus, 159, 160, 161, 162
management, 32, 45, 65, 72, 78, 84,
    119, 127, 128, 134, 151,
    161, 171
  brand, 142, 165
  construction, 10, 90
  crisis, 101
  frontline, 69
  general, 9, 86
  health care, 176
  innovation management
    practices, 154–7
  and leadership, 89, 100, 107, 122,
    125, 128
  middle, 11, 62, 100
  product, 13, 81, 169
  project, 10, 14, 36, 40, 56, 114,
    117, 133
  risk, 142, 177
  self-management, 128

senior, 12, 69, 95, 100, 144
staff, 19
team, 12, 120, 133
time, 90, 115
manufacturing, 100–1, 108
market expansion, 175, 178
Martinez, Rebecca (case study)
     see under domain
     generalists (D)
mash-ups, 4, 50
masters *see* specialists
maturity curve, 91
media, 14, 57, 108, 165
     see also social media
Medici effect, the, 101
medicine, personalized, 109
mediocre performance myth
     regarding generalists, 11
mentorship
   encouraging, 114
   informal mentors, 50
   for lateral growth, 106
   myths regarding, 10–11
   opportunities, creating, 155
   and peer-to-peer coaching, 114
   skill generalists, 77
mergers and acquisitions
     (M&As), 75
meta focus, 160, 161, 162
meta-learning, 87
meta-skills, 22, 80
   ultra generalists, 83, 85, 87
micro focus, 159, 160, 161, 162
Microsoft, 114, 165
minimum viable knowledge
     (MVK), 154
minimum viable product (MVP),
     140, 147
Miro Electronics (case study) *see*
     under skill generalists (S)
multidimensional skill set of gener-
     alists, 9, 13
multidisciplinary approaches,
     124, 150
   collaboration, 86

defining, 120
domain generalists, 137
expertise, 86
industries, 88–9
problem-solving, 120
programs, 81
SDSU framework, 122, 137
teamwork, 42, 50, 123
multi-hyphenates, generalists as,
     xxv, 4
multi-potentialities, generalists
     as, 4, 56
Musk, Elon, 4, 56, 84, 113, 156
MVK *see* minimum viable knowl-
     edge (MVK)
MVP *see* minimum viable product
     (MVP)
myths of generalists, debunking,
     8–13
Nadella, Satya, 165
nanotechnology, advanced, 110
Near Future Readiness Index
     (NFRI), 20, 24–5, 26–7*t*, 28
   application to individuals,
     organizations and indus-
     tries, 28
   competitive scores, 26
   deriving TGA through, 28, 29–30*t*
   eight indicators, 25*f*, 31, 44
Near Future Readiness (NFR), 19–23
   agility of thinking, 21
   anticipation, 20–1
   cultivation of, 22
   defining, 20–2
   examples, 23, 24
   expertise, 19–20
   and generalists, 23–4
   individual and organizational
     levels, 22
   magnitude of change, 19
   near future versus future, 20
   negative readiness, 28
   open-collar jobs, 19
   positive readiness, 28
   resilience, 21

Near Future Readiness (NFR)
(*Cont.*)
  role of generalists, 23, 24
  scenarios, 23–4
  speech of change, 19
  type of industry, 22
  white-collar jobs, 19
  workweek concept, 19
Netflix, 165
networking, 50, 69, 73
  decentralized social
    networks, 109
neurotechnology, 109
new product development, 32
NFR *see* Near Future Readiness
  (NFR)
niche leaders, 6
nongovernmental organizations
  (NGOs), 84
nonprofit sector, case study, 171

online forum lurking, 50
OpenAI, 15
optimization
  advertising campaigns, 45
  business results, 96
  generalist, 98, 99
  organizational performance, 96
  process, 153, 155
  productivity, 98, 99
  supply chain software, 176
organizational culture, 178
organizational renewal, 131
Ortiz, Adele (case study) *see under*
  ultra generalists (U)
outlier events, attending, 50
outside inspiration, 13, 150
outside-in innovation, 151, 152,
  153, 154
outside-the-domain skills, 102–3
  adaptability, 101, 103
  assignments, problem-based, 106
  contributions made, 104–5
  culture shift, 105
  development opportunities, 106

examples, 103–4
external knowledge building,
  supporting, 106
how organizations can encourage, 105–6
importance of, 103–5
lateral growth, mentorship
  for, 106
leadership actions, 106
making connections, 106
opportunities to tackle issues differently, providing, 106
peer-to-peer coaching, 106
project design, 105–6
rotation of roles, 106
start-ups, 103
wicked problems, solving,
  103–4, 105
see also domain and skill variation among generalists
overengineering, 147
oversight, 132–5, 136
Page, Larry, 156
paradigm shifts, 141
patterns
  big-picture patterns, recognition
    of, 14, 25, 31, 56
  recognition of, 46, 87, 137
  seeking, 24
peer-to-peer coaching, 106, 114
Peloton Interactive, 15
personal growth, 104, 113
personality, issues of, 56, 57, 136
  see also traits of generalists
perspectives, SDSU framework
  based on, 61
planning, 20, 159, 169
  contingency, 148
  development, 127
  endless, 138
  future, 48
  mid-term, 21
  and perfectionism, 169
  planned exploration, 99
  proactive, 134

strategic, 21, 23, 100, 142
POC *see* proof of concept (POC)
Polman, Paul, 164
polymaths, generalists as, xxv, 4, 83
portable skills, 39–45, 128
   communication and influence, 40
   critical thinking, 41
   and cross-industry adaptabil-
      ity, 59
   defining, 39
   developing, 42–5
   growth opportunities, seeking, 43
   identifying existing strengths, 43
   investing in, 41, 42
   problem-solving, 40–1, 42, 43
   and professional resilience, 41–2
   SDSU framework based
      on, 58–60
portfolio careers, 57–8
precision execution, 46
predictability, 28
problem-solving, 14, 29, 48, 50, 51,
      61, 126
   anticipating problems, 22
   assignments, 106
   case studies, 148–9, 164–6, 174–5
   cognitive skills, 125
   collaborative, 77
   complementary skills, 35
   complex problems *see* complex
      problems, generalists
      tackling
   contexts, 38
   contrasting skills, 37
   creative, 174
   creativity, 31, 42, 72, 85, 171, 174
   deeply seated, 99
   defining, 157
   domain generalists, 75, 122
   emerging skills, 128
   functional, 46–7
   generalist-led, 131–66
   generalist-specialist debate, 18
   highly informed, 72
   innovative, 11, 38, 88, 113

interdisciplinary approaches, 32
iterative problem-solving
   mode, 157
messy problems, 5
modes, 157–66
multidisciplinary approaches, 120
multi-domain expertise, 177
Near Future Readiness, 21
new problems, 7, 8
niche problems, 98
nuanced, 35
perspectives, 18
portable skills, 40–1, 42, 43
real business, 9
reframing, 56
skill acquisition, 112
skill generalists, 76, 78
soft skills, 117
technology-adjacent, 126
ultra generalists, 85
uncertain events, 131–41
unconventional perspectives, 4,
   12, 30
unfamiliar, 101
unstructured problems, 32
wicked, solving, 103–4, 105
zooming in and out, 158
see also innovation
procrastination, 21
Proctor & Gamble (P&G), 165
product development, 32, 81,
   100, 118
product differentiation, 175
product management, 13, 81, 169
productivity, 137, 149–50
   AI-driven, 45
   and career lifespan, 96–7
   diminishing, of specialists, 95,
      96, 98–9
   enhancing over time, 99
   generalist, 97, 98
   long-term, 98
   optimizing, 99
   productivity myth, debunking, 9
   specialist, 97, 98

productivity (*Cont.*)
  technology proficiency, 117
  trends, 97
  of ultra generalists, 97
programming languages, 115
project management, 14, 56, 114, 133
  design, 105–6
  general projects, 99
  hard skills, 117
  intentionally hybrid teams, 105
proof of concept (POC), 49
prototyping, rapid, 150, 171, 175
Python (programming language), 115

qualitative data (interviews), 25
quantitative data (surveys), 25
quantum computing, 109

R&D (research & development), 23
related skills *see* complementary
  skills
Reliable Systems (case study) *see*
  under shallow generalists (S)
Renaissance thinkers, xxv, 83
research and analysis, 118
resilience, professional
  building, 139
  career resilience, 42
  case study (Adele Ortiz of
    FusionTech), 176
  championed by generalists, 14–15
  developing portable skills, 42–5
  Near Future Readiness, 21
  portable skills essential for, 39–45
re-skilling, 110–11, 114–15
rotation, job, 106, 115
Rowling, J.K., 112–13
sampling mentality, 79
"sandbox spaces," 155
scanners, generalists as, 56
Schultz, Howard, 164
scope, issues of, 56
SDSU (shallow, domain, skill, ultra)
  framework (2x2), xxv,
  57–64

ability to work outside
  domain, 102–3
based on expertise and
  perspectives, 60–1
based on portable skills and cross-
  industry adaptability, 58–60
based on skills and domains,
  61–4
complex problems, generalists
  tackling, 142–3
disciplinary interaction, 120–2
focus approaches, 161
foresight, 135–6
four types of generalists, 61, 62*t*
hard and soft skills, 118–20
hindsight, 135–6
innovation ins and outs of
  generalists, 152, 153*f*
insight, 135–6
multidisciplinary approaches, 122
new skills, ability to acquire,
  111–12
oversight, 135–6
see also domain generalists (D);
  shallow generalists (S);
  skill generalists (S); ultra
  generalists (U)
self-development, 38
serendipity, 88
service industries, 108
Shaikh, Ali *see under* skill
  generalists (S)
shallow generalists (S)
  beneficial environments, 69–71
  case study (Ben Bennett of
    Reliable Systems))
    analysis till paralysis in
      disruption, 167–8, 169
    discussion questions, 170
    early success, 168
    emerging disruption, 168
    fear of failure, 170
    indecision, cost of, 169
    iteration over perfection, 170
    opportunity cost, 170

perfectionism, dangers of, 169
  results, evaluating, 169–70
characteristics, 60, 68
deep focus, 162
defining who is, 66–8
detailed prototyper, 163
expertise, 61
health care, 70
highly regulated industries, 70
how not to become, 68–9
hyper-specialists, as, 63, 66
industry sectors suited to, 70
innovation management
    practices, 154
large corporations, 70
pros and cons, 68, 69*t*
quadrant of, 61–2, 65
R&D, 70–1
science, 70
silo thinking, 144
staying informed, 69
technology, 70
uncertainty, 135, 137
workplace environments suited
    to, 70–1
see also domain generalists (D);
    SDSU (shallow, domain,
    skill, ultra) framework (2x2);
    skill generalists (S); ultra
    generalists (U)
silo thinking, xxii, 141–2, 144
skill generalists (S)
  beneficial environments, 80–2
  bricoleur, 163
  case study (Ali Shaikh of Miro
      Electronics)
    applying unrelated skills, 173–6
    benefits of unrelated skills, 174
    creativity, 174
    cross-functional agility, 175
    cross-team collaboration, 175
    discussion questions, 176
    early influences, 174
    empathy, 174

experimentation, 175
    hack days, 175
    hands-on approach, 174
    human-centered design, 175
    innovation, 174–5
    market expansion, 175
    power of unrelated skills in
        dynamic environment, 173–4
    problem-solving, 174
    product differentiation, 175
    results, evaluating, 175–6
  characteristics, 60, 78
  cognitive adaptability, 76–7
  collaboration, 78
  communication, 78
  creative industries, 81
  curiosity-driven exploration, 79
  customer services, 81
  defining, 76–8
  diverse skill sets, 78
  documentation of process, 80
  education and training indus-
      tries, 81
  executive coaching, 82
  flexibility of, 78
  foundations, focus on, 79–80
  freelance work, 82
  hard skills, 76
  how to become, 79–80
  industry sectors suited to, 81
  innovation management prac-
      tices, 155
  learning mindset, 79
  mentorship, 77
  micro focus, 162
  micro opportunities, seeking, 80
  problem-solving, 76, 78
  product development, 81
  project mindset, 80
  pros and cons, 78, 79*t*
  quadrant of, 62
  sampling mentality, 79
  soft skills, 75
  strategic skill development, 80

skill generalists (S) (*Cont.*)
  "teach as you learn" approach, 77
  teamwork, 77
  technology and digital indus-
    tries, 81
  transferable skills, 80
  uncertainty, 136, 137
  workplace environments suited
    to, 81–2
skills
  AI interaction, 125–6
  aligning skill development with
    career advancement, 114
  balance between specialist and
    generalist skill types, 38
  cognitive, 125
  communication, 36, 43, 81
  complementary, 36, 38
  complex problems, generalists
    tackling, 141–9
  contrasting, 37
  creating clear pathways and
    certifications, 114
  data literacy, 125–6
  defining, 35
  educational technology, 36
  emerging, fit for AI era, 128
  encouraging a culture of upskilling
    and re-skilling, 110–11, 114–15
  execution, 127
  growth acumen, 127
  hard versus soft, of generalists,
    76, 115–20
  importance of acquiring new
    skills, 112–14
  impression management, 127
  leadership, 78, 115
  leadership excellence, 126–7
  meta-skills, 22, 83, 85, 87
  new, ability to acquire, 110–15
  portable *see* portable skills
  SDSU framework based on, 61–4
  significance of acquiring new
    skills, 112–14

skill set of generalists, 9, 13
skillful masters, 145
skills pyramid for generalists, 44–5
  soft, 75
  strategic development, 80
  technical, 115
  technology-adjacent, 126
  top 40, for developing
    TGA, 125–8
  transferable, 39, 80, 116
  universal, 39
  unrelated, applying, 173–6
  video editing, 81
  see also SDSU (Shallow, Domain,
    Skill, Ultra) framework (2x2)
Slack, 164
social intelligence, 46
social media, 78, 104, 109
  see also media
societal needs, 110
Socratic inquiry, 120
soft skills, 75, 115–20, 128
Software-as-a-Service (SaaS), 168
space resources/commercialization,
  109
specialists
  brick wall, 99
  chance of becoming top manage-
    ment, xxiv
  communication gap between, 56
  complementary skills, 36
  defining, 6
  distinguished from generalists,
    17–19
  expertise of, 101
  generalists distinguished from
    specialists, 3
  hyper-specialists, 63, 66
  as masters, 6
  productivity, 97, 98
  saturation, 98
  specialism and mastery, 8
  on specialization, 96
  tunnel vision, 13

specialization, 31, 80, 100–2
  connecting to wider context, 102
  deep, 96, 150
  deliberate, 99
  excessive, 98
  highly specialized projects, 99
  and identifying skill sets, 123
  intentional, 99
  laser-focused, 8
  and Law of Specialist Saturation
    (LOSS), 96
  overspecialization, 96
  rewards, 49
  specialization-heavy cultures, 85
  specialized knowledge, 6
  traditional, 45
  versus versatility, 18
Spotify, 156
Starbucks, 164
start ups and small businesses,
  12, 75
statistical tools, 115
strategic focus, shifting, 140–1
strategic foresight, 21, 24
superpowers of generalist, 13–15
surveys, 25
sustainability, 110
synthetic biology, 109
systems thinking, 30, 80, 125, 162

tactical adaptability, 21
teamwork, 4, 10, 13, 77
  adaptable teams, building, 178
  communication, 165
  intentionally hybrid teams, 105
  interdisciplinary approaches, 42,
    112, 156
  management, 12, 120
  multidisciplinary approaches, 42,
    50, 123
  soft skills, 116
  synergists, 25, 31
  team building, 38
  trans-disciplinary approaches, 124
  translators, 13

technology
  development of TGA, 107
  disruption, 5, 9, 14, 110, 111, 164
  health care, navigating rapid
    change in, 140
  proficiency, as hard skill, 117
  technical knowledge, 6, 56, 98
  technical skills, 115
  technology proofing, 42
  technology-adjacent skills, 126
10,000-hour rule, 8
Tesla, 56, 113, 156
TGA (the Generalist Advantage),
    xxiii, 28–33
  benefits of cultivating, 32
  defining, 29, 31*f*
  deriving through the NFRI, 28,
    29–30*t*
  framework, xxv
  "how" one can be a generalist, 55
  paths possible, 64–90
    switching companies early in
      careers, 64–5
    switching companies later in
      careers, 65–6
  top 40 skills for developing,
    125–8
  top 60 domains for developing,
    106–10
  top forty skills for develop-
    ing, 128
  Type I (shallow generalists) *see*
    shallow generalists (S)
  Type II (domain generalists) *see*
    domain generalists (D)
  Type III (skill generalists) *see*
    skill generalists (S)
  Type IV (ultra generalists) *see*
    ultra generalists (U)
  see also generalists; SDSU (shal-
    low, domain, skill, ultra)
    framework (2x2); skills
"thinking ahead" feeling *see*
    foresight
threats, assessing, 138

3M, 156
timebox decisions, 147
traits of generalists, 3–4, 11
trans-disciplinary approaches,
  120, 122
  defining, 120
  power of trans-disciplinary mind-
    set, 123–4
transferable skills, 39, 80, 116
  see also portable skills
translators
  complex problems, generalist-led
    case study, 148
  generalists as, 4, 56, 148
  for innovation, 150
  learning to translate between dis-
    ciplines, 124
  team, 13
  ultra generalists, 163–4
trend analysis 23, 138
T-shaped professional, 4–5

UK Research and Innovation
  (UKRI)
  Made Smarter Innovation Net-
    work, 64
ultra generalists (U)
  beneficial environments, 88–90
  case study (Adele Ortiz of
    FusionTech)
    adaptable teams, building, 178
    discussion questions, 178–9
    disruption, anticipating, 177
    empathy, 177
    ideas, cross-pollination of, 177
    industry recognition, 178
    market growth, 178
    multi-domain expertise, value
      of, 177
    organizational culture, 178
    resilience and adaptability,
      leading with, 176–9
    results, evaluating, 178

  uncertainty and resilience,
    177–8
  characteristics, 60, 86
  cross-disciplinary approaches, 83
  cross-functional skills, breadth
    of, 86
  cross-paradigm exploration, 86–7
  curiosity, 86
  defining, 82–5
  entrepreneurship, 89–90
  examples, 84
  exploration, 88
  flexibility of, 86
  foresight, preparing for uncertain
    events, 137–9
  future-focused industries, 89
  holistic thinking in leaders,
    complex problem-
    solving, 146–8
  how to become, 86–7
  idea synthesis, 87
  innovation management
    practices, 155
  intellectual play, 86
  intentional but nonlinear path, 88
  key questions, 82–3
  leadership and management, 89
  macro purpose, connecting to, 88
  meta focus, 162
  meta-skills, 83, 85, 87
  multidisciplinary expertise, 86
  multidisciplinary industries, 88–9
  nonlinear thinkers, 84
  pattern recognition, 85, 87
  polymaths, 4, 83
  problem-solving, 85
  productivity, 97
  project-based work, 90
  pros and cons, 86, 87t
  pure idea generators, 85
  pursuit of knowledge, embrac-
    ing, 86
  quadrant of, 63, 65

rapid knowledge acquisition,
85, 87
Renaissance thinkers, xxv, 83
rigid workplaces, not adapting
well to, 85
serendipity, embracing, 88
translators, 163–4
uncertainty, 136, 137
unconventional career paths, 84
versatility, 86
visionary industries, 89
uncertainty
case studies, generalist-led, 139–
41, 176–9
collaboration, 132
defining, 131
generalists dealing with, 131–41
comfort with the unknown,
15, 24
organizational renewal, 131
retail, adapting to market disruption in, 139
ultra generalists leaders
case study (Adele Ortiz), 177–8
foresight useful for, 137–9
Unilever, 115, 164

universal skills, 39
see also portable skills
upskilling, 110, 114–15
user experience (UX), 36
versatility, 45–8
celebrating versatile thinkers, 105
developing, 69
power of, 46–8
versus specialization, 18
ultra generalists, 86
vertical farming, 109
Virgin Group, 165
visionaries/visionary strategists,
generalists as, 5, 57
visionary industries, 89
VUCA (volatile, uncertain, complex
and ambiguous) environ-
ments, 136, 144
web design, 36
what-if questions, 4, 138, 155
WhatsApp, 156
wicked problems, 103–4, 105
wildcards (power moves), 23
Winfrey, Oprah, 4
workplace strategies, xxv

SDSU Framework
for the Generalist Advantage

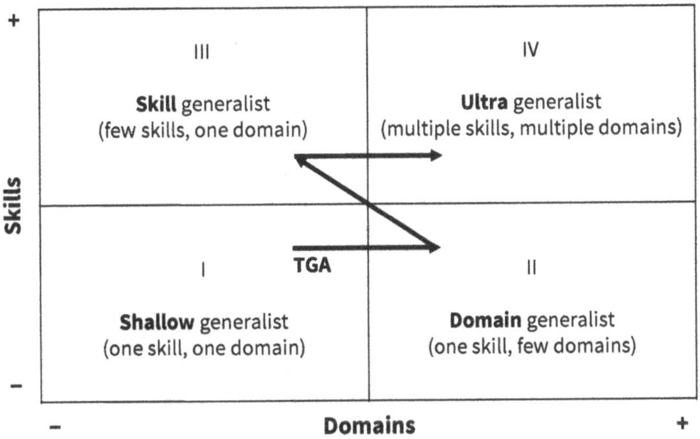
+
III
Skill generalist
(few skills, one domain)
IV
Ultra generalist
(multiple skills, multiple domains)
Skills
I
TGA
Shallow generalist
(one skill, one domain)
II
Domain generalist
(one skill, few domains)
–
–
Domains
+

SDSU: Shallow, domain, skill, ultra (framework classifying generalists into four types)
TGA: The Generalist Advantage (represented by arrows, cascading from shallow to ultra)